THE SHADOW SYSTEM

THE SHADOW SYSTEM

MASS INCARCERATION AND THE AMERICAN FAMILY

SYLVIA A. HARVEY

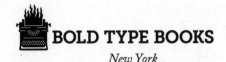
BOLD TYPE BOOKS

New York

Bold Type Books
116 East 16th Street, 8th Floor New York, NY 10003
www.boldtypebooks.org
@BoldTypeBooks

Printed in the United States of America

First Edition: April 2020

Published by Bold Type Books, an imprint of Perseus Books, LLC, a subsidiary of Hachette Book Group, Inc. Bold Type Books is a co-publishing venture of the Type Media Center and Perseus Books.

The Hachette Speakers Bureau provides a wide range of authors for speaking events. To find out more, go to www.hachettespeakersbureau.com or call (866) 376-6591.

The publisher is not responsible for websites (or their content) that are not owned by the publisher.

Print book interior design by Trish Wilkinson.

Library of Congress Cataloging-in-Publication Data has been applied for.

ISBNs: 978-1-56858-880-3 (hardcover), 978-1-56858-882-7 (e-book)

LSC-C

10 9 8 7 6 5 4 3 2 1

For my father, and my brothers

Contents

PROLOGUE

An American Family?

One weekend, my mom is making biscuits from scratch. The heady, sweet aroma of her homemade syrup wafts through our Oakland apartment. She stands at our kitchen counter, wrapped, as usual, in my father's blue robe, flour coating her spice-toned hands. She has pulled her kinky black hair into a bun; her face is smooth, free from the Fashion Fair foundation she puts on when my father takes her dancing. She sways gently to the sound of the O'Jays on our record player. My father slips into the kitchen and dips a fork into the side of the skillet, taking the crispy edge of the potatoes. Before he can sneak a bite of bacon, my mom rallies her troops. "Kiiids," she calls. My dad knows this playful tone. "Come get your father." I abandon my cartoon, my brothers quit wrestling, and we dash into the kitchen. Surrounding my dad, laughter chopping the air, five sets of hands push on him. He stumbles, pretending the small shoves are powerful. Finally, we're successful—we drive him from the kitchen and into the living room with us. My mom, shaping the biscuits, laughs and looks at him victoriously. My dad smiles. He scribbles a note to his childhood sweetheart, "I'm sorry, can I have a piece of bacon?" and sends me to the kitchen with it. At three, I am their only daughter and the baby of the family. My father knows I will return with a treat for him.

Our clan had a rhythm: my dad rose early for work, my brothers went off to school, and my mother and I were left to explore our day together. I was by her side as she baked cupcakes, made Halloween costumes, and attended PTA meetings for my brothers. The weekend, void of work and school, was prime family time. After Saturday's big breakfast, we always went on an adventure: fishing on the pier, to the zoo to gaze at the monkeys, or on a two-hour mini road trip to the Santa Cruz Beach Boardwalk. In between all the joy and excursions, my mother had bouts with being sick. Labored breathing, coughing, and wheezing seemed to be normal parts of my mother's life, my brothers' too—they all had horrific asthma. The doctors suggested my mom slow down, but she couldn't, she wouldn't. Engaging and taking care of us gave her life.

My tiny four-year-old hand slams against the doctor's barren face when he tells me my mother has died. Asthma, a formidable foe, had greedily sucked away her last breath. The familiar buttery scent of homemade biscuits fades. Missing her and the aroma, I ask my dad for God's phone number, so I can tell him to send my mom home. My dad's hazel eyes well up. Finally, I sense my mother is gone forever.

Eventually, I settle into the idea of a new duo. My father and I become inseparable. I relish the mornings he gathers my thick, intractable curly hair and struggles braiding it. I don't mind the days he simply tucks my uncombed locks under a baseball cap. He asks his signature question, "Why are you so pretty?" I have the answer memorized, "Because my father's so handsome!" I lock onto his right leg, and he carries me on his journeys—even to work. He's determined to ward off the vulture-like swoop of Child Protective Services. He parks his car on the dead-end block where the construction site begins, and I sit in the back seat playing with my Cabbage Patch doll, while he's banging on nails or laying bricks. He checks on me often, sometimes giving me snacks and asking, "How's my angel?" A few days later, his supervisor realizes I'm in the car and tells him it's not allowed.

He doesn't return to work.

That same year, following my mother's death, my father's life as widower and doting dad fuses with that of fledgling drug dealer. He lets my mother's death break his sense of self. Every time my brothers and I tell him he doesn't do something "like Mommy," he loses a measure of himself. He believes selling drugs is the perfect solution to earning his lost income, feeling worthy, and being present in our lives. I am just happy to be spending the same amount of time with him that I had with my mother. He helps my brothers with their homework, takes us to the doctor, and makes dinner on the nights we don't devour our favorite Kwik Way hamburgers.

A year later, still delighting in my alone time with him, I place one small foot in front of the other, proudly calling out, "Dad!" My cheeks tip to the sky and my eyes shut. I laugh. "Look, Daddy, look!" Finally, after days of practice, I've mastered the art of skipping. He watches me skip down the street. That's when a cruiser turns onto our block. My father senses trouble. The police approach. He ushers me to the house. "Baby, go inside." He's parked his blue Nova backward on the wrong side of the street, and more than eighteen inches from the curb. Maybe the police are going to ticket him or tell him to move his car.

My dad is arrested, but not for violating parking laws. Being a drug dealer meant he was thrust into street life and all that it encompassed. He was implicated in a drug-related homicide. Eventually, my brothers and I go live with my maternal grandmother. I cry every day for a year. I prepare to keep doing it until my father returns to pick me up.

He never does. He seems to vanish.

In 1986, MY FATHER WAS convicted of second-degree murder. At twenty-nine years old, he began serving sixteen years to life in prison.

I was five years old. I thought I was the only kid with a parent in prison. I was wrong. It took decades for me to realize my father and I represented sobering statistics. Back then we were among hundreds of thousands of families who had a relative in prison. Now we're among millions. Only as an adult was I able to reflect on the oppressive conditions mauling my community or how the sudden ubiquity of crack cocaine was changing the complexion of my community.

In the 1980s, Oakland was marginalized, many of its residents excluded. My family lived in "the flatlands," not "the hills"—a more affluent section of Oakland. Redlining systematically denied black people access to credit and home and business loans, which ensured housing segregation for decades to come. We were relegated to a poverty-saturated, resource-depleted, racially segregated community shaped by structural racism. These racist exclusionary practices perpetuated poverty and economic insecurity, which made people, especially men, in neighborhoods like mine ripe for offending, arrest, and extreme sentencing, ultimately decimating families.

My brothers and I had once played red light, green light and hide-and-seek in front of the apartment, while my mother watched us from the window. Music pumped out of screened doors, little girls played double Dutch, and a grandmother poured buckets of hot water on men shooting dice on her porch. A few blocks away, in the same kind of public housing complex, known as a village, kids who appeared to be lounging on the roof or playing hopscotch were in fact runners and spotters in a drug kingpin's heroin empire. An eight-year-old boy who saw signs of a suspicious outsider entering their complex grabbed the whistle hanging from his thin neck, wrapped his small lips around it, and blew with vigor. The kid, often an addict's child, earned up to $300 a day. A mother pocketed $1,500 for turning her apartment into a safe house by allowing the village drug dealers to store drugs and eat sandwiches in her apartment during their lunch break. Oakland police rarely entered our village, except to drag dead bodies away. It was mostly crack cocaine, but heroin, prescription barbiturates, and bennies also floated through our neighborhood, ghosts entering black and brown bodies in the night. If drugs didn't end their lives, incarceration did.

Oakland was not unique in its deterioration. From Baltimore to Memphis to Miami, the crack epidemic ravaged inner cities across America, exacerbating structural and social problems. In need of jobs, adequate housing, drug treatment, and thoughtful public policy reforms, poor neighborhoods throughout America were abandoned by the government. Residents were left to solve their own problems, and then were over-policed. The government didn't recognize drug abuse as being the debilitating root of the problem, as being a dire public health issue that was further destabilizing poor, urban neighborhoods. Instead, they criminalized it, invoking a more punitive system that aimed to be tough on crime. The War on Drugs, a government-led initiative, enacted policies that increased and enforced penalties for drug-related crimes, and broken windows policing argued that cracking down on minor crimes and quality-of-life offenses—like selling loose cigarettes or loitering—will prevent serious crimes from occurring. Those were not race neutral policies; they put racial minorities in a chokehold.

Poor communities of color were under siege. Targeted, subject to escalating racial harassment, and arrested in droves, African Americans felt the blows of the 1986 Anti-Drug Abuse Act, which issued unimaginably long mandatory minimum sentences for first-time drug offenders. Furthermore, the sentences for possessing the drug that was plaguing black communities, crack cocaine, which was inexpensive and accessible, were one hundred times more severe than sentences for powder cocaine possession, which was more expensive and more commonly used by affluent whites. James, a black man on the corner in Oakland, caught with five grams of crack cocaine (equivalent to five packets of sugar), got five years in prison.

Meanwhile, a white executive in Portland had to have five hundred grams of powdered cocaine (comparable to over a pound of sugar) to get the same sentence. Indeed, US Sentencing Commission statistics report that blacks are more likely to be convicted for crack cocaine while whites are more likely to be convicted for powder cocaine.

This type of racist policing led to the disproportionate incarceration of racial minorities and helped birth the phenomenon of mass incarceration. In 1986, before the enactment of federal mandatory minimum sentencing for crack cocaine offenses, the average federal drug sentence for blacks was 11 percent higher than for whites. Four years later, it was 49 percent higher.

It didn't end there, as a broad array of tough-on-crime policies at the national, state, and local level followed. This broken-windows policing for minor street-level drug and quality-of-life offenses, and the expansion of the inherently racist stop-and-frisk policies, meant that more people came into contact with the criminal justice system. At the same time, the criminal code was expanded and harsher sentencing guidelines were enacted, including mandatory minimum sentences, three-strikes laws, truth-in-sentencing (TIS), laws that severely reduced the possibility of early release, and habitual offender laws. Once arrested, blacks are far more likely to be convicted. Upon conviction, they are far more likely to receive harsh sentences. Today, they are locked up at nearly six times the rate of whites.[1]

America is the world's leader in incarceration, with 2.2 million people behind bars.[2] Since 1980, the American incarceration rate has more than quadrupled. There were periods when the increase was particularly explosive, such as in the late 1980s. Starting at 329,000 in 1980, it doubled under the Reagan Administration and was 627,000 by the end of his presidency in 1988. Over the last decade, public conversation around mass incarceration and its impact has increased. Some reforms, such as sentencing reductions, policies, practices, and changes at the state and federal levels, have contributed to the decline in the national incarceration rate. From 2007 to 2016, the incarcerated population decreased by 18 percent, from 3,210 to 2,640 per 100,000 adult residents. While incarceration rates have dropped, overrepresentation of people of color persists: reform for some, harsher results for others. But we need to pay more attention to the families, especially the children, whose lives have been altered by it.[3]

When people are incarcerated, we as a society rarely consider the lives—and the people—left behind. But their former lives don't simply vanish. For their children, those prisoners remain parents. The collateral effects of mass incarceration cut through the immediate family fabric first, then penetrate the entire extended family for generations. The most fragile of those impacted are the children.

Alongside the rise of incarceration, the number of children with an incarcerated parent has skyrocketed. According to a 2010 study (the most recent data available), 7 percent of American children, or over five million children, have had a parent locked up at some point in their lives. Four percent of American children, or 2.7 million, currently have an incarcerated parent; that's one in twenty-eight kids. Thirty years ago, that number was one in 125. Unsurprisingly, there are stark racial disparities, which have widened significantly. While one out of every fifty-seven white children (1.8 percent) had an incarcerated parent, one in twenty-eight Hispanic children (3.5 percent) and one out of every nine black children (11.4 percent) had a parent behind bars.[4]

Structural inequality, biased legislation, and racism ensure parental incarceration continues to hit poor and racial minorities the hardest. Researchers have found that independent of preexisting social inequalities, children of incarcerated parents experience more negative social, economic, behavioral, and health outcomes. Families, no matter their race or class, are forced to deal with the costs of incarceration, as well as the rules and regulations that dictate their ties to their loved ones. All families, in different ways, are ripped apart at the seams, and some cases more brutally than others, but all suffer.[5]

From the moment my tiny beige hand touched the scratched glass partition, my father's hand covering mine from the other side, the separation was real. Like the millions of kids who would come after me, I leaned my face into the receiver and whispered, "When you coming home?" My brothers, tucked in the booth with me, waited for the answer. "I don't know baby. As soon as I can." My eldest brother, as usual, wailed uncontrollably. He was the only one old enough to understand that this separation could be permanent. A reality that would haunt millions of children.

As a child, I got used to the barbed wire gates and the officer holding a rifle in the gun tower. I knew prison guards would make me undo my hair in the hopes of finding heroin tucked in the folds of my braids. It was merely the price I had to pay the prison deities. In exchange for surrendering my freedom, I was allowed to see my father. Our future together would be in the hyper-supervised, limited-contact prison visits. For this, we were lucky; in subsequent years, even that sliver of connection would be robbed from families because of new visiting restrictions, new cutbacks to family programs.

Living at my grandma's meant I couldn't sleep with the boys. But each night I would slip out of the bed I shared with my aunt and two cousins and lie in a sleeping bag on the floor, nestled between the two sets of bunkbeds where my four brothers slept. I knew I could no longer climb in bed with my parents, but I yearned for the days when I slept next to Domonic, my youngest brother. I was grateful just to be in the same room as my brothers. There, on the floor, at least I was close to them. I'd try to return to the bed I shared before anyone noticed I was gone.

My aunt and grandmother could have gone with the original plan to divide my brothers and me up among family members, or worse—let us get caught in the web of the child welfare system. Many children of incarcerated parents do not have a family member who is willing or able to take them in, so they are placed into foster care, where they are more likely to be permanently separated from their parents as well as their extended families. But the effects of parental incarceration are dogged. They take jabs at kids beyond the barbed wire of prison grounds, beyond busy courtrooms, and beyond crowded foster homes. They tap their shoulders in school, a reminder, "I'm still here."

Having a parent locked up pushes children, children who are already vulnerable because of systemic racism and structural inequality, further into the margins. Moreover, geographic location and socioeconomic status disparately impact how families fare in the face of mass incarceration. Politics, history, public health, public policy, and economics create varying realities for families across the country, dictating which families float and which families sink.

MASS INCARCERATION IS a national issue impacting millions of families in every state across the country. *The Shadow System* investigates the various systems, policies, programs, and practices that touch the lives of these families, not just inside the prison walls, but in every part of their lives. It illustrates ways that our nation's most important social institutions, namely the criminal justice system, child welfare system, and education system, all have a hand in shaping the outcomes of children and families with an incarcerated parent.

This book follows families in Florida, Kentucky, and Mississippi who must navigate the different regulations, programs, and economic realities as they learn to cope (or not) with impossible situations. Some families are white, some black, and they come from varying economic backgrounds. Some have young children, others have adult children who have been affected by incarceration since childhood. Some prisoners who come from these families are convicted of serious, violent crimes while others are in for minor drug-related offenses and status crimes. Experiencing varying degrees of damage, each family is stuck in the shadow of America's criminal justice system.

In Miami, Florida, we bypass the drop-tops cruising down Ocean Drive and follow the palm trees to the prison where a twenty-year-old man is incarcerated, sentenced to life without parole (LWOP) before his daughter was born. His daughter, now ten, has become his reason to live, but she's struggling to understand what it means for her father to be gone.

In Louisville, Kentucky, we meet mothers fighting to overcome opioid addictions and regain custody of their children after incarceration. Serving time behind bars is especially consequential for mothers, as even a short stint in jail can jeopardize their parental rights. As a returning citizen, a mother learns what it means to be labeled a felon and how a drug conviction makes securing a job, renting a place to live, and regaining child custody especially hard. As the criminalization of addiction persists, the rate of incarcerated women has risen sharply. At 15 percent, Kentucky has the second highest parental incarceration rate in the country. Where are these children going when their mothers are locked up?

In Jackson, Mississippi, where the Confederate Battle Flag still blows in the wind, we meet a family dealing with decades of incarceration. A wife, still at her husband's side as he steels himself for his thirty-ninth year in prison, is also a mother raising sons in a country where she's seen repeated evidence that their lives matter the least. We meet her sons, who endure the impact of pervasive racism, structural inequality, an unforgiving parole board, and the threat of intergenerational incarceration.

CRIME AND THE NEED for safety is touted as a reason for increased incarceration, yet studies have found that increased incarceration is not making us safer and has little if any impact on crime. Since the 1990s, we have seen a drop in crime somewhere between 75 and 100 percent. This drop is due to our population getting older; increases in graduation rates, wages, employment, consumer confidence, law enforcement staff; and changes in policing strategies. In 2012, federal, state, and local expenditures totaled $80.7 billion a year on incarceration, without considering the economic and social costs to children, families, communities, and society. At every turn the prison industrial complex makes an enormous profit from mass incarceration, and prisons get a kickback from many of the contracts. Correctional phone companies, prison health-care companies, prison commissary suppliers, and the bail industry all exploit families of the incarcerated.[6]

In 1984, thirty-four thousand people were serving life sentences in American prisons, and that number had increased nearly fivefold, to 162,000, in 2016. One out of every nine people in prison is serving a life sentence, and one out of every twenty-eight prisoners are serving LWOP. LWOP is now known as "America's new death penalty." Although long prison terms have not been proven to increase public safety, we continue to use them, raising questions over our nation's ideas about correction, rehabilitation, and the lie of justice.[7]

Our current criminal justice system is not true to its name. It is seeking justice only for some. Ignoring racial bias and structural inequality in our criminal justice system means an entire segment of our population continues to be treated as disposable. And the policies, programs, and practices that impact the families of the incarcerated carry a cumulative social, emotional, and economic cost, not just for those families, but for all of us. It's not sufficient for those who are directly affected, their allies, and criminal justice reformers to be conscious and fight for an equitable system. All families, not just those affected, need to think about and reckon with how these systems impact society. The current system is not only broken, it's brutal to far too many families. These families are experiencing something that has become an all-too-common American experience. Too many of us have become comfortable with this reality. But in writing this book, my hope is that we won't look away. We'll get closer to humanity, and in turn, justice.

1

THE RED HAMMER
Mississippi

R uth Anderson's gray Nissan cruises along the highway. The rain falling from the gunmetal sky sounds like hurried knocks from a stranger seeking shelter. The windshield wipers push back slowly, never fully clearing the downpour. For a minute, she wishes she had driven her GMC Yukon truck instead. Ruth can barely see the signs ahead, but even if her lane weren't clear, she could make this drive wearing a blindfold. She's heading to meet her husband, William, for their weekly Saturday morning rendezvous. When the rain does beat down on the city like this, William suggests his wife stay home, and sometimes she heeds his concern.

The rain slows as she nears her exit to Pearl, Mississippi. The quiet gospel song playing on her radio resurfaces. She's just a few miles away. She passes sprawling, lush fields, rows of wet trees, and a few small houses. Once she sees the gun tower, it's time to hide her phone from view. Ruth makes a right into the lot and stops at the first security checkpoint, where a group of officers wearing green circle her car. She hands one officer her driver's license, then pops her trunk at another officer's prompting. He looks in the car—the back seat is clear—and then nods for her to proceed. She's cleared and pulls into the prison's parking lot. She parks near the gate, then removes her white Apple watch and gold hoop earrings. She leaves on her wedding ring, a gold ban dotted with diamonds—the only jewelry, aside from a religious medallion, visitors can wear inside the facility. She tucks her Dooney & Bourke purse in the trunk.

Ruth's face is bright and smooth, the color of peanut butter, and this week she's sporting a sable-brown, straight bob haircut. She doesn't like too much fuss. Her eyes are calm, alert even, despite just leaving a twelve-hour night shift in the psychiatric department of a local hospital. She's still wearing her navy blue scrubs and sneakers. The seasoned registered nurse isn't a stranger to long nights. "We didn't get no admissions last night," she offers. "But got a boy that wanted to fight a huge guy," she tells me. He was likely a schizophrenic who'd gone off his medication.

It's just after 9:30 a.m. "I'm later and later now," she says slowly. "Sometimes it'll be about ten." Mornings aren't her favorite and coming later means she avoids waiting in a long line with the throng of other visitors. She'll have just over two hours to spend with her husband. She jogs past the rows of barbed wire fence and the electric door, out of the rain. A few other latecomers join her. Some are carrying children in their arms, and they sprint inside. Others walk slowly with jackets sprawled over their heads and join the short line outside the pale-yellow entry. Ruth checks in, handing the guard her license and car keys, and receives a silver coin in exchange. She removes her shoes and walks through the metal detector and X-ray machine.

When she enters the visiting room, William is already sitting in their usual spot—the back corner against the wall. He always faces the door to keep an eye out for anything happening and to see her arrive. Each day before the sun has a chance to yawn awake, William is up. He's in his cell stirring his instant Folgers into a cup. He gets up by four o'clock every morning. He'll take a shower and get dressed, his clothes already laid out from the previous evening.

These days, an officer shortage means offenders don't have a set ride to the visiting room. They catch a ride wherever they can, sometimes it's on the canteen truck or the food truck, whichever is passing by. By 8:00 or 8:30 a.m., he's sitting patiently waiting for his wife.

William, who looks taller than his actual six feet, stands up before Ruth reaches the table. He grins like he alone knows the secret to maintaining a marriage for over forty years. He's still giddied at the sight of his ladylove. She approaches the table and he wraps her in his long arms, closing the one-foot gap between them. They share a familial embrace and brief kiss, the kind shared by a couple wed for decades, still crushing on each other, but with nothing to prove to onlookers.

His head is freshly shaven, his chestnut skin is alive against the bright white of his crisp button up. Green stripes march down his starched and creased white pants. His white Nikes look brand new, standing out from the black boots the other men are wearing. It's the one day to pull out all the stops. "It's fashion day," he declares seriously. "Don't want to look like no slouch. Got to represent."

WILLIAM IS ONE OF THE more than 2.2 million people confined in America's correctional facilities. Central Mississippi Correctional Facility, CMCF, has been his home for well over a decade. Like with thousands of families across the country, collect phone calls, pictures, and letters have been the fibers that have kept the Andersons connected. The moments when families get to touch, however, are the most coveted. Prison visitation varies from state to state and prison to prison. The warden is in charge of running the prison, and the one who approves the policies and procedures for their facility. But those practices must conform with the laws, rules, and standards of their state.

Typical visits, called contact visits, take place in designated areas with tables, chairs, and in some cases vending machines filled mostly with junk food and the occasional frozen food item. In some facilities, there are books to read and games to play. These visits take place under strict surveillance and allow extremely limited physical contact—usually just a brief hug and a kiss, lasting less than ten seconds, upon entry and exit.

The visit that William and Ruth are experiencing today is bare bones compared to what they once had. A few years ago, the Andersons had access to something else entirely: Mississippi's Extended Family Visitation program, widely known as the Family House, which started in 1974 and lasted nearly a half-century. It was a real-life dream. The program allowed unsupervised visits that lasted for three to five days and took place on the facility grounds, in small apartments. They also had conjugal visits where; as a married couple, they could spend one private hour together once a week. The visits were cut due to reported budget cuts and racist, classist ideas about families of the incarcerated. Prison officials in Mississippi didn't like the idea that they couldn't police the number of babies being conceived, arguing it was unfair for a child to be brought into existence to a single parent.[1]

Now, they're left with a four-hour slot once a week on Saturday, which is more than other prisoners are allowed. William is minimum custody and so receives more visits per month. For William, the visits remain the highlight of his week. "That's what you have to look forward to."

The worn beige walls are home to prison rules, notices, and a clock. Dozens of families, black and white, gather around white tables, sitting in blue or mauve chairs. At one table, a kid motions for his mom to open the clear plastic bag of food sitting at the center of the table. The hum of families catching up, the sound of soda cans popping, the ruffle of chip bags opening are thick in the air. Ruth and William are happy with the Styrofoam cups of water at their table. In the past, families visiting Mississippi prisons had their choice of purchases from vending machines: frozen burritos, chicken wings,

Lunchables for kids, and more. But now the only vending machine in this visiting room is for prison staff.

Now, Mississippi prisoners must use the commissary—a store inside the prison—to buy a $10 bag of food one week in advance of visitations. William says it comes with the same items every week: two sodas, cookies, popcorn, peanut butter crackers, potato chips, and mixed nuts. Content with their cups of water, William and Ruth are holding their silent protest of two. They talk about the high costs of the food inside prisons.

Many of the items sold in the commissary are more than four times the retail price outside prison because private companies set their own prices. Prices can fluctuate and vary from facility to facility as contracts are negotiated between corrections departments and their vendors. So, depending on the state and facility, some commissary items are priced the same as they are in the free world. They're what some would consider reasonable, but reasonable for whom? Paying $4 for a tube of anti-fungal cream, which isn't a luxury item but a medical treatment, is prohibitively expensive for many in prison. Incarcerated people can't afford to pay these *reasonable* prices on their own; even those who work in prison would have to save several days' pay to fork over $4. In 2016, people incarcerated in Massachusetts prisons purchased over 245,000 bars of soap, at a total cost of $215,057. Although the department's policy is to supply a free bar of soap weekly, each person spent an average of $22 for soap that year. When an incarcerated person has to buy items such as cough drops, eye drops, or an extra roll of toilet paper, the burden falls on their families to put money in their account. Nationally, families spend $1.6 billion annually on commissary items.[2]

"Between canteen, collect calls, and visiting, don't ask me how much I've spent," Ruth said. "I know it's enough to buy a car or a small house." William doesn't even want Ruth to buy him the Christmas box for the holiday; he thinks it's overpriced at $100. Instead, his friend, who is free but served decades with him in the MDOC (Mississippi Department of Corrections), is going to send it. Years ago, Ruth was able to purchase all of William's favorites and make a care package that she would then mail directly to the prison. She could shop at discount stores or buy in bulk to keep the price down. A jar of peanut butter, or a can of instant coffee or tuna, let William know that Ruth cared. These food items were also supplements to the unappealing, and often unhealthy, small portions he was served behind bars. Since then, however, Mississippi prisons prohibited families from sending care packages directly to their loved ones, and instead required them to buy care packages through a privatized service.

Prisons across the country have stopped accepting care packages directly from families, arguing that it's the best way to prevent drugs and weapons from entering facilities. More and more facilities have in turn privatized care packages, forcing families to purchase expensive, preapproved products through private vendors. Companies that sell care packages often combine multiple services, such as phone and commissary, into one contract with a corrections facility. In 2012, the Keefe Group, which is contracted with Mississippi facilities through its affiliate companies Keefe Commissary Network and Access Securepak, reported net sales of over $375 million from care package, commissary, and technology programs. In 2017, the New York State Department of Corrections piloted a program that used a secure vendor program for care packages, a practice they said was used in nearly thirty other states. After outrage from families and reform advocates, New York governor Andrew Cuomo instructed the department of corrections to "rescind its flawed policy."[3]

The cost is only part of the issue for the families. The Andersons feel it's too early in the morning for a bag of junk food. "We don't need that mess," Ruth says. Sitting tall in his chair, William leans back and grabs his kangaroo pouch of a tummy. "This is my only problem," he teases. "I know," Ruth shoots back. "That's diabetes and high blood pressure," she predicts. Ruth is right. Long-term health consequences can be a result of prison diets. Menu analysis at prisons across the country found incarcerated people were served diets too high in cholesterol, saturated fat, and sodium, and were too low in fiber—all factors linked to an increased risk of heart disease. Researchers have found that incarcerated people suffer disproportionately from hypertension, heart problems, and diabetes—all preventable with a healthy diet. This unhealthy diet reduces life expectancy by two years for every year of incarceration and is part of the reason why black men are less healthy than white men. And the habits of a prison diet are hard to break, even after release: The Whole Shabang chip that was once only sold in prisons, and has 90 percent of the daily recommended sodium, is now sold online by stores outside of prison because former prisoners missed them so much. A six-pack case of six-ounce bags sold directly from the Keefe Group costs $18.99, while the same size variety pack can be found on Amazon for $59.99.

Ruth stays in William's ear to make the best decisions he can with what's offered. That means staying away from chips, candy bars, and ramen; limiting canned meats; and avoiding some parts of his prison meal if it has too much salt. Ruth recognizes that her husband doesn't really have a choice and that poor eating is an unfortunate part of prison life. "You have to work on it," she tells him. William does have high blood pressure, but Ruth knows eating healthy behind bars is nearly impossible. "They don't have very much to choose from." She wants him to live long so they can restart their clock one day. William, the more lighthearted of the two, chuckles, then takes a sip of his water. When their three sons were young, the Andersons indulged in snacks because they were there for hours and the kids needed to eat. But those days are long gone. It's just her and William most Saturdays. Occasionally, she'll bring their grandchildren.

The conversation pivots toward William's new look. He's sporting a longer-than-usual goatee this week, and it's far more salt than pepper. "Uh-uh," Ruth says shaking her head with a smile.

She knows when her husband is trying to sneak a new look by her. This time he's giving away their age. "If you were home, I'd brush through it with Gray Away," she teases. William shakes his head, grabs his wife's hands in his, rubs it, and grins. He likes it and plans to keep the new look, but Ruth usually gets what she wants. The Andersons use the time alone to catch up, though much of it is spent talking about their three adult sons and six grandchildren. Two of their grandchildren wanted to come on the visit, but it meant Ruth would have to go forty minutes in the opposite direction to pick them up. It would have been too much of a strain for her this week.

Since 2004, Ruth's commute has been shorter because William put in a request to transfer and was moved fewer than twenty miles away from home, so it's just a thirty-minute drive. It's a relief from the earlier years when Ruth struggled to stitch together her separated clan; visits—no matter how far—were the seam.

William went to prison in 1981. Ruth was pregnant, and they had a nine-year-old son, Kevin. William was held at the Mississippi State Penitentiary in Parchman, located over 140 miles away from Ruth. Across the country, families of prisoners often make long treks for that fleeting visiting moment. The majority of people in state prisons are held over one hundred miles away from families (and five hundred miles for federal prisons). Most prisons aren't accessible by public transportation, thus limiting a family's ability to visit altogether.

Ruth found a few options that helped her make the commute in the early days. She used a bus service that picked up riders at a mall a short distance from her home. She remembers paying the driver about $25 to join the nearly thirty other passengers. Before the sun came up, she boarded the bus, Kevin by her side, and the baby, Robert, in her arms. The bus chugged out of the city onto the highway, past several towns and through a countryside dotted with catfish farms, cotton fields, and cow pastures. Sometimes the bus took far longer than the expected two-and-a-half hours. But Ruth bonded with other families during the ride or over a breakfast stop at a Mc-Donald's. The return trips were the longest. Sitting in traffic, many families asleep, Ruth watched day ease into night.

"I met so many people on that bus," she reflects. Over the years, she watched families come and go as their loved ones got released from prison. Eventually, she met a new set of people and saw the same thing happen. After a few years, she says, the bus service stopped and she joined a community shared-ride service. A man named Andrew drove a van and picked everyone up at their homes. He started out around four o'clock in the morning, which was earlier than the bus. Ruth always hoped she'd be the last pickup, so she could sleep in a little. The bus and van, if they could afford it, were rides that families could rely on. They paid, boarded, and relaxed until they arrived.

Ruth speaks slowly and deliberately, making each word feel pertinent. "I was younger and all that time . . ." she says, trailing off, captive in her own thoughts. "I didn't know these many years was gonna pass 'cause it was just starting out. I could take it better," she remembers. Ask Ruth how she's survived and she'll point to God, to her faith, to the love she and William share, and most important, to her family.

NEITHER WILLIAM NOR RUTH could have envisioned their current life when they met as teenagers at a movie theater in 1970. William was sixteen, Ruth was fourteen. "I just happen to see her sitting over there by herself," William recalls blissfully. He was there with a few friends, a weekend tradition. He can't remember the movie. "We didn't go there for the movies," he jokes. "We were going to *try* to meet girls." It didn't always work out in their favor, he admits. Ruth was sitting by herself, her slanted eyes fixed on the big screen, her copper-toned skin bright under the screen's flashes, her billowing red Afro the show stopper. William had to say something. Ruth appeared to be alone at the movie theater, but her mother always made her older brother go with her. Lucky for William, he was somewhere else in the theater, so he made his move. He approached the girl with the red hair and asked if he could sit down. She agreed.

Like most lovers whose story began long ago, William tries to say, "We started from there," and end the retelling of their love story there, implying that the rest of how they became a couple is history and the details didn't matter. But it wasn't that easy. Ruth and William sat and talked for a while at the theater and he scored her number, or so he thought. When William got home the night they met, he unfolded the number from the girl now coined the Red Hammer. He dialed the number and got a disconnection signal. "She gave me the wrong phone number," he recalls, shock still lingering in his voice. "She wrote the right phone number down, then she scratched through it, and gave me a wrong number." Holding the piece of paper up to the light, then peering at it from different angles, he was able to see the number she'd scratched out. He called it, and it was the right one.

Ruth's mouth fell open when she heard his voice on the other end of the phone. "I thought I had dogged him," she tells me playfully. "Then he all of a sudden called me and I'm like, how did you figure that out?" At the time, Ruth was seeing another boy and she wasn't buying someone else claiming to be moved by her. "Nah, I don't really know about him," she recalls thinking back then. "Naw, I don't want him to have my phone number," she concluded. She realized he might see her at the theater again, as it was the only place to catch a movie in Jackson, but she took the chance of giving him the wrong number anyway. "I just didn't take him serious. Really, I was like, I'm finna get rid of him," she says laughing. She doesn't laugh easily, but when she does, it's authentic, traveling from her stomach, and it's usually about a memory of her and William.

But back then there was no *je ne sais quoi.* "It wasn't like instant, first sight. He grew on me," she remembers. "For real." Ruth was smart, and a popular majorette. "She had all them lil boys runnin' behind her," William recalls. "I had stiff competition." During their conversation, Ruth mentioned she was going to The Jackson 5 concert the next day. William thought it was the perfect opportunity to see her again. "It was something about her and I wanted to find her," he recalls. He and a few friends snuck in the back door of the concert and William started on his mission to find the Red Hammer. "I looked for her. I couldn't find her in no coliseum with all them people," he says, bemused at his youthful desire. "From then on, it was just like he was stalking me," Ruth adds, laughing. "A coliseum?" she asks rhetorically, baffled at William thinking he could find her in a stadium that held ten thousand people. He didn't find her that day.

"I tell her right today, 'Well, you know I fell in love with you the first day.' She don't believe it, but I'm telling her the truth," he insists. Ask him how he knew it was love at first sight and uncertainty dances in his voice. "I don't know. It was just *something* about *her.*"

That *something* fueled his pursuit of Ruth. There was also a small detail about the movie theater meeting that Ruth had first left out. "I did kiss him," she admits with a giggle. "So I guess he thought I was gonna be his girlfriend."

Ruth tells William it was the kiss that put a spell on him that day. He disagrees, saying a man gets one chance to meet the right woman, and when he does, he better be prepared to do everything in his power to get her.

He did.

William took Ruth to the movies, out to eat, and on picnics by the reservoir. They shared secrets, went to sports matches, cut class, and then made up the missed homework together. Ruth began taking his romantic interest seriously.

Soon they were inseparable. "I said, well, he real serious about it, maybe I have to go with this boy," Ruth said matter-of-factly. William hitchhiked and sometimes walked the nearly three miles to Ruth's house. "William hung on to me like glue and I said, well maybe this is the one," she says. "I'm just blessed I won out," William concludes.

They didn't attend the same school or live in the same neighborhood. Ruth's family was middle class. She lived in a new house in a neighborhood called Georgetown with her mother, siblings, and father, who was a disabled veteran and cab owner. Her neighborhood was home to the same teachers who taught her in school, and to other black working professionals.

William was an only child and lived with his mother, who worked in a nursing home. Their apartment was in West Jackson near the historically black Jackson State College (now Jackson State University) and steps away from the local NAACP office. His parents separated before he was born, but he saw his dad often. "He still used to come over. My momma let him in, they spent the night. I used to go over to his house sometime. They had that type of relationship."

Ruth couldn't have company at her house, so William snuck into the side entrance. He did this for months. Soon, his mother went with him to a jewelry store. "I had bought her a lil ole cheap promise ring. You couldn't even see the diamonds in it," he says chuckling. "You would call it a bubble gum ring nowadays," he admits. "Back then it was *something*." It was enough for Ruth.

William's mother died in early 1971, which brought the couple together even closer. Soon the teenagers found themselves sitting on a curb talking about getting married. Later, William asked Ruth's mother for permission to marry her daughter. "I don't know about that," Ruth recalls her mom saying. "You have to ask her daddy." William was terrified of Ruth's father, who was stern and known to give scorching lectures. He would repeat himself over and over, Ruth remembers. It started with, "Look here boy, marriage is a huge responsibility. . . . Boy, you know this is a big responsibility. It's a big responsibility." William was trembling. The preaching continued for a while. "It's a big responsibility, you ready for that?" William was nervous, but he said, "Yes sir, I know it." Ruth remembers peeking from another room at a nervous William sitting at the table with her father. She burst into laughter at the memory.

In July 1972, still in high school, when he was eighteen and she was sixteen, they got married. They had a rustic, outdoor ceremony in a neighbor's backyard near Ruth's home. His mother had left him the apartment and her car, which was paid off, and he was receiving a Social Security check, which helped him provide a life for his bride. As a new husband, he also began working. He found a job on the night shift at a meat packing house, where he loaded trucks until the early morning hours. These hours resulted in him dozing off during class. He didn't finish his last year of high school.

Ruth was completing her senior year when she got pregnant. They welcomed their first son, Kevin, in 1973. The young couple was just living, trying to be happy, and make it in the South. "Basically, trying to keep our lil heads above the water," William recalled. William continued working. After they had Kevin, Ruth started working at Shoney's, a drive-in restaurant. She worked the cash register and bussed tables, and when it was her time to clean the parking lot, William came to help her. When they weren't working, they had family outings: trips to the reservoir, movies, the countryside, or the zoo. They took a drive to Vicksburg to look at the statues. They had friends over for BBQs and went to concerts when they could.

William continued working at the packing house at night and worked at a gas company during the day, until he got fired from his night job. One day, a white associate who worked in the receiving side of the warehouse, scanning packages, referred to him as *boy*. William got upset, shot a few choice words at the man, and was fired. "It just didn't sit well with me," William reflected. The man was in his fifties and William was the youngest male there. He felt like he was doing hard physical labor and wanted the same respect as his colleagues. Ruth's mother lectured him when she found out, reminding him you can't leave a job because someone calls you a name. It was a bad time to lose a job—their apartment had just burned down and he had recently purchased a new car that he had to make payments on.

William had reason to attach meaning to the incident. Living in Jackson was a constant show of volatile race relations. He'd seen racism, discrimination, and flat out disregard for black bodies. He lived within walking distance of Jackson State College, and his mother shoved him under the bed at the tattering of gunshots when police open fired on the campus. Lynch Street, a major street that bisected the campus and linked West Jackson to downtown, was said to be the site of confrontation between black and white residents. Black students said they were harassed by white motorists who drove through the campus yelling racial slurs from their windows. On May 14, 1970, black students reportedly responded to the harassment of the white motorists by throwing rocks at their cars, according to reports.

Tensions escalated after a false rumor spread of the murder of Charles Evers, a local politician, civil rights leader, and the brother of slain activist Medgar Evers. A non-Jackson student set fire to a dumpster. When firemen arrived, they called for police backup to control the crowd that started gathering. When police arrived, the crowd reportedly threw rocks, bottles, and bricks at the officers. Police advanced and opened fire for thirty seconds, letting out 150 rounds into Alexander Hall, a women's dormitory. Two young black men were killed and twelve others were injured. Officers claimed that there was a sniper in the dorm, but investigators found insufficient evidence of that claim.

William went to school with the brother of one of the slain men and was reminded that black lives weren't valued by all. William's mother was scared after that. She wouldn't let him out of her sight. National Guard tanks and soldiers stood ready in his neighborhood, and a curfew was enforced.

William knew that racism was real, and he tried to push back when he felt it. Losing his night job was collateral for standing up for what he believed. He stayed on at the day job and Ruth also continued working. She eventually got a better job at a local blood bank. But she wanted to eventually earn more, so she decided to stop working to attend a one-year program to become a licensed practical nurse, LPN. William supported them while she attended classes. Ruth got pregnant with Robert in 1981. So, now, Ruth was in school, the couple had a son, and they had a baby on the way. William struggled to support his family.

THAT LIFE FEELS SO far in the past now. Today Ruth tries to accept the life they will share until William is released. As their visit comes to an end, Ruth shrinks behind William's body and says goodbye. They wait until the last few minutes, then William walks away slowly, his right knee still bothering him. He also has two knots on the calf of his leg. He needs an MRI, an impossible ask in prison, where it's common for medical complaints to be ignored and go untreated, and for patients to receive shoddy treatment. William has been having problems with his knee for years. In 2010, after a year of waiting, he had a procedure to repair his left knee. Still, he's been having problems with his right knee for several years. Most recently he received steroid shots for the pain. Most prisons require offenders to pay co-pays to see the doctor. Mississippi prisoners are charged a $6 co-pay per doctor visit, unless a waiver is made for a chronic issue, mental health treatment, or a "true emergency," and they must make a separate visit for each issue. These costs are often paid by the family.

Claims of medical neglect are common in prisons across the country. Corizon Health, one of the country's largest for-profit prison health-care firms, treats more than three hundred thousand prisoners nationwide, earning about $1.4 billion in annual revenue. It has been the subject of several investigations, and in 2013 the *Florida Bulldog* reported that the company had been sued 660 times in the preceding five years for malpractice.[4]

Finally, William joins the line of other prisoners waiting to exit. Some men wear shirts with "convict" stamped on the back, while others read "offender." Ruth stands in a separate long line of visitors. Directly in front of her is an older white man with gray hair. He's holding a small boy with a head of blonde curls. The boy raises his head from the man's shoulder and looks across the room at his dad. Waving, he shouts, "Daddy, Daddy!" His father, a young man with a baby face and straight black hair, joins his index fingers and thumbs and places them around his eyes to form pretend binoculars. He's letting his son know that he can see him from across the room.

Ruth's line starts to move. She returns the silver coin and gets her car keys from the guard. As she drives out of the parking lot, she joins a line of cars. When you leave you have to open the trunk again "to see if you brought 'em with you," Ruth shares. "I would like that, so I can sleep on Saturdays when I work. I wouldn't have to go nowhere." The rain has slowed; just a few sprinkles dot her windshield now. She eases on the highway and heads home. She'll do all this over again next Saturday.

The Anderson family was part of the first wave of families fractured by mass incarceration, and they've watched the prison system change over the years. They have no idea when, or if, William is ever coming home. He is due to go before the parole board in the summer of 2020. Now, after so many years, even his teenage grandchildren need answers. "What did Grandpa do?" Whenever they ask, Ruth replies, "They say he killed a white man."

2

IN THAT PLACE

Florida

Niyah stands over the stove, shaking taco seasoning onto the browning ground beef. Eager for another step, she calls out to her paternal grandmother, Cynthia Johnson. "Can I add water?" No, Cynthia replies from the living room. "The beef will make its own juice," she informs the ten-year-old girl. Niyah moves on to the next task. Her small, untrained hand tries to steady the head of iceberg lettuce. After a few tries, she gets it, forcing the trimming knife down, cutting wedges. Her eyes widen with pride. She smiles to herself. Her mother, Ayana, doesn't allow her to use a knife at home, or cook. Cynthia sits down at the dining room table to dice the tomatoes, pausing only to check in on her granddaughter. That Sunday evening Niyah, an only child, is making her cooking debut. Later, Ayana wouldn't take the news seriously when she learned her daughter had made a meal. "So now she's gonna come home thinking she knows how to cook," she says. Ayana doesn't have plans to grant her daughter stove access just yet.

Niyah remains in the kitchen, excitedly stirring the meat as if it were a sauce. Whenever she hears her grandmother cough, she goes

to check on her. Cynthia has a defibrillator and chronic obstruct-
ive pulmonary disease (COPD), an inflammatory lung disease that
makes it hard for her to breathe sometimes. Cynthia has spent the
entire day running around with Niyah and another small child she
was babysitting. Between laughing and joking or fussing at them, by
evening she has exhausted her lungs. She takes a break from chopping and sits back on the couch. Now that Niyah is older she can
help her grandmother more.

Once the meat is cooked, Niyah takes a spoonful to her grandmother in the living room. Cynthia chews it, then closes her eyes to
think of what is missing. After the taste test, Cynthia goes to the
kitchen, grabs the seasoning from the cabinet, and shakes it on the
ground beef, while Niyah gives it a stir. Without a second tasting,
Cynthia says, "Now *that's* it, baby!" Cynthia takes the box of soft-
shell tortillas and makes three open-faced tacos. A little mountain of
meat, lettuce, tomatoes, and cheese neatly sits at the center of each.
She heads to the living room, sits on the worn faux suede couch,
places her plate on her lap, and says her grace. She continues watching a movie from her phone, which is propped up on a wooden
barstool. Niyah makes her tacos, piling on toppings until they spill
over when she tries to fold them. She sits at the dining room table
and plays a game on her iPod.

Cynthia has played a central role in raising Niyah from the beginning. Randall, Niyah's father, is Cynthia's youngest son. He
went to prison before Niyah was born. She watched her for long
stretches when she was a baby, and she kept her many summers
through the years. They still spend a lot of time together, and it's less
of a strain on Cynthia now because Niyah is mostly self-sufficient.
They watch movies with Niyah cuddled underneath her grandma,
or they take trips to Overtown, a neighborhood of Miami where
Niyah's grandmother and father grew up, to take a dip in the public
pool. Most times Niyah shares random facts with her grandmother:
something she saw on the news, read in a book, or learned in class.

They can range from why the rapper Childish Gambino featured a man shooting up a church choir in his music video, "This Is America," or how many bites one must take to properly chew their food. "She loves to talk," Cynthia says, her eyes widening. "Talk, talk, talk." Niyah has a lot of energy and will talk about most things as long as she has an audience. "I told her; she needs to do more listening than talking. That's a talking child," Cynthia says, laughing. "I told her, you learn from listening. She so advanced, I tell her, she out of line." Although the girl's precociousness can overwhelm Cynthia, she raves to her friends about Niyah skipping a grade and earning an academic scholarship to a private school.

Cynthia and Niyah make it an early night so that they're prepared for their early morning. They're going to see Niyah's father in prison. He is serving time for a first-degree murder conviction. The duo participates in quarterly prison visits with a program called Children of Inmates (COI), which was started with a planning grant in 2005 to provide services to address the unmet needs of children of incarcerated parents. It is similar to programs in New York and California. Niyah has visited her father through the program consistently for a little over eight years.

COI also makes it easier for Cynthia to see her son. She worked a host of jobs in her youth, but due to serious health problems she no longer works, so she relies on Social Security Disability Insurance (SSDI). She doesn't have a car, which makes getting to the prison to see Randall difficult. COI takes hundreds of children and their caregivers living in Miami, Jacksonville, Tampa, and other parts of Florida to more than a dozen correctional institutions quarterly. In addition to these Bonding Visits, the organization connects children of incarcerated parents with wraparound services—including support groups and crisis prevention—that aim to ease the burden of having a parent in prison.

Beginning in 2005, COI was initially funded by the Children's Trust of Miami-Dade County to lead a Service Partnership of twelve community agencies. The organization has received contracts and grants, totaling over $2 million per year, to support services for two thousand incarcerated parents and their families. Their funding sources span the board and come from funding provisos from the State of Florida through the Florida Department of Corrections, the Florida Department of Children and Families, the US Department of Justice Office of Juvenile Justice, Palm Beach County Youth Services, and Miami-Dade County.[1]

In 2016, Niyah was one of more than three hundred thousand children in Florida who have experienced parental incarceration. In 2015, 34.4 percent of Florida's 99,485 prisoners reported having 64,848 minor children. Fathers, like Randall, accounted for 89 percent of the parents. Only 15.8 percent of those prisoners reported that their children lived in the same county or a county close to the facility they were held in. This severely limits the opportunities for in-person visits.[2]

Soon, even more incarcerated parents in the state could be held farther away from their children. In 2018, the Florida Department of Corrections proposed a new policy that would prevent prisoners from being housed in prisons within their home county. Prison officials argue that this policy prevents the prisoner from becoming friendly with staff, which they say creates security risks. Moreover, they argue that creating physical distance between prisoners and potential visitors reduces the likelihood of contraband (drugs, cell phones, weapons, and so forth) entering the facilities.[3]

The influx of drugs, specifically the synthetic marijuana known as K2, into Florida prisons has proven deadly. But creating even more barriers between the incarcerated and their families is not the solution. Placing insurmountable distance between prisoners and their families isn't going to lower the risks of drug abuse in prison and might even have the opposite effect. Some studies have shown that prisoners fare better when they have access to their families. Visitation has been proven to reduce recidivism and to facilitate successful

reentry upon release; and when prisoners are moved farther away
from their home, visitation decreases.[4]

IT IS 7:15 A.M. and Cynthia and Niyah are barely awake. They
fumble around the apartment grabbing the last of their things for
the trip. A COI volunteer, who has been waiting outside for over
ten minutes, is starting to worry that they aren't coming. They finally emerge, hurrying to the car. The volunteer drives them to the
St. James A.M.E. Church in Liberty City, Miami, which is not far
from Cynthia's home. At the church they have a warm breakfast.
Kids, volunteers, and employees hug, talk, and joke with one another. Everyone looks forward to the visits, even if it does mean they
have to get up early in the morning. Cynthia and Niyah will sit for
at least another two hours before it's time for the buses to depart. It
is no small task for the organization to ensure that all families are
picked up from different points throughout the city. Cynthia sips on
her coffee and tries to wake up fully.

On the bus, most of the kids are mellow. Only a few are energetic so early in the morning. Niyah sits next to her grandma, and
as usual her oversized Beats headphones hide her ears. Soon she will
be asleep. About an hour cruises by, and then the buses pull into the
prison parking lot. The families gather at the picnic tables in front of
the facility entrance and wait for their surnames to be called. Small
children are restless, and they run into the open green grass until
guards tell their parents it is not allowed. The families are eager to
enter, with some prematurely standing in line. They chat among
themselves or complain about the wait. Though the program has
existed for over a decade, getting into prisons still comes with com-
plications. One time the guards couldn't find the written approval
for COI to bring in soil for the activity of the day. In celebration of
Earth Day, the families were to pot tomato plants that the children
would take home and watch grow. Most times it's because a few
visitors are wearing clothing that is prohibited. Visitors must follow

the institution's dress code. No camouflage or clothing with metal for the men. For girls and women, the list is longer. No spandex, leggings, tube tops, tank tops, fishnets, sheer or see-through clothing, open-toed shoes, skirts or shorts more than three inches above the knee—nothing that can be perceived as explicit. Sometimes it's the new visitors who do not listen to COI's warning about proper attire, other times a visitor might be wearing something they have worn to the prison before, only to get stopped this time. Approval remains at the discretion of the corrections officer, meaning that what might have been allowed on one visit by a staff member could be restricted by a different one. COI staff and volunteers often bring extra clothing in case families need to change.

Cynthia and Niyah don't expect to have any issues with what they are wearing. They wait in line, happy they are about to see Randall. At one point in time, they had to get up at 4:00 a.m. for a long bus ride across the state. The Dade Correctional Institution is the closest Randall has ever been to home, and they hope it stays this way. When Randall first went to prison nearly a decade ago, he started out at Desoto Correctional Institution, in Arcadia, Florida, nearly two hundred miles away from home. Then, after getting an institutional adjustment transfer, which happens when the facility wants to shake up the prison population, he was transferred to Okeechobee Correctional Institution in Okeechobee, Florida, which was a tad closer at 150 miles away from his daughter. Then, because he had stayed out of trouble for several years, he received a Good Adjustment Transfer, a reward for good behavior that granted him a transfer closer to home. Now, the current commute is fifty miles, just under an hour drive. Wherever he was housed in Florida, however, Niyah was still able to see him through COI's Bonding Visits.

Finally, Cynthia and Niyah are next in line. Niyah is calm, walking barefoot through the metal detectors with familiarity. Then, Cynthia and Niyah enter a small room with white walls, a blue door, and sheets of paper covering the window that separates them from the families who have been through security and are already in their visits in the next room. A black female corrections officer, who wore white gloves, prepared to pat them down. "Turn to the left, take your bra, pinch it," she directed Cynthia. Decades ago, in most prisons underwire bras were not allowed; all female visitors had to wear a sports bra whether it was supportive or not. Here at this facility, female visitors can now wear an underwire bra if they submit to an extra search. Even today, many prisons still do not allow female visitors to wear underwire bras, and they don't offer the extra search as an option. "Hands out toward the wall," she says as she waves a black, Garrett brand handheld metal detector over Cynthia's body. When it is Niyah's turn, she giggles as the guard passes her hand up her legs and arms. She's ticklish and can't keep from laughing. Her straight, white teeth are a striking contrast to her black skin, and her braids move along with her as her body shakes with laughter. On some visits she encounters a guard who is familiar with how ticklish she is, so the guard will *search* her until she is on the floor, buckled in laughter.

Niyah doesn't associate the searches with surrendering her freedom in exchange for seeing her dad. These Bonding Visits have helped ensure that Niyah doesn't feel the real restrictive nature of visiting her father in prison. They are nothing like the visits that hundreds of thousands of other children across the country experience. Niyah has never experienced a prison guard's watchful gaze following her as she moves around on her father's lap. Her mother and her grandmother have never been told that they're too close to Randall.

The Bonding Visits last from three to four hours and provide a different kind of access for children and their incarcerated parents. Unlike visitation in regular correctional settings, here these children are able to touch, hug, and be held by their incarcerated parent without consequence. They receive new toys, have scheduled learning and bonding activities, can play games, and are served a warm catered family meal with dessert.

When the children enter the visiting room, they see several long, adjoining tables topped with toys and games that COI staff and volunteers have brought from their massive arsenal. Staff believe that allowing the children to select a toy or game of their choice gives the parents insight into their child's interests. The last time Niyah went to visit her father, she picked the game Jenga. This visit, her father has already picked something for her: Scrabble and a three-in-one game of chess, checkers, and tic-tac-toe.

Cynthia and Niyah meet him at the table and embrace. They hug and chat among themselves for a few minutes before sitting down. Randall has dark skin and a slight build and stands five foot ten. The thirty-one-year-old sports a goatee and mustache. The crown of his head is slightly balding. He has a small white towel in his right back pocket. He wears a blue chambray top and bottom. He's written his nickname, Box, with a blue marker on the white square nametag on his shirt. His serious demeanor melts when he sees his daughter, his cheeks lifting, his white teeth revealed.

The visiting room walls are vibrant with prisoner-painted murals. The space provides an intentional escape for children and adults alike. The children's corner has a scene out of Walt Disney, full of princesses and princes. On another wall, there is a replica of the Mount Rushmore National Memorial sculpture, with precise depictions of former US presidents George Washington, Thomas Jefferson, Theodore Roosevelt, and Abraham Lincoln. Elsewhere in the room are images of Rosa Parks, Martin Luther King Jr., former president Barack Obama, and the Statue of Liberty.

At the table, Randall has already opened the Scrabble board. He and Niyah sit side by side. When he explains that she can make up a word, Niyah, already suspicious, turns toward her grandmother for confirmation. Her father continues explaining the rules. Niyah twirls her braids in her hand as she listens. She leans into the table; her green school uniform sweater hangs off her shoulder. Soon they will be playing an intense game of Scrabble, a father challenging and building his daughter's vocabulary. Niyah's eyes are fixed on the board, but she is noticeably stiff as she tries to focus to impress her dad. She tries to make a word and Randall reminds her, "It's my go. You just went." Cynthia chimes in. "She's anxious."

The last visit, three months ago, was all fun and games. Jenga, a game of physical skill, and Uno, the kids' card game, reigned. It was Randall, Niyah, and his sister April. Whenever Niyah removed a wooden block, her dad followed, pushing the wooden blocks back together to fix the unstable structure or giving her tips on where to pull the next block to prevent the tower from falling. After making it to the next round, Niyah rewarded herself by eating a vanilla Grandma's cookie she got from the vending machine. For lunch, they had BBQ chicken, rice, and veggies. Watermelon was a healthy dessert. Randall has told Niyah how awful the food is inside the prison, so she often gives her dad food from her plate. She can always have a good meal at home, but she knows that he can't.

The visit on this summer day is more about developing her skills. Once they have had enough of Scrabble, Randall pulls out the chess pieces. "Oh man, you're gonna make her play that?" Cynthia asks. He tells his mom and daughter that checkers and tic-tac-toe are too easy. Randall is always looking for something to stimulate him while in prison, and his daughter is always ready to be challenged herself. Niyah, again, leans forward in her chair, ready to listen to her dad.

Randall is fiercely curious about child development and tries to nurture Niyah's talent. When she was an infant, he asked COI staff for literature on infant brain development. Niyah was born prematurely at six months. She was one pound, one ounce and doctors didn't expect her to survive. If she did, they said, she would have severe learning disabilities and be visually impaired. She wasn't. Instead she's seen as gifted in the eyes of the many adults who engage her, including her teachers at school.

Randall's question about brain development helped motivate COI to establish a program called Babies N' Brains, a nine-week course that teaches prisoners about infant brain development and child wellness. The program offers benefits to more than parents in prison; it offers comprehensive support services for their children through age five, conducts family home safety and wellness checks, creates individualized case plans, and enrolls the kids in health insurance plans. At the time, the program had seen three infants of parents in their COI program die from preventable causes within six months of one another, which encouraged them to start the Babies N' Brains program to teach parents about their infants' development.[5]

Emerging research had studied the importance of the first three years of a child's life, during which 80 percent of the brain is developed. As such, the first half of the course teaches the parents the theory of brain development, and the second half is an applied learning laboratory in which COI brings the children and incarcerated parents together for a visit. These visits allow the incarcerated parents to organically interact with their kids and apply what they learned in the class. The visiting room is outfitted with baby mats, developmental toys, and a puppet theater. COI staff observe the interaction and then take that information to work with the incarcerated parents to help them improve on any parenting weaknesses they might display.

As a two-year-old, Niyah started saying she wanted to be a doctor. The desire grew from the mornings she sat in front of the TV watching the Disney show *Doc McStuffins*. The show's protagonist, Dottie, is a black preschooler who plays doctor in her playhouse clinic. As Dottie places her stethoscope on her toys, dolls, and stuffed animals, they come to life and she can communicate with them. Dottie's mother is a real doctor on the show.

Ayana, Niyah's mother, started nurturing her talent early. She enrolled Niyah in a private preschool. It wasn't until several people continuously questioned her about paying for private school that she even considered public school for Niyah. They argued that public school was just as good and, what's more, it was free. People thought it was financially unsound for a single mother to pay for school when her child was so young. So when the time came for Niyah to go to kindergarten, Ayana enrolled her in a public school. Ayana didn't like it.

Soon, Niyah's teacher began reporting her in-class behavior. "The kindergarten teacher was harassing me every day, saying, 'You know, Niyah does her work and starts drawing,'" Ayana recalls. She would tell the teacher, "Okay. Well, she's bored. Can you give her more work?" The teacher refused, saying she had premade study plans that were set for all students. Ayana began sending Niyah to school with a workbook to keep her occupied when she finished her assigned class work. By the second quarter, someone from the school's administration called Ayana in and asked if they could place Niyah in the first grade class next door. She agreed, and Niyah moved to the first grade class. The new class was more on par with her learning ability. Afterward she earned a scholarship to attend a private school to start second grade.

SEEING HIS DAUGHTER ONLY four times a year is challenging for Randall. As each visit approaches, he's "excited" but admits, "It feels like business sometimes. I don't get to probe into her personality." In one visit he's tasked with covering a lot of ground. "I want to show her I love her, maybe teach her some lessons. I have to encourage her. I have to reprimand her. I try to fill so many things in one visit." Because Niyah is advanced in many areas, it has led her to think she knows more than she actually does, her father says. Once he was reviewing math problems with her, which got a little complicated. When he tried to break down the mathematical formula to one of the problems, she rejected it, but without sound reason. "She believes in her own smartness," he says. "It might be hard to change her mind, even when she's wrong."

In the end, he thinks, she enjoys the back and forth dynamic he permits. "No one else allows her to express herself in that kind of way," he says. "They always like, 'shut up' and 'don't talk back.'" Her mother doesn't offer her the same latitude. When Niyah starts asking too many questions, she's met with her mother's, "Because I said so." Her father agrees that she can be hardheaded. "She don't know when to listen sometimes." But he wants to allow her the flexibility to think and challenge him. Making sure she doesn't go overboard is a juggling act. "Sometimes I be conscious of risking making her mad during a visit," he says. "It's so little time."

Randall and Niyah have developed a close relationship despite his incarceration. He is sentenced to life without the possibility of parole (LWOP). Prisoners sentenced to LWOP remain in prison for the rest of their lives. His relationship with Niyah has thrived in part thanks to the cell phone he's managed to get behind the walls. He went in when he was twenty years old and has been in prison his daughter's entire life. Niyah doesn't know her father's crime or sentence. She just believes he's coming home "soon."

THE FATHER AND DAUGHTER chess match is interrupted by count time. Prisoners are counted multiple times a day, every day, to ensure no one has escaped. On this day, the men line up in the back of the visiting room and each loudly calls off a number in the suddenly quiet room. Some have their hands crossed along their chests, others sip their coffee, a few wave at their kids still sitting at the table playing games. Once count is cleared, they're back to visiting.

Niyah, her dad, and her grandmother get in the line to take Polaroid photos, which cost $2 each, that they'll get to keep. The father and daughter momentarily escape their surroundings for the photo. The background, framed to exclude the visiting room, is a mural of a beach: green palm trees under a bright sun, birds in flight, a multicolored blanket on the sand for parents, a sand castle next to a kid's pail and shovel. The mural is next to a blue door with a small window to the outside world.

The trio negotiates who will take which picture home. Soon, a voice announces, "We're about to do the hard part. The 'see you later' part." The room erupts into simultaneous sighs. They have about ten minutes left to visit. The families don't want to part, and they talk loudly about how quickly the time has gone. A mother rubs her son's back; a little girl says "Bye, Daddy," walks away, but then runs back for another hug; one dad gives his teenage son a pep talk; one husband pulls his teary-eyed wife in for an extended embrace; a large family forms a prayer circle and bows their heads.

Randall picks Niyah up, hugs and kisses her. When he puts her back down, she knows the affection isn't over. He tickles her, her deep-set eyes close, and laughter ensues. Soon, as the final moment arrives, Randall says, "Give Daddy a hug." At this point, Niyah is still afraid he will tickle her again, and she moves in for a hug with her underarms pinched tight against her sides.

ONCE THE FAMILIES LEAVE, the room is quiet. The men lean their heads down over a sheet of paper as if taking a test; they are summarizing their visit for COI staff. One man tells a staff member that he learned about his son's fifth grade chess tournament, another man says he played Uno with his grandson, who proclaimed he was his hero. The visits "make us feel real good," says another man. "When we step out the door, we have to hold it all in." COI staff remind the men to write to their children.

While the men are reflecting on their visits, the kids are trying to wipe away any possible sadness. Instead of going straight home, the program takes the kids to a bowling alley, a jumping gym, or a skating rink as a way to ease their anxieties from separating again from their incarcerated parents. Throughout the trip, counselors are around to help the children work through any emotional difficulties that arise.

Niyah still holds on to a story her parents told her when she was younger—that her father was away at school. Today, she knows he's not in school, and anytime she hears people stereotype prisoners she defends those who are locked up. But she still avoids saying the word "jail" or "prison," and instead uses the phrases "in there" or "in that place." She doesn't talk explicitly about where her dad is. Even when speaking to her mother, she simply says, "I'm going to see my dad" or "My dad is going to call my cell phone."

Randall explains how he thinks she's processing the knowledge. "She knows where she's going. But she has kinda dealt with it in her mind, the way we have dealt with it, by saying that I'm in school. So she's at a point now where she knows she's supposed to say 'school,'" Randall admits. The explanation isn't just for the outside world. "Not even for the public, for private too. Like, it's a way of not dealing with that reality so much. We're not really dealing with it in its nature."

Niyah takes aim and rolls the bowling ball down the aisle. She doesn't feel sad, exactly. Unlike other kids, she knows she can call, text, or video chat with her father anytime she needs him.

3

WHAT ADDICTION
LOOKS LIKE
Kentucky

L atonya McNeal sits behind the desk and shuffles through piles of papers while she simultaneously fields requests from different women. Some want to buy a half-priced bus ticket, a few need to have a private conversation with her, others just want to say "hi." One woman needs a visitor's pass to attend Happy Hour, a twelve-step meeting that will start in fifteen minutes. "Are you in compliance?" Latonya asks. The woman is, so she approves the pass.

Latonya's brown face is makeup-free, her dark hair in a straight bob that falls just past her shoulders. She is wearing a matching dark purple top and bottom, and a thin gold chain with a cross pendant. She walks from behind the desk, her wide brown eyes peering out over the dozen or so women in nonmedical detox. The detox requires pure abstinence, so the women have to let the drugs go out of their systems and feel the symptoms of withdrawal. There is nothing to stave off sickness.

Some women are asleep, wrapped in blankets in their twin-size beds; one is responsible for the sound of gentle snoring. One woman carries dishes and puts them in a cabinet near the kitchen. One can be heard vomiting in the restroom. Others mill about, while some sit talking to each other. Posters and drawings on the wall send the women messages. One, with a fist revealing a nail polished thumb, reads "Fight Like A Girl"; another has a drawing of a woman with wings and reads, "Let That Shit Go." In the back corner, there is a soda machine, a snack vending machine, and a closet full of bed linens. The machines are not far from a section of the room where the women have created the Death Wall, a wall that features framed photos of the women who have left the program and overdosed. A memorial of sorts and a cautionary tale wrapped in one.

Latonya works at the women's campus of a long-term recovery program in Louisville, Kentucky. The Healing Place (THP) is a nonprofit, with both male and female campuses in Louisville. It receives court-ordered clients and those who check in on their own. THP has a contract with the Kentucky Department of Corrections (DOC), which provides beds at their women's campus for those sent to the program from prison. In 2018, approximately eighty clients at the women's campus were there because of the DOC. A probation officer works onsite at each campus.

Latonya has supervised the overnight homeless shelter and the detox department of the women's campus for about three years. She also teaches her own class, called Sucker Free Sunday. In the class she explains parts of the Big Book, the basic text for Alcoholics Anonymous (AA), and asks clients to give self-disclosures in which they tell the group what their life was like, what happened, and what it's like today. A young woman who looks like she is in her twenties, her pale face littered with red scabs from picking at her face while high, asks Latonya if she can speak with her. The woman tells Latonya that she wants to leave detox and spend Christmas with her children. She will return after the holidays. This woman isn't DOC ordered, so she can leave if she wants. But Latonya knows leaving is a bad idea and encourages her to stay. "You already know what's going to happen when you go home," she tells the woman. She reminds her that she can invite her family to come have Christmas lunch or dinner while she is still in the program. "What if you go home for Christmas and overdose?" she asks.

Looking at the young woman's face, Latonya reflects on her own battle with addiction. Eight years ago she had shown up at the Healing Place, one of her brown irises turned gray from picking at her eye while smoking crack. "We get so selfish that we think our kids want to be around us, but they sick of us," Latonya says to herself. She wants the young woman to make it, not end up with her picture on the Death Wall, another mother permanently taken away from her children. She knows that the women miss their kids, but she believes they need to be clean in order to effectively be present for them. She knows from experience. "My daughter was probably so glad when I left Chicago," Latonya says. "She ain't gotta worry about me and my momma arguing and her having to pick a side."

The majority of women who work at the Healing Place are themselves in recovery. Latonya retreats to her office and lets out a deep sigh. On her desk, a framed photo reveals a mugshot of her during her addiction, her body thin, head nearly bald, eyes wide. Then a current photo, her in professional attire, a smile dapped with lipstick, her straight hair hanging long. Her office is loaded with bags of donations, boxes of women's hygiene products, stacks of pillows, and Christmas gift bags for the women. She knows detox is a tough part of the journey, but she can also see the rewards because she's living it, clean and sober. Before she checked into the Healing Place, she bought methadone, a narcotic used to wean people off drugs, on the black market. She had refused to be balled up in a fetal position, burdened with diarrhea, vomiting, and shaking with chills as she experienced the symptoms of withdrawal. Feeling like she wanted to die. But she also wants the women who have made it far enough to check into the program to push through the rigors of a pure absti-nence detox.

Latonya works with women of all ages, but the majority are be-tween the ages of twenty and forty, many of them addicted to heroin or prescription opioids. Most of them are white. This marks a huge demographic shift for THP, which up until the mid-2000s, accord-ing to the women who lived and worked there, was predominately serving black women battling crack cocaine addiction.

Neighborhoods like the one Latonya comes from—poor, black, and urban—never received the resources they needed to combat the crack epidemic, and many have never fully recovered. Today, Latonya works in an environment where mostly white women are being treated for drug addiction. Latonya met Melissa Huff and Dawn Abbott, who are white women, when they were in treatment at the Healing Place. Now, they are all a part of a Louisville-based advocacy group com-posed of formerly incarcerated individuals fighting for prison reform. While she is friends with them and they're seeking criminal justice reform together, she knows the response to drug addiction looks different based on the color of a person's skin. "See, the crack wasn't killing people, and then it was like more of a black people's [issue]," she says. "I was telling the people in Louisville that the whole epidemic with the overdose happened ten years ago in Chicago. It's just hap-pening here, but that already happened where I come from because I got caught up in that," she says. "The only thing that made them do something about it in the projects that I was in is because the white people were coming over into the projects buying the heroin, and they were dying from it," she says. Police weren't kicking down the door to the drug house that Latonya got high in. There were no efforts to solve the crack crisis. Instead, the focus was on policing black communities, particularly young black men. "The police came through and kicked in everybody's door. Door to door until they found, or thought they was gonna find, who was selling this heroin," she says. "So they went to everybody's apartment trying to look for the people selling this dope because white people were dying from buying the heroin, you know, and that's when they first started putting that fentanyl on the heroin. Now, when I get here, it start happening here."

Kim Moore, a mother of four who is twenty years sober, says she experienced the disparity firsthand in Louisville. Twenty-two years ago she slept on a mattress in a crack house and had few resources to combat her addiction. "I didn't have a crack pipe exchange," she recalled. "All these services were not available because people didn't look like me. When the black community was ravaged with AIDS in the late 1980s, they didn't get clean needles, they went to prison." They were locked up with mandatory minimums and stiff drugs sentences. "We still got people we love in jail now who got locked up in the eighties," Kim declares.

Kim beat her addiction after receiving private medical treatment and completing a sixteen-month residential program at the Beacon House in Old Louisville. After getting sober in 1998, Kim ran a halfway house for six years, where she first noticed the increased use of heroin. Today she believes the drug epidemic needs to be viewed as an issue that impacts everyone. "We all affected and it's no longer 'not in my backyard' for white people because their kids are the ones dying. And it's in their backyard."

In the 1990s, the number of opioids prescribed to patients began to grow and the number of overdoses and deaths from the drugs increased. The rise is attributed to the company Purdue Pharma, which introduced and aggressively marketed OxyContin in 1995. OxyContin, a long-acting formula of oxycodone that slowly releases the drug over twelve hours, was said to be a safer way to manage pain. It turned out to be highly addictive and lit the match for the opioid epidemic.

When states began to crack down on the abuse of prescription pain pills by monitoring and regulating the prescription of opioids, more women turned to heroin, a cheaper, easier-to-access drug that is chemically similar and provides the same effect.

For Latonya, an addiction to pills, even one that grew from an addiction to prescription medication, was a new phenomenon. It wasn't something she saw in her home on the South Side of Chicago. "I was a dope fiend for sixteen years, hardcore on the street, and I have never done a pill before. I've never been around people that was hooked on pills before," she says. "When I got here, it was like everybody was doing pills or everybody was shooting." By the time Latonya made her way to Louisville, she'd already spent well over a decade addicted to crack and heroin and says she had cycled in and out of jails and prisons throughout Illinois nearly fifty times.

A lot of the women Latonya works with are not only trying to beat an addiction but also trying to reenter society with a drug conviction on their record. Incarcerated women now constitute a larger proportion of the prison population than ever before, showing an increase of more than 700 percent, from 26,000 to 225,000, between 1980 and 2017. In 2016, almost two-thirds of women incarcerated in state prisons were in for nonviolent offenses, many of them drug-related crimes. Sixty-two percent of women in prison, and nearly 80 percent of women in jail, are mothers.

As a result of the laws that criminalize drug use, Kentucky is among the states that saw a surge in women going to jail. The state incarcerates women at a rate that is nearly twice the national average. The opioid epidemic has also driven an increase in white women in prison. Between 2000 and 2015 the imprisonment rate of black women declined by nearly 50 percent, whereas the white female rate increased by 53 percent. The racial disparity between black and white women's incarceration was once 6:1, but it was 2:1 at the end of 2016. Tougher sentencing for drug crimes accounts for the growth in the number of incarcerated women, and while crack use, which ravaged communities of color, has declined, the use of methamphetamine, heroin, and opioids has risen. These drugs are more widely used in white rural areas and have disproportionately affected white women. Local news reports show that Kentucky zip codes with the highest overdose rates in 2017 were in the majority-white area of south Louisville, and that more than 90 percent of people participating in Louisville's syringe exchange program were white.[1]

Women, black and white alike, from across Kentucky see the criminalization of substance abuse as an assault on women, on mothers, on families. Latonya, Melissa, and Dawn all have stories of recovery and reentry that overlap. They all see the criminalization of addiction as the wrong solution to a dire problem. As women in recovery, they have all been incarcerated for drug-related offenses and must deal with the impact of a criminal record upon release. The greatest challenge, however, for them and many women, is child custody. When mothers are imprisoned, their children are often displaced. Nine in ten fathers in state prison report that their children live with their mother, while only about one in four mothers in prison says child's father is the current caregiver. When mothers are incarcerated, children are more likely to go into the foster care system, with the lucky ones being placed with relatives. Latonya, Melissa, and Dawn have all experienced the loss of their children in some capacity. Some, years later, are still trying to regain custody or visitation rights.

DAWN LAUGHS EASILY AND is high energy and spunky. She's still a small-town girl, one who traded in the narrow roads and vast woodlands of eastern Kentucky for a bustling section of Louisville. She lives in a prewar, rustic cherry, multifamily home that is reminiscent of a medieval castle. She has an entire floor to herself, and despite the beauty of the house and how far she's come, she still considers the place to be a stepping stone. This afternoon she is sitting on the couch in her living room, her pit bull terrier quietly lying in the back room. Her gray eyes are noticeably tired as she gazes at the dozens of records that make an art piece on an accent wall.

She is on a work break from a local restaurant where she worked a number of positions before becoming the general manager. The last few years have reminded her that finding a job with a criminal record is a privilege. "I don't care if I have to shovel shit or flip burgers," she says. The owner of the restaurant has allowed Dawn to unofficially turn the tavern into a second-chance hiring business; almost all of the staff, like Dawn, are recovering addicts.

This day her face is bare, not even a touch of lip gloss or eyeliner. Her hair is now a quiet golden brown, not pink or purple as it's been on other occasions. She wears a blue polo shirt with a black-and-lime–lined Champion zipper hoody and black pants. Still, her punk style peeks through the tameness of casual work clothes. She wears black nail polish and her hands are adorned with three oversized silver rings, the most notable one portraying an eagle flying.

Before she returns to work, she checks her mail and smiles when she sees a Christmas card from her youngest daughter, Hannah. Dawn lives a few hours away from her five children—between the ages of twelve and twenty-two—who are spread across East Central Kentucky, living with family members or her ex-husband. For Dawn, part of maintaining her sobriety and successfully reentering society means she has to continue living hours away from her kids in a city couched in resources compared to where she comes from.

Dawn has plenty of story to tell, and she does so no matter how unfavorably she might appear. She is unapologetically real and raw. Her voice is consistently energetic, the tone of someone humbled by life, and proud to be alive to tell it. When she thinks about her battle with substance abuse and the impact it has had on her kids and her ability to maintain a family, she reflects on the time she lost her own father. Though it was a defining moment in her life, her memory of it remains fragmented five years later. It was 2013. She woke up on a beach in Florida, and memories sans cohesion flashed in her head. What she could piece together was that three days earlier she had driven her BMW all the way from Mount Sterling, Kentucky, a thirteen-hour drive. She was high on Xanax, a medication used to treat anxiety and panic disorders, so she couldn't remember how she washed up on the beach. Her recollection of the drive was blurry. There was a fight with a friend, a blown tire on the highway, and the knowledge that cancer had killed her father.

"I'm like, holy shit. I'm in Florida," Dawn recalls. She was deep in her addiction, and she was always taking off. But she had always made her way back to Kentucky, thanks to her dad. "I knew if I had serving shoes and black pants, I could go anywhere in the world I wanted to," she says. Dawn was a self-defined hustler. Once she rode her motorcycle to Tennessee, purchased a tent, slept in it for a week, and earned enough money serving at restaurants to get an efficiency hotel room and do what she wanted. Ever since she was a teenager, she'd felt like a gypsy. A girl, then a woman, searching for something to make her feel alive, wanted, valuable. Her father was the one person she worshipped, and after he died she was lost. She was also tired of running. "Before I would always end up somewhere and I could call my dad and he always made sure I got home," she reflects. But this time was different. "I was just sitting there stuck, don't know what to do . . ." It was the first time she seriously considered getting sober. "I was already on my way to jail and didn't even know it yet," she would later say.

By this point, Dawn had fallen all the way through the cracks—an opioid addiction that had started off as something recreational had successfully ripped her life to shreds. It ultimately resulted in her children being taken away. She wasn't the only casualty of the opioid epidemic that hit Kentucky hard, especially rural Kentucky. Drug education, prevention programs, and treatment and recovery options were limited, even nonexistent, in many parts of Eastern Kentucky's rural counties and small towns, which was where substance abuse first shot up. Addiction had ravaged much of the state.

With law enforcement stretched thin, their response was "Lock 'em up or forget it," according to Dan Smoot, a former state police narcotics officer. In 2011, a few years before Dawn washed up on the beach, news reports noted funding for drug abuse prevention was being cut despite the growing crisis.[2]

4

BOY, THEY GON FRY YOU
Mississippi

R uth Anderson lives in a terra-cotta brick single-family home with a sprawling, manicured green lawn. She pulls into her garage, parking her youngest son Naeem's gray Nissan next to her truck, a GMC Yukon. Her oldest son, Kevin, recently repainted her truck a shimmering burnt umber color, then he put tires and rims on it that were far too big for Ruth's liking. "Mama, you need those," Kevin told her. She wasn't sure. She felt like they were too masculine, that they were tires for young people. Kevin, who is planning to move to Maryland, said the tires were safe, insisting that he wanted to be sure she was okay. The neighborhood is peaceful: the streets are lined with trees, cars are neatly tucked in their garages. Since all her sons have left the nest, it's quiet inside as well. It's usually just her, but today her brother shuffles from a back room to peek in on her. The bedrooms no longer have owners, so she welcomed him to stay temporarily.

Ruth's home is filled with vintage decor. In the living room, there is a lived-in blue suede bench with wooden legs; behind it, a blue framed picture of a blossomed white rose; and gold wall plates cover the light switches. The center of the walnut-stained wooden hutch is a flat screen television, flanked by framed family photos, antique vases and plates, signs that read "hope" and "believe," a white cross, and Naeem's football trophies. Ruth manages to keep her home organized; the signs of clutter are limited to a small section in the living room where she has hand weights, a pile of folded laundry, and a Black & Decker drill—all signs of a woman moving through life quickly, always running, always working.

She walks around the house, looking in drawers and boxes to gather documents she's collected over the last three decades. The walls of the hallway to the bedrooms feature framed photos of her family: a tall standing photo collage of her parents, her children from infancy to adulthood, a forty-year-old picture of her and William, her wearing a turquoise plaid shirt and orange vest, him in a black button-up shirt. After she finds all the paperwork, she returns to the living room, folders in each hand.

She flips through the contents of each folder. Her eyes are steady behind her glasses, and she makes separate piles and places them on the coffee table in neat stacks. On the top of one stack are black-and-white copies of 1980s newspaper clippings. "It saddens me," she mumbles, about the articles on William. "I don't want to read it." It's a sure way to dampen her spirits, and today she's in a good mood.

William has an easier time recalling the day that irreversibly changed his life, but he hesitates because he believes his truth is part of the reason he hasn't been paroled. At this point, thirty-nine years later, he'll tell the freedom gods whatever they want to hear if it means he'll have a chance at getting home to his family. "I'll say the moon is falling," he admits seriously.

William loved the outdoors. As a boy he played on his family's ninety acres of land in a town just northeast of Jackson. The woods stretched farther than the eye could see, and he explored every inch of the land with his grandfather, sometimes by foot, but most often by tractor. His grandfather took him along to plow the land, taught him how to pick corn, milk cows, make syrup, cut hay, and even how to slaughter a hog. As a young adult, he took Ruth and his son, Kevin, and they sat in the quiet, inhaled the fresh air, watched the sunset, or took long walks in the woods. In 1981, William invited his friend Paul Reed, a white man he worked with doing plaster, to the land for an outdoorsy adventure. William knew Paul shared his love for wilderness, for hunting and fishing, so he was excited for him to join. The peace that seemed to live on the land was a welcome change from the noise of the city and a nice departure from their usual routine. He and Paul would hang out at William's home for dinner, and they'd watch a game, or shoot the breeze, or they'd go out as a group to house parties. Young and exuberant, they'd often block out what was happening around them. Paul was a quintessential liberal hippie, but William and Paul didn't go out together often because they knew it wasn't publicly acceptable. When they arrived on the land, they would walk and walk until they disappeared. They talked about life in Jackson, shot their guns, sometimes practicing on cans.

On the ride back to Jackson one day, Paul, who was driving, ran a stop sign. About twenty yards away, William saw, was a constable parked on the side of the road. The officer promptly pulled them over. They were an unlikely duo for 1980s Mississippi: a young white man and a young black man in an old-school Mercedes in a small white town. It was a quick way to get pulled over. William just hoped it didn't escalate. The constable told the men he smelled marijuana and asked if he could search the car. Paul agreed. He popped the trunk, where a rifle and pistol lay visibly.

The pistol belonged to William and Paul owned the rifle. William thought for sure he was going to jail. A few years earlier he had served a year on a burglary charge, and as a convicted felon he wasn't legally allowed to carry a weapon. Paul offered to tell the officer that the gun belonged to him, but William knew that wouldn't work. The gun was registered in Ruth's name. William wasn't arrested, but the constable confiscated the hand gun and gave him a ticket for carrying a weapon. The two men drove back to Jackson.

But the day William went to the police precinct to pay the ticket, he was met with metal handcuffs. "They locked me up," William recalls. Everything moved in quick succession afterward. "It just went downhill." Soon, he was moved from the general holding cell to the back of the jail, where he was interrogated by a group of officers. They said they had run ballistics on William's gun and that it had been used in an unsolved murder from a year earlier.

He called his wife. "You ain't comin' home?" she asked, perplexed. No, he was not coming home. "I was in a daze," Ruth recalls.

The police were referring to the murder of a service employee who had been killed at a trailer home not far from the town William and Paul visited that day. The man was shot twice with the pistol, once in the shoulder and once in the head, by someone said to be burglarizing the trailer home.

During the interrogation, William saw his past running behind him, wrapping its hands around his throat. William said he was at work the day of the murder, but the construction site didn't have a punch clock to sign in. He told the officers he'd loaned the gun out to a friend a year earlier. That friend had since been killed. Without a provable alibi, and a dead man as an alternate suspect, trying to tell his version of what could have happened was like talking to a steel bed frame.

William sat behind bars nearly two months before getting legal representation. His public defender arrived the day he was set to go to court. William, again, tried to explain that he had loaned the gun out. He asked his public defender, who was accompanied by a young junior lawyer, to investigate the alternate story of the murder. "'I don't get paid for investigating,'" William remembers him declaring. "'I get paid to take you to court.'"

There, William was a twenty-seven-year-old black man with one conviction on his record, and he was the owner of a gun used to murder a white man in a small town. His fate seemed sealed. William seems to transport back to the jail all those years ago when he recalls the lawyer and their haunting conversation. The white attorney leaned back in his chair, kicked his legs on the table, and crossed his cowboy boot–clad feet at the ankle. He puffed on his cigar, looked at William, and said, "Boy, they gon fry you."

"I'll never forget him," William breathes. "'Boy,'" he repeats, pauses. "'They gon fry you,'" he says each word slowly. The lawyer's image, voice, and name are seared into his memory, still haunting him, though the man's been dead for a long time.

William feared he would be executed. Going to trial and being convicted of capital murder, committing homicide during the course of a felony, meant he could be sentenced to capital punishment, meaning the state would kill him in retribution for his crime. He could also get life in prison or life without parole (LWOP).

If convicted, William would be going to the Mississippi State Penitentiary at Parchman. Parchman is Mississippi's oldest prison. Built in 1901, Parchman is massive and remote, sitting on twenty thousand acres of sprawling plantation in the Yazoo-Mississippi Delta, surrounded by uninhabitable swampland. Given its location and vast size, prison officials didn't see the need for building walls or electric fences to prevent escape. It became known as "the prison without walls." In addition to the white sergeants who operate the prison, prison officials select the most violent offenders they deem trustworthy and arm them with shotguns and rifles. Known as "trusties," those prisoners serve as guards and are separated from the rest of the prison population.[1]

Although Parchman was supposed to be an improvement on the statewide convict-leasing system, a barbaric practice in which state officials sold the labor of black prisoners to private contractors, the prison became notorious for its nearly uninhabitable conditions, exploitation, and inhumane treatment of its prisoners. Prisoners worked ten hours per day, six days a week. Male prisoners often picked cotton or worked in the brickyard, sawmill, cotton gin, or prison hospital. Female prisoners made clothes and bed sheets for the prison. Prison labor made the prison profitable. In 1918, Parchman collected $825,000, or about $800 per prisoner, from their work in their farming operations.[2]

Prisoners were housed in long, single-story buildings called cages and weren't separated by offense type. The water supply was contaminated, and a subpar sewage system led to the spread of infectious diseases. Inadequate medical staff and facilities meant sick prisoners did not receive proper exams or treatment, and they were even punished if they appeared healthy after an exam.

Offenders were segregated by race, which meant black prisoners lived under more crowded conditions than their white counterparts. Additionally, blacks were not given equal access to vocational training and were disciplined more harshly than whites for violating the same prison rules. Prisoners were subject to corporal punishment: beatings with a whip called Black Annie, beatings with blackjacks, electric shocks from cattle prods, and confinement in the dark hole sans clothes, hygiene materials, a shower, or adequate food for up to seventy-two hours. Finally, they could be shot by trusties.[3]

In the 1970s, members of the Freedom Riders, a group of civil rights activists who went to the southern states to work for desegregation, were imprisoned at Parchman. It was during this time that Roy Haber, a civil rights lawyer, heard of the conditions and treatment. He described Parchman as the last legal vestiges of slavery and filed a class action lawsuit against the prison on behalf of prisoners. In the 1974 landmark case, Gates v. Collier, the Fifth Circuit Court of Appeals found Parchman had violated the Eighth Amendment and lacked modern standards of decency. Over the next decade, the prison was forced to desegregate, end the trusty shooter system, eliminate Black Annie and other unconstitutional forms of punishment, and end forced field labor. The state then began building facilities with physical cells and walls and hired professional guards and administrative staff.[4]

FACING THE PUNISHMENT OF DEATH was not far-fetched in 1980s Mississippi. By then the state had come a long way since its first known capital punishment case: the hanging of George H. Harman in the summer of 1818. He was a white man, punished for "stealing a Negro." In 1940, hanging was replaced with a portable electric chair—it was death that could be carried from county to county. It brought dark distinction to Mississippi, as it was the only state to use such a machine. By the late 1940s, efforts to replace the electric chair began. In 1955, the gas chamber was introduced. The first man to be executed in the gas chamber at Parchman, where William would go if convicted, was Gerald Gallego. He's said to have "coughed, choked, and wheezed on a less than lethal cloud of cyanide poisoning." He banged his head against a steel pole in the gas chamber while prison officials, reporters, and witnesses looked on.[5]

In 1964, state-sanctioned executions in Mississippi paused amidst litigation that challenged the death penalty at both the state and national level. There were no executions in the country between 1967 and 1977. In 1972, the US Supreme Court struck down capital punishment statutes in *Furman v. Georgia*, reducing all death sentences pending at the time to life imprisonment. Four years later, the death penalty was reinterpreted as a matter of states' rights. In 1983, death by state started up again. The gas chamber was replaced by lethal injection in 2002.

To date, 80 percent of the state's executions have been of black men. Since 1818, Mississippi has executed 794 people, 639 of whom were black men. Seventy-seven percent of the seventy-three people executed between 1940 and 1955 were black: fifty-six black men, sixteen white men, and one black woman. In the years that followed, the number of executions decreased but blacks continued to be the majority. From 1955 to 1972, thirty-one men were executed, and 77 percent of them were black.[6]

FACING THE DEATH PENALTY, William couldn't breathe or imagine a way out. He had to reflect on the ways his lifestyle had led him to this unexpected and devastating reality. By day he had put on his hard hat and steel toe boots and laid gas pipes for a local gas company. He earned an honest $2.10 per hour.

He felt it wasn't enough, especially after his apartment caught fire. Even though he was working and had moved out of his old neighborhood, he still popped in to hang out with old friends. When things felt financially too tight, they offered him a solution. This solution pulled William into a neighborhood and lifestyle he'd known but thought was history. He sold drugs sometimes.

"When you got a family to feed, either you do that or go hungry," he recalls. Some nights he showered, changed clothes, put on his cap, adorned his fingers with diamond rings, sprayed a dash of cologne on his neck, and hopped in his freshly detailed car. He drove into the night where the wild things were. He pushed PCP and marijuana alongside his now-adult childhood friends. He danced with a life he never fully escaped, despite how far away he moved with his family. "I was a hustler in the street, trying to make a dollar," he says, thinking about decades past. He never fully embraced the life he dabbled in. The times, he believed, required stepping outside the line. His wife cautioned him though, telling him, "Money ain't everything." She wanted him home with his family.

Life wasn't easy for the couple. "We were def struggling, we were a young couple," Ruth recalls. Despite both of them working, they had their car repossessed and faced other financial hardships. What they earned wasn't enough. Dabbling in selling drugs was common in the neighborhood; it was a way for folks to ensure they could make ends meet. Still, Ruth didn't want her husband hanging out in the street. And he didn't tell her everything he was up to. "I guess he was keeping some things from me," she admits.

William knows that his decisions weren't sound, no matter how common it was in his community. "See, that's living two lives," William admits. "You can only live one. You can only prosper at one. The one you live in the street, eventually get took away from you. Going down the wrong road is gon end up in trouble. Always."

William had served a year behind bars on a burglary charge, but facing the death penalty or the thought of LWOP, of leaving his family for that long, was not what he fathomed would happen to him.

Now, a man was dead, and someone had to pay. He remembers the lawyer saying, "Now, I'm gon go try to get you a deal." He returned with an offer. William could admit to being a "habitual offender," essentially a career criminal, and get 120 years without parole. "Habitual offender?" he recalls asking. "I'm not no habitual offender. I ain't gon cop-out for that." The lawyer approached the district attorney for another deal. When he returned, William recalls, he said, "Okay, I done went and talked to him. I done made him mad."

The offer seemed better.

If William pled guilty, he would get a life sentence. "'You can come on and get on out in about ten years,'" he recalls the attorney informing him. "'Because if you take it to court, they gon fry you.'" William believed him. "I said, I might as well take it. I can do the ten years," William remembers. He had to take responsibility for loaning out his gun. "So, I went on and confessed." Usually, when you plead guilty you must describe the events of the crime and say exactly what you did, but William wasn't required to.

After a year, the town finally got their answers on the unsolved murder, and a satisfactory conviction. Newspapers identified William as a black man who was under the influence of rum, marijuana, and Valium during the burglary and murder.

When William went for sentencing, he got far more time than his public defender said the district attorney agreed to. William received a life sentence for the capital murder, five years for carrying a concealed weapon, and ten years for burglary. With the two added charges, he would be eligible for parole in fifteen years instead of ten. Parole is a conditional release of a prisoner who, after serving a portion of their sentence, is released from prison before completing their entire sentence. Parole itself is not guaranteed; it's up to the discretion of a parole board and the laws of the state. In William's case, parole depends on the complete discretion of the Mississippi Parole Board. They consider the crime itself, criminal history, sentence, victim opposition, and a long list of other matters. William has been denied parole nine times so far. In Mississippi, prisoners aren't even allowed to go in front of the board in person anymore. Their hearings are relegated to video conference. In some instances, they're not even allowed to be present via video. Mississippi doesn't release its parole records, so there's no way to determine how often parolees are denied by the board.

"They lied about everything they said," William says with a hint of lingering disbelief. "Now, I know that's what they do, but back then you wanted to believe." At the time William was sentenced, murder carried a mandatory life sentence in Mississippi, which was presumed to be at least thirty years. So if William had been charged for only the murder, then sentenced to life, he would have been eligible for parole after serving ten years, which is what his attorney had told him.

That has since changed in Mississippi in favor of more punitive laws. Today, anyone convicted of a homicide on or after June 30, 1995, and who has a prior serious offense, is ineligible for parole. Those previous crimes include arson, drug trafficking, robbery, burglary, and others.

THE NUMBER OF PRISONERS NATIONWIDE started to rise rapidly in the 1970s, going from 196,441 in 1970 to 481,616 in 1985. When William was convicted and sentenced in the early 1980s, people of color were already overrepresented in prisons. But after he entered the prison system, the crackdown on crime only got more intense, policies became stricter, and services and opportunities for rehabilitation disappeared. From inside Mississippi's prisons, William has seen firsthand the explosion of the prison population and the effects of increased sentencing, the results of a series of crime bills that have fueled mass incarceration.

In the 1990s, violent crime was seen as being out of control. Robbery and assault rates had exploded, beginning in the late 1960s. The murder rate peaked at 10.2 deaths per 100,000 people in 1980, fell four years later, and then started to rise again. In 1987, the murder rate started to increase about 5 percent each year, reaching 9.8 deaths per 100,000 people in 1991. Many of those victims were young and black. Families wanted to feel safe, and they called for economic investment in their communities, a reduction in crime, and safer neighborhoods for their children. In the name of safety and community and social preservation, the 1990s brought an unparalleled kind of legislative punitiveness in the form of harsh crime bills that would impact families for decades to come.[7]

In 1994, President Bill Clinton signed the Violent Crime Control and Law Enforcement Act. At $30 billion dollars, the package was the largest crime-control bill in US history. The bipartisan bill, which legislators proclaimed would be tough and smart on crime, included the Violence Against Women Act, provisions for drug treatment programs, prevention programs, gun regulation, and funding for one hundred thousand new police officers. The aim was to reduce crime rates and protect families. But the rest of the bill ensured some families would be ripped apart and some communities would be decimated. In 1993, when the bill was introduced, the National Association for the Advancement of Colored People (NAACP) predicted its devastating impact, calling it a "crime against the American people."[8]

The bill implemented mandatory-minimum sentencing enhancements, expanded the death penalty to include sixty new offenses, and added three-strikes laws, including mandatory LWOP for federal offenders with three or more convictions for serious violent felonies or drug trafficking crimes. This paved the way for states to introduce their own versions of the three-strikes laws. It also allowed the prosecution of children over thirteen as adults for certain violent crimes. It granted states $9.7 billion in funding to build or expand prisons if they passed truth-in-sentencing laws, which required people convicted of violent crimes to serve on average 85 percent of their sentence. The funds were divided between two programs: the violent offender incarceration (VOI) grants and the truth-in-sentencing (TIS) grants. States could seek funding from either program as long as they implemented laws that guaranteed offenders convicted of violent offenses serve 85 percent of their time. Between 1996 and 2001, more than $2.7 billion was allocated for the programs.[9]

After the crack epidemic of the 1980s, being seen as weak on crime was political poison. Democrats feared being painted that way and so they were willing, along with Republicans, to push through harsh crime bills. Joe Biden, then the chair of the US Senate Judiciary Committee, was a fervent proponent of the 1994 Violent Crime Control and Law Enforcement Act bill. He argued for families, but only some families. He said the societal conditions that led people to commit violent crimes were irrelevant, and that criminals needed to be immediately locked up. In his 1993 speech in support of the bill, he roared:

> The consensus is A), we must take back the streets. It doesn't matter whether or not the person that is accosting your son or daughter or my son or daughter, my wife, your husband, my mother, your parents, it doesn't matter whether or not they were deprived as a

youth. It doesn't matter whether or not they had no background that enabled them to become socialized into the fabric of society. It doesn't matter whether or not they're the victims of society. The end result is they're about to knock my mother on the head with a lead pipe, shoot my sister, beat up my wife, take on my sons.[10]

Biden declared that something had to change, arguing that we would be "absolutely stupid as a society" if we didn't act. He wasn't alone. Some black leaders supported the bill as well. For example, Kurt Schmoke, Baltimore's first black mayor, rallied his community to support the bill because it was imperative, as he put it, to "send a signal" that "if there is evil manifested by actions taken by individuals who choose to prey upon our residents that that evil will be responded to quickly and correctly."[11]

Some opponents predicted the laws would be catastrophic. US Representative Kweisi Mfume, chairman of the Congressional Black Caucus (CBC), argued the bill would "find better ways to incarcerate people" and "give us a sense that we are more secure as a result of the new prisons and the tougher sentences." Black community activists, criminologists, civil rights lawyers, and members of Congress all fought against various provisions of the bill. Other members of the CBC resisted parts of the bill, but they ended up voting for it out of fear that the next proposed bill would be worse. A group of thirty-nine black pastors wrote a letter to the CBC saying, "While we do not agree with every provision in the crime bill, we do believe and emphatically support the bill's goal to save our communities, and most importantly, our children." In the end, the bill passed by a fairly wide margin: 195 members of the House and four senators voted against it.[12]

But this crime bill didn't just drop from the sky; it was built on ones that came before it. The Comprehensive Crime Control Act of 1984 was the first comprehensive revision of the US criminal code since the early 1900s. It established the US Sentencing Commission, which ushered in an era of mandatory minimum sentences and the reduction of good time and parole options, reinstituted the federal death penalty, and increased penalties for the growing, transfer, and possession of marijuana. President Ronald Reagan signed the Anti-Drug Abuse Act of 1986, which established five to ten years, without parole, mandatory minimum sentences for first-time drug offenders (marijuana offenses included), and a 100:1 sentencing disparity between crack and powder cocaine, respectively. This disparity disproportionately impacted black Americans. That law also removed options for parole in lieu of federal supervised release, meaning it imposed a more punitive form of supervision on people released from prison instead of the more rehabilitative system of parole.

Families are still paying the costs of legislation from decades past. For many inner-city communities, the new law meant more surveillance, punishment, and incarceration. Many of the provisions had a huge impact on mass incarceration and crime. The 1980s War on Drugs legislation ensured that people of color were already under attack and overrepresented in jails and prisons. The 1994 crime laws were more like blows to a man already on the ground. From 1990 to 1999, the number of police officers rose 28 percent, from 699,000 to 899,000. While this might have contributed to a modest drop in crime, it served to increase surveillance, create an uptick in stop-and-frisk actions, and result in more arrests for people of color, especially for those in poor communities of color. As states were financially incentivized to enact harsher sentencing, prosecutors leaped at the opportunity to dish out long sentences. An offender didn't have to commit a violent crime to receive a third strike. Even small infractions could generate big sentences. In California, for example, a man was sentenced to fifty years to life for shoplifting $153 worth of video tapes. Passage of the 1994 crime-control legislation ensured an explosion in the prison population, more criminal prosecutions, longer sentences on average, and more and more people touched by the criminal justice system in some way. Families and neighborhoods paid the cost along with those locked up.

WILLIAM WAS SENTENCED in the 1980s, just before the wave in which nearly all of those convicted of crimes started to receive longer prison sentences and more of the convicted began receiving life sentences. But the political shift toward more punitive policies ended up affecting him anyway. Since 1984, the number of lifers (people serving a life sentence or a "virtual life," a term of fifty years or more) has more than quadrupled—a faster growth rate than the overall prison population. The number of lifers continues to grow despite the decline of serious, violent crime over the last twenty years. Currently there are nearly 160,000 lifers, and almost 50,000 of those people are serving LWOP and will never get out. Since the 1980s, the average amount of time lifers serve for murder convictions has doubled, going from 11.6 years for those paroled in the 1980s to 23.2 years for those paroled between 2000 and 2013.[13]

Half of all people serving life and virtual life sentences are black; in William's home state and Alabama, Georgia, Illinois, Louisiana, Maryland, and South Carolina, the rate is two-thirds.

In many facilities, prisoners serving life sentences have less access to programs, receive limited or no visitation, and are rarely considered for rehabilitation. According to the ACLU of California, "Prisoners condemned to die in prison are not given any special treatment and, in fact, have less access to programs than other prisoners."

"Sometimes people make a mistake and they get a chance to shake it off and improve their life," William says. "Sometimes, you can make the wrong mistake and you spend the rest of your life trying to pay for it. In this case, I made a mistake and I've been paying for it a long time." William isn't the only one paying for his mistake. "My family paid the ultimate price. My kids paid it without a father, my wife paid it without a husband."

5

A NORMAL CHILD
Florida

Cynthia wakes up around seven o'clock in the morning, watches a bit of news from her full-size bed, then rolls over and chases a few more hours of sleep. The summer morning is hot. Miami's sun pours through the opening in her curtains and finally lures her out of bed around eleven o'clock. She puts on a red-and-white T-shirt, blue jean shorts, and flip-flops that match her Fourth of July–inspired nails. She sits at her dining room table, closes her eyes, and slowly sips from her small McDonald's coffee, the scent of two creams and ten sugars sailing up to her nose. It's just what she needs to lean into her day. She saves half of her coffee for later so it doesn't steal her appetite.

Later, she bows her head, adorned in a blue-and-yellow rayon scarf, and says grace over her scrambled eggs, sausage patty, and hash browns. She has a few things on her to-do list for the day: get quarters and detergent, do laundry, plan her Sunday dinner, and send her son Randall $50. She lives alone and doesn't cook often. This day, she pulls out a package of pork chops from the freezer to defrost, but recalls how she feels after she eats pork and considers putting it back in the freezer. "I don't want to be draggin'," she says. "I want to wash and feel good. If I eat that, it kinda makes my head hurt. That pork is something else." Cynthia opts for chicken and potatoes.

She's new to the pastel-yellow apartment complex. Outside, the green grass is manicured and trees are scattered throughout the courtyard. She knew everyone in her old building, but she doesn't socialize much here. There's one neighbor she sits with on the concrete bench and talks about life. The last time they bonded over missing their loved ones in prison. The woman told her about her brother who served time in a Mississippi prison and faced severe mental deficiencies once he was released. From the story, it was unclear if the man had existing problems before going to prison, but Cynthia thought about the mental impact of being imprisoned and worried about her son. She'd heard enough stories of men who didn't survive incarceration.

A golden-oak curio cabinet with a metal leaf trim is the focal point of Cynthia's living room. Candleholders, a vase, a praying black angel, and a small Bible with curled edges are some of the extras to the two dozen photos spread across three shelves. The photos, which she carries to each place she calls home, are a snippet of her family's journey throughout the years. On the bottom row are pictures of Niyah as a baby, side by side with one of her donning a red cap and gown from her first graduation.

Cynthia sits on her sofa with a stack of letters clasped in one hand. The other hand flips through a pile of papers and old photographs resting by her side. Finally, she lands on pictures of her youngest son before his neighborhood tugged at him, before he began to drift, before his life irreversibly changed. "Randall was a normal child," she says, holding a few of her favorite photographs of her son. In one photo, Randall is a boy, holding an oversized crayon; in another he's at a neighborhood park feeding a duck. In others, he's shooting a basketball at dusk or lying in a hospital bed being greeted by Santa.

She reminisces about the smart, savvy, respectful boy she knew her son to be. The boy who planted a tree in his neighborhood, got an award for perfect attendance, and cried when he couldn't make it into the school parade. She proudly holds his student of the month award and his high school diploma, as clean and crisp as when it was awarded in 2006. She holds copies of his pay stubs from jobs he worked over the years.

The only pictures of her son from the last decade are captured in prison visiting rooms. There are different backgrounds, but her son is in the same chambray top and bottom, his baby face never quite aging. His face is either speckled with a beard or not. His daughter, Niyah, grows taller in each photo, him holding her, both waving at the camera, and her always smiling.

Cynthia has two sons and three daughters. Randall is the young-est, born seven years after his last sister. She never purchased a crib for him. Instead, he spent his first years tucked under his mom, sharing the same bed, mother and son growing closer by the day. The children don't share the same father. Randall can use one hand to count the number of times he saw his father in the flesh while growing up. "His father was incarcerated half the time," Cynthia says. "In the streets, wasn't coming by. Maybe on a birthday, he might bring one present." Randall didn't have grandparents on ei-ther side of his family. His father's parents died before he was born. Cynthia was raised by both of her parents alongside her two older sisters until her third birthday, when her mother was killed inside their home. Her father, a laborer, then raised her alone. He died in his sleep from cardiac arrest before Randall was born.

Over the years, Cynthia had some support from partners in re-lationships, but she carried the brunt of the work of raising her five children and relied on them to care for one another. Adrienne, who is the oldest, had the most responsibility for watching her siblings. Adrienne recalls, "My mom is only thirteen years older than me. So I was a child. I was being raised by a child. And pretty much when my mom had her kids, I pretty much was the mom. I used to have my sisters and brothers. I used to have to miss school watching them."

Cynthia's priority was keeping a roof over her children's heads, which meant she worked multiple jobs with long hours. She rose early in the morning to take multiple buses for her 1.5-hour commute from her home in Overtown to a wealthier suburb to work her first job at Checkers. She worked as a crew manager there, but she needed more income, so she picked up another position as a manager at a nearby Wendy's. When she finished one shift, she went into the bathroom, changed uniforms, and headed down the block to the next gig. Each day came with at least sixteen hours on her feet. By the time she reached home, night had fallen.

When Randall was around ten years old, Cynthia took him to work with her. She taught him how to use public transportation so he would know the bus route to her job. Sometimes he would meet his mom at work and help her. She would have him pick up litter in the parking lot or clean the dining room area. Once she let him take orders in the drive-thru at Wendy's. She would give him whatever he wanted from the menu or give him a few dollars. For Randall, it was the only time he could spend with his mom. "She was gone all the time, so I wanted to know what she was doing," he recalls.

As he got older, Cynthia would return home to find Randall missing from his bed. His older siblings, unaware of where he'd gone, would say, "He was just in here." Adrienne remembers Randall taking off a number of times when he was younger. "He used to get missing," Adrienne recalls. "This is elementary school. We're talking eight, nine years old and we couldn't find him—one time all day. We got crazy." Adrienne's daughter, Tika, was the same age as Randall and attended the same school. They were more like brother and sister, and they got competitive sometimes. During their school's candy sales program, which was meant to raise money for a school program, Adrienne helped Tika with her sales by getting her colleagues at work to buy the candy. Tika became the top candy seller at their school. As a prize she won an evening out with her teacher, which included a limousine ride. Adrienne said Randall wanted to beat Tika, so he came up with an innovative way to sell more. After being gone all day, Randall returned home having sold all of his candy. He had taken a jitney express bus across town to 15th Avenue in Liberty City, a well-known area for drug dealing. He had sold all of his candy to the men in the neighborhood.

Randall always sought ways to be self-sufficient, even in middle school. With no stable support system, Cynthia relied on Randall's school to be a guaranteed babysitter. While he was in school she could work an uninterrupted first shift. That plan was thwarted whenever she got a call from Randall's school to tell her that he'd gotten into trouble. "I'm finna go out there and take my belt," she'd say. "Randall, I hear you cutting up," she'd say. "I'm not going to no schoolhouse behind y'all. The teacher betta keep y'all," she recalls, slapping one hand on the backside of the other. "If I gotta leave my job and come there, what the hell I'm sending you to school for?" she asked him, perplexed.

Cynthia recalled that after Randall had gotten in trouble a few times at school, her daughter Adrienne, who worked with at-risk youth, told her she could get Social Security disability benefits for Randall. She suggested that perhaps he had attention-deficit hyperactivity disorder (ADHD). Adrienne doesn't remember telling her mother this, but it's seared in Cynthia's memory. Cynthia didn't like the idea of labeling Randall and couldn't fathom receiving money from the government because of it. "A who, a what?" Cynthia asked, her nose turned up at the perceived insult. Sure, he was hyper, but in her eyes that was normal boy behavior. Medicine, she feared, would have Randall moving like a robot, his eyes wide as saucers, his mouth dropped open. Medication, even if he had ADHD, which she didn't think he did, would send her little boy off somewhere. He just needed some discipline. "I got his medicine. This belt." She would manage her son's misbehavior in-house. "I ain't getting no medicine, he ain't gettin' no check," she remembers, leaning back in her chair like a gangster, proud of her decision. "Ain't nothing wrong with Randall. He just needs a good ass whooping," she says, then erupts into laughter, stomping her feet from the chair. "He's a boy, just leave him alone."

But Randall's problems in school didn't stop. As a teenager, he complained to his mom about how he was being treated at school. "Man, these people prejudice," he reported to his mom. At the time, he was being bused to a predominately Hispanic school. Back then, Cynthia didn't have the bandwidth to honestly consider her son's observations. She told Randall to sit down, pay attention in class, and be quiet. She brushed it off. "What prejudice is you talkin' 'bout?" she'd ask rhetorically. He'd get mad at his mother sometimes, saying, "Man, you make me sick 'cause you don't listen. I'm tryna tell you." Cynthia would tell him "to shut the hell up and get going." In hindsight, relieved of the burden of working to survive, she thinks she understands what he was talking about. "You have to listen to the kids," she says. "You have to listen to both sides." Randall was young, but he observed and was acutely aware of racial and class disparities in school and his neighborhood.

What Cynthia didn't know was that racial bias was real and could have contributed to Randall's experiences. Children of color, especially black boys, who attend public schools have long since faced racial bias in school. The bias starts increasingly early too. A Yale study found preschool teachers are more likely to expect young black children, especially young black boys, to misbehave. The researchers used eye-tracking technology and found that as teachers watched video clips of children in a classroom setting, the teachers showed "a tendency to more closely observe black students, and especially boys when challenging behaviors are expected." Black preschoolers are 3.6 times as likely to be suspended as their white classmates. While they make up only 19 percent of preschool enrollment, they account for 47 percent of preschoolers who have been suspended one or more times.[1]

It only gets worse as these students grow older and are monitored through a prism of bias. At five years old, their actions are penalized; later as they move through the school system, their adolescent behavior is systematically criminalized. Eventually, they're punished or pushed out for school incidents, be it by expulsion or referral to police. In 2016, the US Department of Education Office for Civil Rights released data revealing the racial disparities in public schools. The study reported that during the 2013–2014 school year, black students were nearly four times more likely to be suspended than their white counterparts.

"Randall was not a bad child," Cynthia insists. "You know, normal bad." Randall was guilty of the kind of mischief she'd come to expect of growing boys. But the trouble she was accustomed to wasn't the kind of trouble school teachers or administrators were willing to deal with. Cynthia's school experience had been different. Although the 1954 *Brown v. Board of Education* verdict ruled racial segregation in public schools unconstitutional the same year Cynthia was born, school segregation persisted. Though the Court ruled that segregated schools were inherently unequal, the Supreme Court did not instruct schools on how to integrate and asked for additional arguments. The following year, in 1955, the Court issued a second opinion that sent future desegregation cases to lower federal courts and instructed district courts and school boards to desegregate "with all deliberate speed." The Court's decision didn't prevent "local judicial and political evasion of desegregation."[2] So, many Southern states were slow to integrate their schools. "I stayed in black schools," she recalls. Her father enrolled her in black, private, Catholic schools. It was his way of protecting her from what he said were "bad kids," mostly ones hailing from the neighboring public housing authority complex. She remembers hopping in her teacher's

Cadillac, being driven to ballet practice, then going to her teacher's beautiful home, where she would have dinner alongside a few other students. She thinks the teacher showed her more attention because she was being raised by a single parent. But that reality was nonexistent for Randall.

The idea of being alienated at school was foreign to Cynthia. She didn't recall students being tossed out of school, nor did she experience having police officers on campus. If she or her classmates disobeyed their teacher, they had to hold their hand out and receive a smack on the palm with a paddle. It wasn't until she started to have kids of her own that she noticed truant officers cruising around, picking up kids, and taking them to the detention center. Things started to change. "Teachers don't even want to look at the children while they sitting in the class," she says. "Talkin' 'bout take 'em to they house? A lot has changed."

THE FIRST TIME RANDALL FELT the metal handcuffs tightening around his wrists, he was in seventh grade. One day, he noticed that a new security guard had joined the other campus guards. He stood out to Randall because he had only one arm. Randall found his missing arm peculiar, and he stood one day staring at the security guard. "I guess I watched him too long," Randall recalls of the incident. "So I was watching this guy and I guess he was uncomfortable with me watching and he took it as an offense or something." The new officer reported Randall's behavior to a senior guard who had a rapport with the black students. Randall saw him as a liaison between the black and Latino students, who had a tense relationship. The senior security guard approached Randall in what he perceived to be "a very threatening manner, like he wanted to get physical." Randall, a young teenager at the time, admittedly had no experience with male authority figures. "I wasn't fond of males or men wanting to put down on me," he recalls. "I wasn't prone to male leadership, and male guidance. Especially in that threatening, dominant manner. I wasn't used to that. I grew up with my mom."

Randall didn't know how to respond once the security guard grabbed him. Randall pulled away. As the security guard approached again, Randall picked up a rock and threatened to hit the officer with it. The officer came closer and Randall reacted. "I threw the rock with every intention *not* to hit him," he recalls. He was sure the officer knew he wasn't serious. "He seen it. It was a bluff. I was really like telling him, 'Don't put your hands on me.'" But what Randall intended wouldn't matter. The very fact that he threw the rock meant he would be punished. "I was a young kid, I had great aim. If I wanted to hit him, I could have hit him. He knew it. I guess you could say it was a power struggle. He wanted to show me that he was running things, he's the security guard. And I wanted to show him, ain't nobody gonna pick on me or put their hands on me."

Randall made the mistake of believing that he would be treated like a child disobeying authority. In his mind, at worst, he might be sent to the principal's office, assigned detention, or be suspended. "I end up being carried away. In a police car. In hand cuffs." Randall sat in jail for a few hours until his mother came to pick him up. Randall didn't think the security guard intended to have him arrested. He was the most approachable and likable of them all, but he had a job to do. "He was just trying to make a point. I could see it in his eyes that he didn't want to follow through with the process." But once the police arrived, it was out of his hands. After the incident Randall moved to another school.

Randall's on-campus incident was a decade after schools began subscribing to the 1990s narrative of the super predator, juveniles who, as First Lady Hillary Clinton put it at the time, have no conscience and no empathy, and need to be brought "to heel." The idea infected everything from school discipline to neighborhood policing. Schools began enforcing zero-tolerance school discipline, which helped shape the lives of kids like Randall. Such strict school disciplinary policies favored suspension, expulsion, and school-related arrests for minor offenses. School security guards, often referred to as "school resource officers," were first introduced in Flint, Michigan, in the late 1950s. They were meant to foster relationships between local police and youth, and officers visited schools on a part-time basis. A proliferation of campus-based officers came in the 1990s in response to a number of school shootings and the fear of school violence. Members of Congress began calling schools "increasingly dangerous places to be." The Gun-Free Schools Act, passed in 1994, mandated a yearlong out-of-school expulsion for any student caught bringing a weapon to school. Funds allocated for community policing in the 1994 crime-control laws were spent on school security. The federal Office of Community Oriented Policing Services (COPS) was formed to develop the programs that were meant to "advance public safety through community policing." In 1999, just days after the Columbine High School shooting, when thirteen people were killed, President Clinton announced the first round of COPS grants, which would allow schools and police to form partnerships that were focused on "school crime, drug use, and discipline problems." Over the next two years, COPS awarded 275 jurisdictions more than $30 million for law enforcement to partner with schools.

Having officers on campus increases the likelihood that students will interact with law enforcement and the juvenile justice system. By the 2013–2014 school year, suspensions had increased. And a student who is suspended or expelled during preschool or elementary school is up to ten times more likely to face jail time later in life. A single suspension in ninth grade doubles a student's risk of dropping out, which is a major predictor for incarceration. Nearly ninety-two thousand students were arrested in school during the 2011–2012 school year. These policies significantly increase the chances that students will make contact with the juvenile justice system, creating a national trend that has been dubbed the school-to-prison pipeline.

Children spend the majority of their time in schools, a social institution meant to be a great equalizer because education is the bridge to economic mobility. That opportunity is given only to those who aren't pushed out. The school-to-prison pipeline is mass incarceration's cousin—they are closely related. They share the same "lock 'em up and think later" philosophy, and both boast strict policies meant to preserve safety. Zero-tolerance school discipline, especially with its inequitable distribution, is a version of a tough-on-crime policy for children. Having cops in schools increases the likelihood that students, especially those of color, will be more harshly punished. Such policies criminalize children for minor infractions of school rules, which result in these children being relegated to inferior alternative schools or, worse, sent to juvenile hall. A schoolyard scuffle that should land two students in the principal's office instead has children standing in front of a judge. More and more kids have their first serious run-in with the criminal justice system from a school incident.

Being referred to police for a school-related incident can be profoundly detrimental to a child because that initial contact with the criminal justice system puts a mark on the child's record, making their pathway to future incarceration easier. Much like with Randall after his first incident, once kids are labeled as being bad kids, they're expected to get into trouble. It becomes normal to punish them. Furthermore, the first mark ensures the child will be surveilled more closely on school grounds and not presumed innocent if another incident occurs. This first contact with juvenile justice is comparable to the mark of a misdemeanor for adults. The school-to-prison pipeline creates a direct pathway to mass incarceration.

Today, in 51 percent of high schools with high concentrations of black and Latino students, cops freely stop, frisk, detain, question, and arrest students on campus. School security officers dot the halls and campuses of 24 percent of elementary schools and 42 percent of high schools. Randall's own middle school was a mere two-minute drive from the police precinct.

Over the last thirty years, the issue has gotten worse. Examples are everywhere: a teenager at a Virginia middle school was arrested and charged with disorderly conduct and petty larceny for allegedly stealing a $0.65 carton of milk, despite the fact that he was enrolled in the free lunch program. In Louisiana, an eighth grader was arrested and charged with simple battery for allegedly throwing Skittles at another student on a school bus. A ten-year-old autistic girl was handcuffed and tossed to the ground after climbing on desks, knocking over chairs in her classroom, and retreating to a tree outdoors.[3]

Students who are suspended or expelled from school are twice as likely to be arrested as those who remain in school. When Randall got into trouble in 2000, more than 102,000 juveniles were in out-of-home placement, a foster home, group home, residential treatment center, or juvenile correctional facility.

In 2002, black youth, which made up 16 percent of the US youth population, accounted for 28 percent of youth arrests and 33 percent of court cases resulting in out-of-home placement. The number of juveniles locked up rose 11 percent, from 33 percent in 2002 to 44 percent in 2015.[4]

In 2015, over forty-eight thousand young people were locked up on any given night. Sixty-nine percent of those incarcerated were youths of color. Forty-four percent were black, despite the fact that they still make up only 16 percent of US youths. And although the actual number of juveniles locked up has decreased, racial disparities have risen.

THE ALTERCATION WITH the security guard on campus resulted in Randall's first arrest, but when his mother was forced to move to the Overtown neighborhood of Miami he started encountering the police more frequently. Cynthia and her kids had previously lived in a better neighborhood, in a home she had inherited from her father when he died. When she lost the house, she was forced to move someplace more affordable. In moving to a neighborhood she could afford, she had also found an area where there was little public financial investment—except in the form of police officers.

By then, Randall's view of and relationship with law enforcement had started to change. As a boy, Randall wanted to be a police officer. To him, they were "actual heroes that you can see and touch." The verified good guys. He saw them in his neighborhood and remembered them from TV shows he watched with his mom. On a few occasions when he was young, officers allowed him to get in their police cruiser, run his small hands across the seats, place the mic up to his mouth, and pretend to call something in. He can't remember when his admiration melded with fear and ultimately transformed to an "us against them" mentality. Instead of being invited to peek into the back seat of a police car, he was being shooed away enough by officers to know that he wasn't welcome there. Around when he turned ten, he stopped being perceived as an innocent boy. He was seen as suspicious to many cops. Randall's observations weren't far off. According to an American Psychological Association study, black boys as young as ten are more likely to be mistaken as older than they actually are, perceived as guilty by police officers, and face police violence if accused of a crime. The research found that "black boys can be seen as responsible for their actions at an age when white boys still benefit from the assumption that children are essentially innocent."[5]

Unlike the majority of his friends, Randall didn't learn about racial bias, discrimination, and profiling until he was older. "I came about late, realizing that police officers were capable of a particular type of behavior or a particular attitude . . . that officers behaved this way or thought this way. Or treated a certain people this way. That came to me late," he says. It was when he moved to Overtown as a preteen that he started to pick up on what his playmates had learned or had been told since they were young children. "I was maybe twelve years old, versus my friends, who maybe grew up in the midst of things, maybe acclimated with this type of thinking from the age of five." It was also in this new neighborhood where he learned how some officers viewed him. The stereotypes—violent, threatening, up to no good—that follow black boys in urban neighborhoods had descended upon him. As he moved through the neighborhoods, each one getting a little tougher, his new friends taught him to run at the sight of an officer. "Even when you a young kid and have nothing to run about, to be afraid about, you be like, 'Oh, there go the police.' They became, or I guess, I became, the opposition."

Randall describes Overtown, the neighborhood where he grew up, as a "typical, inner-city community, affected by drugs and violence and stuff like that." Today, where he hung out a decade ago, there are young men hanging on the corners dealing drugs, old men sitting on milk crates drinking beers and playing cards, and homeless people sitting beside boarded up buildings. In the span of a few blocks, one can buy a loosie, or single cigarette, from the corner store and a $2 alcoholic drink from a house that runs numbers. In one section, restaurants and new construction are popping up as gentrification moves in on the neighborhood.

Overtown, often referred to as "historic Overtown," is one of the oldest neighborhoods in Miami. It has a rich cultural history of perseverance that was ultimately met with disenfranchisement. Henry Flagler, oil tycoon and railroad magnate, was one of Miami's first developers. Relying on the work of mostly black laborers, in the late 1800s he built the city's first highways, luxury resorts, and the overseas railroad connecting the Florida Keys to mainland Miami. In 1896, Miami was incorporated as a city with the help of black men, who accounted for 168 of the 362 votes. They stepped in to replace white voters who didn't turn out. But that didn't guarantee them any say over what the city would look like, or where they might live. Due to restrictive covenants in the Jim Crow era, black people were forced to settle in a community just northwest of downtown. It was one of two places they could live in Miami until the late 1930s. After the city's incorporation, separate but equal laws meant the neighborhood would be designated as "colored," and eventually the area would be called Colored Town.

From the 1930s through the 1950s, Colored Town was a thriving neighborhood, and it served as the center of black culture and life in Miami, as the city itself became a national destination. Hotels, restaurants, theaters, and lounges dotted the streets and attracted black artists, politicians, and celebrities. Billie Holiday, Nat King Cole, and Josephine Baker were some of the renowned musicians who performed all over Miami. They weren't allowed to sleep or dine in the upper income, white neighborhoods like Miami Beach where they performed, so they went "over town." That's how the neighborhood got its new name. It became the go-to spot for black intellectuals like W.E.B. DuBois, Supreme Court Justice Thurgood Marshall, and Zora Neale Hurston. It wasn't just a happening cultural, social scene, it also satisfied all the health, commercial, and social needs for black people. They had their own black police precinct, courthouse, clerk, and judge. The community bustled with small businesses, grocery stores, churches, schools, and a library—all by and for black people.

Although black residents created a vibrant community for themselves, the neighborhood was overpopulated and it suffered from neglect by the city, which meant there were subpar roads, public schools, sanitation, plumbing, and electricity. Although black laborers played a vital role in building Miami, segregation ensured they didn't have a vote in crucial matters of the city's future. In the 1960s, local officials voted to build the I-95 highway overpass in the center of the neighborhood, which broke up the neighborhood and ultimately caused severe economic decline. At least twenty thousand homes were torn down, wiping out 80 percent of the neighborhood's population. Colored Town went from fifty thousand residents to less than ten thousand.

The black residents were displaced in droves and forced to move to other parts of Miami—with no compensation from the city for moving costs. The area's property values tanked, businesses shuttered, and the neighborhood continued to decline. In 1989, the police killed two black men in Overtown, sparking several days of riots. For the next few decades, Overtown continued to be plagued by over-policing, drug problems, disinvestment, and poverty. While many parts of the neighborhood still struggle with high crime and high unemployment, the last few decades have brought some revitalization, including the restoration of the historic Lyric Theater, the creation of community gardens, and the growth of bustling small businesses.[6]

Still, even the revitalization has come at a cost to Overtown's residents. Outside investment is creeping in and it has sparked fears of widespread gentrification and ultimate displacement. Overtown is considered a hotbed for investment by real estate groups. Home prices have risen dramatically, going from $20 a square foot to $150 a square foot as developers and investors purchase apartment buildings and vacant land in the area.[7]

In 2019, soccer superstar David Beckham and his investing partners purchased six acres of land for $19 million to build a new major league soccer stadium in Overtown. He has said he will include a youth soccer academy. Upon hearing news of Beckham's plans, some British newspapers criticized the neighborhood, calling it a "Miami hellhole" and "bullet-riddled gang ghetto" where the streets are "lined with crack-addled prostitutes selling their wares in the dirty district." Another big-name investor is celebrity chef and restaurateur Marcus Samuelsson, who has plans to open a soul food restaurant in Overtown. Samuelsson, who opened Red Rooster in Harlem in 2010 as the neighborhood was starting to gentrify, says he'll hire within the community.[8]

Some residents, business owners, and activists are keeping a watchful eye on the impending gentrification and taking action to ensure they get to keep at least some of the neighborhood. At least one small business, the Miami Millennial Investment Firm, purchases neglected homes, renovates them, and resells them to community residents at affordable prices as a way to help them maintain ownership of the community before it's too late.

In 2000, when Cynthia was raising Randall, 74 percent of the neighborhood residents were black, and the median household income hovered just under $21,000. The unemployment rate was 22 percent and the poverty rate was 53 percent. In 2015, the median family income dropped nearly $6,000, bringing it to near $15,000.[9]

RANDALL ISN'T SERVING TIME NOW for throwing a rock at a security guard in middle school, but that was his first real brush with the system—and it has a lot to do with where he is now. Less than a year later, at his new school, he got into a fight on campus and was arrested again. Another student had approached him looking for his friend, and Randall says he replied, "Man, get out my face." The boy punched him and ran. When Randall returned to school, his friends, who had heard about the incident, said Randall and the other student needed to fight one on one. The boy was bigger than Randall, so his friend decided to take over the fight for him. The fight ended with all three of the boys sitting in the administration office. Randall, new to the school, and with absences and a prior arrest on his record, was arrested again. "Out of all of us three, they decided I was the problem," he says. He was expelled from school. "I think after that, my life just kinda spiraled out of control."

Not long after being expelled, Randall found himself in the back of a police car again. His friends had been driving up and down the block in an old-school car. He sat, jealous and pouting, and begged for a chance behind the wheel. His friend finally took notice of his moping and allowed him to drive. "'Go 'head and let him drive,'" he remembered his friend saying. "And soon as I get in the car, before I can get good around the block, the police was behind me," Randall recalls. Shocked at how quickly it happened, Randall says he almost jumped out of the car while it was still running. Even though he could barely see over the steering wheel, Randall thought he could plead his case to the officer. He just wanted to try driving. "We all was just taking turns trying to practice, to feel that adrenaline." The officer saw it differently: they were partaking in the crime of joyriding, unauthorized use of a vehicle. "I didn't think I would be in real trouble," he says. "I was just a young kid being mischievous. Like all kids are." But when the police discovered that the car had been stolen, Randall was arrested. Even if he didn't steal the car, even if he hadn't known it was stolen, he would be punished. He was confined to juvenile detention due to his previous two arrests at school.

He attended school while in detention and enrolled in the now-closed 500 Role Model Academy, an alternative school. Many students, like Randall, are transferred to alternative schools as punishment for getting into trouble at their original school. Discipline wasn't always the mission of these schools. They emerged in the late 1960s as less competitive, more child-centered learning environments with the goal of giving flexible instruction to kids who weren't thriving in traditional classrooms. Two decades later, school districts began using them as places to warehouse students who had broken their schools' zero-tolerance policies. Those policies were based on the idea that schools couldn't tolerate students who exhibited dangerous behavior, and so these students were removed in order to maintain order for the remainder of the student population. Later, students started challenging their expulsion or suspension. The courts ordered the schools to find a place for the kids to continue their education, which led to an explosion of alternative schools from the 1990s through the 2000s.[10]

A large number of alternative schools get less funding per student than traditional schools in the same district. They are also often held to lower standards and are exempt from achievement goals, oversight, or reporting rules that other schools must follow. In Florida, where Randall attended school, unlike regular schools that must issue letter grades for performance, alternative schools can opt for less rigorous ratings tied to testing progress. Graduation rates at alternative schools are low. While just 6 percent of regular schools have graduation rates below 50 percent, a ProPublica analysis found nearly half of alternative schools have graduation rates below this threshold. Many students forced into these schools never academically recover.[11]

Black, Hispanic, and low-income students are also overrepresented in alternative schools. Black students make up about 16 percent of students nationally but 20 percent of students in alternative schools. During the 2010–2011 school year, the alternative school Randall attended served seventy-five students in grades six through nine. Of those, 80 percent were black and 20 percent were Latino. The number of students proficient in math and reading/language arts was under 10 percent, which was much lower than the Florida state average of 62 and 68 percent. The student-teacher ratio was 6:1, significantly lower than the Florida state level, which was 16:1, but this did not appear to be an advantage for the students. Across the country, alternative schools serve roughly 500,000 students, putting them at a great disadvantage.[12]

It was in that school that Randall first started selling drugs. In fact, the first time Randall decided to sell drugs, they weren't really drugs. Bored, hanging out in his neighborhood one summer, he and a friend were continuously approached by drug users looking to buy drugs. "I don't know if it was a drought or a major shortage on drugs, but it was like drug users was everywhere looking for drugs," he says. The older guys who usually manned the streets weren't around that day. To Randall and his friend, it seemed like an easy way to earn cash, and so they decided to create supply to handle the demand. They purchased peanuts and cut them into small pieces, and had someone else purchase the small bags to put them in, and they were in business. Selling a dime bag was a quick transaction—purchasers didn't stop to ensure the product was authentic. They likely wouldn't discover the ruse until some time later. They moved from block to block in the neighborhood in the hope that they wouldn't get caught.

Later that day, word got out that someone was selling fake drugs. The older men in the neighborhood learned it was Randall and his friend and gave them a warning. "We did it for one day and made a few bucks, and that was it. We didn't try to make a career out of it," Randall reflects. "We knew it was dangerous. Not only dangerous to the people you're selling it to, but for anybody else's business that you're interfering with."

That window of opportunity they capitalized on gave Randall a taste of a different life. "What attracted me was the fast money. It was right there in your face." At that time, crack was more popular but some people purchased heroin. Overtown's proximity to downtown Miami brought affluent drug users to the area. "People who had *money* were buying drugs. No broke person spending a few hundred a day or every other day. You had a lot of professional people coming through buying drugs. White people come up with their scrubs on."

He was fourteen the first time he got to deal real drugs. An older guy, around eighteen years old, needed someone to "hold things down for him where he could move," Randall says. "I basically begged him. I was like, 'I can handle that.'" At first, the young man told him no. Inducting Randall or any of the younger kids into the drug game held consequences. "He told me he would get in trouble with my mom. My mom would be upset." Some drug dealers respect a parent's wishes and will steer away from kids who are looking to start dealing if they know their parents are staunchly against it. It was the dealer's way of showing respect to the neighborhood. Randall wouldn't take no for an answer, though, and eventually the man obliged.

At that time, Randall was in the alternative school, so he would get out of school late in the afternoon. Then, in the evening, he would go to his supplier, get the drugs, and sell until ten or eleven o'clock at night. This schedule gave him enough time to make it home before his mom returned from work. Any later would be far beyond his bedtime, so he convinced the man he worked for that he had other responsibilities. By that time of night, Randall had already made a pocket full of money, likely more than his mother earned at both of her jobs. "I'd be done made a couple hundred dollars for myself at that time, so I would just go home." Randall was able to make it home before his mom returned from her double shift and long commute. "My mom, she was very, very, very hard working."

Cynthia was suspicious of anything Randall tried to bring into her home that she didn't purchase, so he couldn't sneak name-brand shoes or clothes past her. Instead, he waited until she gave him the usual $100 to buy his school clothes. The fourteen-year-old would buy $400 to $500 worth of clothes and pretend he got a bargain. Sometimes his sister told his mother that the deal he claimed to get was impossible.

Over the next four years Randall was shuttled in and out of juvenile detention centers and juvenile programs. After completing a sentence in juvenile lockup, kids in Florida have to complete an aftercare program, which consists of reintegrative services designed to prepare juvenile offenders for reentry into the community. It's basically probation for juveniles. If the juvenile fails to complete aftercare, they're sent back to a juvenile program of a higher degree. Randall started out in a Level 2 Program then spent a little over four months in a Level 4 Program. From there, he spent more and more time in higher levels, eventually spending close to a year in a Level 8 Program.

A year after his release from that program, when he was twenty years old, he was booked on a murder charge.

6

BAR BABY
Kentucky

Dawn's mom, Jo Arnett, was a teenager when she met Dale Grant in Mount Sterling, Kentucky. He was twice her age. In the beginning, the relationship went well. He was an older man with charm. She got pregnant with Dawn when she was sixteen. Dale, according to Jo, was a known drug lord in Mount Sterling. His most prominent business was a local bar and he ran drugs out of it. Ultimately he'd find himself in prison multiple times. Still, Dawn had been a certified daddy's girl since she could remember, although her version of daddy-daughter time was different than most. When she was in kindergarten, she remembers she was taken to the cafeteria and given a Popsicle. School officials wanted to know if her father sold drugs. "Yeah, but it's okay," Dawn recalls telling them. "He's gonna buy some of those red sports cars, you know, like on the commercial," she told them. "Then he's going to quit."

At a young age she was used to hearing the ruckus of a keg party or seeing piles of cocaine on the tabletops in her father's bar. "We were like bar babies. I was just raised in there and it just seemed normal to me." A quintessential normal childhood escaped Dawn,

91

although she saw glimpses of what it might be like when she spent time at the home of her maternal grandmother, Mawmaw Ida. It was her refuge, the only semblance of structured living she experienced. With her grandmother, she went to the Saturday farmers' market, and learned how to bake pies and shuck corn. But when she was home, she wasn't allowed to have friends over. It also wasn't easy for her to maintain friendships, because she moved to different towns and schools so frequently. When she was about eight years old, her father was arrested and prosecuted for running guns and served time in federal prison. Jo migrated along with her husband, picking up her three kids and moving to the county that was closest to the prison where Dale was held.

Eventually, Jo decided she wanted to leave Dale, whom she says was abusive. Because he was in prison, she thought, "This is my escape." She took her children and left Mount Sterling and moved to Paris, Kentucky, about a half hour away. When Dale was released from prison, he got in touch with his children. Dawn, who was about thirteen years old at the time, decided she wanted to live with her dad and his new wife. "That's when he started his organization back up again. After he got out, he sold the bar and got a little trailer park," Dawn says. She got to live with her father, but she moved between the two parents as it satisfied her desires.

In the new neighborhood, Dawn struggled with belonging. She sought attention in ways she couldn't understand at the time. She was promiscuous, hoping to land on love by giving herself to boys. "I was the neighborhood whore," she says reflectively. "That's what I did. I didn't care," she adds, pausing to recall what it all meant. "I just wanted anybody to pay attention to me or love me." She never really knew love in her relationship with her father; instead he bought her things. It was a love language that she would later pick up as her own. When she was fourteen she met a guy who clung to her, which she appreciated, and she latched on to him too. Soon, she got pregnant with her first daughter, Taylor. In the eighth grade—before she turned sixteen—her parents signed for her to get married. She was off to be a mother and wife. "I just quit school and they never come and look for me," Dawn says, still feeling the disappointment of being an invisible teenager. In hindsight, Dawn says she wished it wasn't so easy to drop out of school and try to be an adult while still a teen. She wished the school had been held accountable, wondering whether her life might have turned out differently if someone—her parents or an adult from her school—had stepped up. "I wish somebody would have stood up for me and been there and said, 'This is not right,'" she says. Jo believed she had been a really good mother and figured that letting Dawn get married was the best decision at the time given the circumstances. Dawn and Noah, her daughter's boyfriend, were already living together.

The young couple made their home in a trailer in Montgomery County. "I was playing house," Dawn says about her young love. Selling drugs became normal too. "We always had some, and my dad let my ex work for him," she says. "We had money and I thought I was doing the right thing because I was raising my daughter. I had a house." After a couple years in the relationship, Dawn started working. At seventeen, she joined her mother, who worked as part of her grandmother's private nursing business. She sought comfort in helping take care of Alzheimer's patients. She later got a state certification and began working long hours, in shifts of twenty-four, forty-eight, or seventy-six hours. She loved the work. "I think, too, it was an escape because I would just work and work and work. It kept me away from [the] reality of stuff." When she was seventeen, she had her second daughter, Annabel, with Noah. They stayed together—living, loving, occasionally fighting—for a little over five years before the relationship fizzled. Dawn felt restrained by the relationship, wondering if she'd gotten tied down too soon. Still, she and Noah remained close friends, something like a family, for years to come.

Over the next decade, she repeated a pattern. Dawn's spirit kept her searching for love and acceptance. "I just worked and I kept having kids. I thought that was the thing to do," she says. Soon she met Jim, a multihyphenate poet-artist–band member. He sported long hair, a bandana, and had pockets filled with sweet nothings. He was a rock star in her teenage eyes. After they got together, he'd randomly turn to Dawn and ask, "Are you my girl?" Her cheeks would redden and she would giggle, insisting, "Oh my God, yes, I am!" She can't tell the story today without laughing wildly. She was sure she'd met her very own Jim Morrison. "This is the one," she thought. Soon she got pregnant with her third daughter, Willow. "I'm having this poet's baby," she thought. He often went to jail for stealing cars, and whenever he did he wrote Dawn love letters. She went to visit him in jail often. It was a short-lived, intense love. Ultimately, he was in and out jail and drank too much for Dawn.

Today, Dawn says she was young and dumb. Still her desire to be loved and valued persisted. "I had a man problem. I guess I thought that we're gonna have a baby and it's going to all work out. We're gonna have this family." It never did fill the void she felt from her own childhood. The relationships never compensated her for the limited access she had to her dad growing up. In between each relationship, she had to show up for her father. In 1998, he was indicted on serious charges of organized crime and trafficking. He was sentenced to eighteen years. His new wife had been arrested with him, so Dawn had to manage everything for him, including digging up hidden money to pay his lawyers.

"I settled back down and I met the next guy, Lonnie," Dawn says, slightly embarrassed by her list of former paramours. She walked into the bar and saw a tall, handsome guy in a black leather jacket. He didn't look like he belonged in the neighborhood and Dawn wanted to know his story. Barely twenty-one years old, Dawn wasn't a serious drinker, but she was up for a cocktail if it meant spending time with the mysterious stranger. She learned that Lonnie sold Norco, a prescription medication containing an opioid and acetaminophen. The drug, which is used to treat moderate to severe pain, is highly addictive. Before she knew it, Dawn was snorting a line of crushed prescription pills courtesy of Lonnie. Then she began using the pills as an excuse to see him. "You got any of those?" Dawn would ask. "Let's meet up."

Dawn had a friend who used pain killers recreationally and was still functional, so she didn't think it would be harmful. There was always cocaine or marijuana around when she was growing up, and she smoked a little weed now and again, but that was it. She knew the cocaine was for the customers. She never knew her father to use drugs, and if he caught a worker indulging he would fire him. She didn't think the same rules applied to taking pills.

Dawn and Lonnie started spending more and more time together, and four months later they moved in together. "He was really, a really good guy," Dawn says. He was family oriented. They planned to have a child together and got married. Soon, she had her fourth daughter, Hannah. Dawn continued to use the pills recreationally, but she worked, made dinner, and took her other kids to ballet and cheerleading and soccer. Lonnie worked for the water company.

A few years into their relationship, Dawn considered Lonnie to be like a father to her girls. When she worked the twenty-four-hour shifts, the kids stayed with Lonnie. That worked for a while. Toward the end of their relationship, Lonnie started using more than the pills. He used harder drugs and would go on a drinking binge sometimes. Little by little she noticed him changing more and more. One night, when she was working with an elderly patient in Lexington, she got a call from police officers. Lonnie led officers on a high-speed chase by motorcycle. He'd left the girls at home alone, saying he was going to the store. Her daughter, Annabel, remembers that night well. She was in bed asleep, until the cops woke her up. There were lights shining in her eyes. "What's going on?" she asked when she noticed the police officers. "I just remember they weren't mad or nothing, they were just like, 'Girls come on with us.'" Their Uncle Jerry picked them up that night from the police station and took them to their grandmother's until Dawn could come pick them up.

But it wasn't until Dawn got into a near-deadly fight with Lonnie while her kids were home that she finally left him. That night, he wasn't the man she'd come to know and love. His drug addiction had reached new heights, and Dawn says he seemed like a demon that night. "He mixed up all these drugs like muscle relaxers and pills and crazy shit and made all this stuff and, like, snorted it. So I don't know if it wiped his head or whatever, because it was not Lonnie."

Annabel remembers being roused from sleep that night too. "He was going crazy. I don't know what he was doing, I was half asleep." Taylor, who was ten or eleven at the time, heard her mother screaming. She told her younger siblings to stay in the bed while she went to see what was happening. She found Lonnie beating Dawn with their marble table top, which he'd removed from its base.

Lonnie later walked into the girls' room with a knife behind his back. "I don't think that he would have hurt us," Taylor says, "because he was kind of crying when he was doing all this." But she was worried about what would have happened to her mom if they hadn't woken up. Dawn managed to get all the girls into her bedroom. Lonnie was on the other side of the bedroom door, stabbing through it with the knife. Dawn put Taylor and Willow out the bathroom window, then handed the baby, Hannah, to Taylor. When she noticed Annabel wasn't there, she panicked. She told Taylor to go on ahead, to take the kids and run down the road and hide, and that a friend would be there to pick them up. "No matter what happens don't come back here," she instructed her daughter. Dawn went back in to get Annabel, who was hiding under the bed. "I just remember seeing Mom come around and her face is bloody and, like, black eyes," Annabel recalls. "And she's like 'Come on!' so we end up running." Dawn and Annabel made it to the front door and ran desperately. "We end up walking down to the very end of the road and sitting in the snow," Annabel recalls. Dawn held as many of her daughters as she could, sobbing, looking at Taylor. "You're my hero," Dawn told her. "You helped me get out." They waited for someone to arrive, and within minutes a truck pulled up. It was Dawn's friend Ethan, who took them to Jo's house.

That night Lonnie tore up the house, spray-painted profanity on the garage door, cut himself, and ended up in a psychiatric ward. Dawn and the kids stayed at Jo's for the next several days, and Ethan continued to come by to check in on her and the girls.

Soon Dawn and Ethan were dating. They got married and she had her fifth child with him, her only boy, Wesley. She was twenty-three at the time. "I *really* loved him," Dawn says. She was still working as a caregiver in the family business and he worked in construction. A year later, they bought their first house together in the up-and-coming neighborhood of Stoner Place. It was an area of Mount Sterling where other young families lived. She was settling into what she describes as a normal marriage; her relationship with Ethan offered the most stability she'd ever experienced. He was present as a father, participating in daddy-daughter dances and stepping up to care for the family. Taylor was doing well in competitive national cheerleading competitions. She had been participating in cheerleading for years, after starting when she was only two. Dawn and Ethan would take the kids across the country for cheerleading events. They spent thousands of dollars a year on trips to Florida, Georgia, Ohio, or wherever the cheerleading circuit took them. Dawn worked nearly ninety-six hours a week as a caregiver, where, she says, she often made close to $2,500 a week. "I was able to give the kids everything they wanted," she says.

Dawn and Ethan both used pills recreationally for the first five years of their marriage. Then a friend introduced them to "what everyone was doing," Roxicodone 15, a stronger opioid than what they'd used before. Dawn had been wary of them. She'd told herself, "no, no, no," but she realized she needed more of the pills she'd been taking in order to feel the effects. "I can just shave you off just a little bit of this and you're going to feel so much better," the friend told her. She did. "I can remember going to work and felt so freaking amazing, and then it did not take a couple weeks with those," Dawn recalls. It was an elevated high that she enjoyed and she was quickly addicted to the new, even stronger, opioid. She was working at a local hospital at the time, and she would lock herself in a bathroom stall and swallow the pill. "I can remember looking at the head nurse, like 'Does she know I'm high?'" Dawn says. It got worse from there. "It was just crazy."

In order to get the new pills herself, Dawn learned, she had to travel to Florida.

EASTERN KENTUCKY IS SATURATED with prescription drugs. Abuse of them is rampant. Until recently, people addicted to prescription opioids traveled throughout Kentucky to go doctor shopping. That is, patients were going from doctor to doctor, illegally seeking prescriptions. Then, as the crisis began getting national attention, Kentucky started to crack down on the epidemic. The state introduced methods designed to prevent doctor shopping.

KASPER, a system that tracks all Schedule II–V drugs dispensed by licensed Kentucky pharmacists, began operating in 1999. It was developed to help physicians, pharmacists, and law enforcement fight doctor shopping. KASPER was Kentucky's version of the prescription drug monitoring programs (PDMPs), which are state-operated databases that collect information on prescription drugs. PDMPs have existed since the early twentieth century, though at the time not all states had PDMPs. As the opioid crisis roared between 2000 and 2010, twenty-seven states implemented PDMPs to curtail doctor shopping and overprescribing.

In 2005, in an effort to stop rampant prescription drug abuse in Kentucky, the system went online as eKASPER. This made Kentucky the first state to offer a self-service, Web-based system for tracking all Schedule II–V prescription drugs.

Many people, Dawn included, resorted to traveling out of state to bypass the new tracking systems. They visited pain clinics known as pill mills, unscrupulous health care facilities that diagnosed and managed pain. Many of these cash-only clinics, which started to pop up in the 1990s, were run by crooked doctors who failed to perform real examinations, or who offered sham examinations. As a result, patients received unwarranted prescriptions for strong painkillers. In order to get the Roxicodone pills they'd been introduced to, Dawn and Ethan traveled to Florida monthly. They followed what became known as the Florida pill pipeline. There was very little regulation in Florida compared to Kentucky. In Florida, hundreds of trailers and small storefront pain clinics operated under lax regulations and without a system to track the dispensing of prescription drugs.

"You have an MRI that might not even be a good MRI. They don't care. You're in and out in ten minutes and you have three hundred opiates in your hand," Dawn recalls. This level of access was unbelievable. Law enforcement officials reported that 90 percent of patients at some Florida pain clinics were from Kentucky. At one point, Dawn would sponsor someone—pay for someone to get a sham MRI, then give them 40 percent of the pills and keep 60 percent. "You're going to get what you need. I'm going to get what I need," she thought.[1]

In 2011, Florida passed legislation that imposed strict regulations on pain management clinics, hoping to drastically reduce pill mills and their impact. They were banned from dispensing drugs and had to provide a medical exam and follow-ups before and after prescribing opioids. In the first year that the clinics had to register, there were more than 900 clinics; by 2014 that number had dropped to 371.

Dawn was traveling a deadly road that was already all-too-familiar to many. In 2012, doctors wrote 259 million opiate prescriptions—enough for every American adult to have their own prescription, with 19 million to spare. Among women, prescription painkiller overdose deaths jumped 400 percent from 1999 to 2010. In 2016, Kentucky had the fifth highest overdose rate in the country at 33.5 deaths per 100,000 people and 1,419 overdose deaths overall. In 2017, Kentucky drug overdose deaths jumped 11.5 percent from the year before. The state had 1,565 people die from drug overdoses, a 40 percent increase over the previous five years.[2]

While opioid use resulted in an increase in overdoses, it also contributed to more people being locked up for drug and status crimes. As most states reduced their prison population, Kentucky did not. From 2008 to 2018, the state saw an 11.2 percent increase in its state prison population. Over the five-year period from 2014 to 2019, Kentucky's prison admissions, fueled by drug offenses and other low-level crimes, increased by 32 percent. House Bill 396, which failed, had plans to reform criminal justice in Kentucky and reduce the steady growth of the prison population and save taxpayers $350 million over ten years. Among other things, the bill would have reduced some nonviolent crimes from felonies to misdemeanors, including first- and second-offense drug possession. This would have dramatically reduced the number of offenders spending time behind bars and would have freed them of the stigma of a felony conviction. Defelonizing drug possession has a huge impact on citizens returning to society. Removing the felony conviction from someone's records opens up more opportunities during reentry. Since 2014, California, Utah, Connecticut, Alaska, and Oklahoma have reduced drug possession offenses from a felony to a misdemeanor. Though the bill's primary sponsor was Republican, some Kentucky lawmakers remained reluctant to adopt or support ideas that appear to be "pro-criminal." The bill's opponents, which included prosecutors and judges, said it tried to make too many big changes to the courts at once. Their suggestion was that lawmakers break up the bill and try to move it over several sessions.[3]

Kentucky's incarcerated population is so high that nearly half of all prisoners are housed in local jails. These facilities are severely overcrowded and do not offer many vocational or educational pro-grams or addiction treatment. According to the Bureau of Justice Statistics, Kentucky ranked second highest for imprisonment of state and federal prisoners in local facilities in 2014. By 2016, Kentucky jails were at 120 percent of authorized capacity and the Kentucky Department of Corrections spent $128 million to house state prison-ers in local jails.

At the time, Dawn didn't notice any of this. She sold some of the pills and kept a stash. The kids stayed with their grandmother often enough that Dawn's monthly trip to Florida didn't seem sus-picious. She bought them trampolines and Power Wheels, paid the mortgage and car notes. "I felt like I had arrived," she says. When her brother got a job in a pain clinic in Kentucky, Dawn and Ethan took advantage of it. But having unfettered access to the drugs was trouble. After a while, she noticed how bad their addiction had be-come. She recalls having to drive an hour to her husband's job to give him a single pill so he could make it through the workday.

Things got much worse when Dawn found out that Ethan had cheated on her. She couldn't reconcile with him, and so she left him. "I thought Ethan had everything he wanted. We had a nice house and cars, but in the meantime, I left my husband alone," she says. Dawn couldn't get past Ethan's betrayal. She kept asking herself how and why. "I was mad at the world forever," she says. "He had raised my daughters, and they didn't know any other dad. It was rough." Jo noticed that Dawn had been hit hard by the end of her marriage with Ethan. "I think that was a little different than any of the other men she'd ever broke up with," Jo says.

After the breakup, Dawn's drug use intensified. "It got to where I couldn't wake up without being sick, and I didn't know what to do because I still had to keep being a mom." When she realized that she had to use drugs to stop her body from feeling sick, she knew her life had started to spiral downward. She would spend more and more time away from her kids. "I was chasing it where I was, like, gone for days, and I thought because I would leave my kids with my mom and I thought, 'Oh, they're with my mom, they're okay. I'm not being bad because they're where they should be.'" Still nursing a bruised heart, she soon found an "I don't give a shit partner" in a man named Walter, who was also using pills.

Dawn often went to local treatment centers trying to get clean, but nothing stuck. Her mother continued to take care of the children whenever she needed to, but she was at a loss when it came to helping Dawn with her addiction. Dawn wasn't the only person close to Jo who struggled with addiction. All three of Jo's children had faced a battle with substance abuse. Jo had never tried drugs; her one vice, as she describes it, is cigarettes. But her father, a Vietnam veteran, turned to alcohol after the war. "He would hear a plane going over and next thing you know, he was throwing us on the ground, jumping on top of us hollering, 'Hit the bunks, hit the bunks.' He thought he was reliving Vietnam," Jo recalls. With Dawn and her other kids, Jo couldn't make sense of it. "I guess I was an enabler. I covered up a lot of stuff. If there wasn't food in the house, I went and bought the groceries and put 'em in there. If they needed the electric paid, I paid it. So I enabled her to do it instead of just saying 'You need to hit rock bottom,'" Jo says. The bottom was on its way.

Dawn moved to Salt Lick, Kentucky, which she describes as country as country gets, with Walter. Her mom had cut her off from working, so she couldn't keep up with her bills. Her electricity got shut off and her car was repossessed. She worked temporary jobs in factories or fast food or serving, but it wasn't enough. She'd take off on a motorcycle with Walter, leaving her teenage girls alone for days at a time. "I just remember there really wasn't much food in the house. We were kind of scrounging around," Annabel says. "Taylor, she's kind of like the chef, so we get some stuff and do some weird stuff. We just throw together." Taylor remembers serving her sister glazed donuts and tuna out of a can for Thanksgiving.

One day in 2010 or 2011, she can't remember exactly when, Taylor got fed up with her mother leaving them alone and told her sister that she was going to call social services. It was a choice that could change the course of their lives. Dawn and Taylor had gotten into an argument about Dawn leaving them alone. "It was almost like a fist fight because she was just erratic about the whole situation," Taylor recalls. She went to the back room and called child welfare services to report her mother. She can't remember everything she told them, just that she said, "Somebody needs to come out here." When the social worker arrived, she questioned both Dawn and the girls, separately. Taylor was a freshman in high school at the time, and her main concern was her mother leaving for days at a time.

To Taylor's surprise, the social worker walked out of their home without taking any action. "I guess she had an excuse for everything that was coming at her," Taylor recalls. Dawn did. Dawn had dealt with social services coming to her home before, and she knew how to work her way out of an allegation. "I was always slick enough," Dawn brags. "I always had a nice house, always had food, my kids always had nice stuff. And I was always able to slide out," Dawn says. As the woman headed for her car, Dawn was relieved. But then Taylor yelled out to get the social worker's attention. She had a request. "Drug test her, then that'll put it all to rest because she can't lie about that. Why don't you drug test her before you leave?" "That was a big mess," Annabel remembers. Dawn was livid at Taylor. "I thought my daughter was the biggest rat." Later she realized that her kids just wanted their mom. "I was just too wrapped up and sick to see. I thought they were okay because they're with me or my mom or something."

Taylor's gambit worked: Dawn was given two hours to arrive at the jail or a testing center for the drug test. She didn't. A few hours later the social worker returned with the sheriff. Dawn had a bench warrant for a cold check, which gave them probable cause to arrest her. They asked her where she wanted her kids to go. Her five children were split up between family members to make caring for them easier. Back at the jail, she tested positive, but she was out within a day after paying a fine for writing a bad check.

The family was upset with Taylor for reporting her mother, but she felt she didn't have a choice. "She had everyone against me because I had called social services," Taylor admits. "It was our well-being that I had to protect." She didn't worry about where they would go, because she knew her grandma would be there to take them in. As for her mom, she hoped it would save her. "I thought she would have to go to some classes, I even thought maybe they'll take her to jail. Maybe that'll straighten her up for a little bit, but it seemed like she got wilder after she got rid of us."

It was 2012, and Dawn was deep into her addiction. "I was addicted. I needed that pill and me being sick overrode everything—my kids, my home, my mom, everything," Dawn says. She says it was like a demon on her back. Her family agrees that she really spiraled out of control during this period. "By this time all the clinics had closed down," Dawn recalls. "It was like a dog-eat-dog world on the street, you know, trying to get one [of] the drugs that I was doing went from like $12 dollars to $45 dollars apiece."

The child welfare case dragged on and Dawn had gained some arrest warrants, so she skipped out on court, afraid that she'd be put in jail. She couldn't meet the child welfare case plan to get her children back. She needed to be drug-free, have a job and transportation, and provide a stable place to live with working gas and electricity. "They write out this big plan with you, and they want you to do all this stuff," Dawn says. She needed services, resources, a treatment program, a ride to court, and more. "There's no way I can do this stuff," she thought. She needed someone to show her, not just tell her what to do. "I can tell you all day this is what you need to do.

But if you don't know what to do and your mind's not set and you're broken and you've just lost—my kids were my world—you know, and I've lost all them. . ... They don't help you get to those resources."

Eventually, her social worker told her that the worse-case scenario, which didn't seem that bad to Dawn at the time, meant her kids would remain with the selected family members if she didn't act. Three of her daughters, Taylor, Annabel, and Willow, were with her mother. Her youngest daughter, Hannah, was with her sister, who had served as Hannah's babysitter since she was a baby. Her son, Wesley, was with his father, Ethan. She thought it was a good scenario. She popped in on the kids in their respective homes and didn't think about how giving up custody could impact her later. The legal guardian of each child would have the final say on whether Dawn could be involved in the child's life. Dawn would no longer have any say in major decisions that affected her children. She trusted her mom, sister, and ex-husband. She assumed she would always be able to see her kids.

The court granted the respective caregivers permanent custody but didn't terminate Dawn's parental rights. Jo uprooted and moved to the county where Dawn lived. She wanted to be sure the three girls in her care could stay in school.

In 2018, Kentucky had the highest rate of children living with relatives in the country. Nine percent of the children in the state, about twice the national level of 4 percent, were living outside of their home. Between 2013 and 2015 more than fifty thousand children were being raised by a relative, and the number nearly doubled from 2016 to 2018, reaching ninety-six thousand children. Some state officials attribute this rise of displaced children to the growing epidemic of opioid addiction. As parents lose their jobs, homes, and ability to parent in the midst of addiction, a vast burden settles on the shoulders of family members.[4]

On any given day, there are nearly 443,000 children in the United States foster care system. In many cases, eager parents are on the other end working hard to get their children back. Dawn could be considered lucky since her family was able to step in and prevent her parental rights from being terminated and her children from being thrown into foster care. But many parents aren't so lucky, and so the outcome can be much bleaker. Parents like Dawn have a more complicated child-welfare journey, because their cases sit at the crossroads of the child-welfare and criminal justice systems. Battling a substance addiction can be messy and complicated, because incarceration and recovery are messy and complicated, and the systems these parents face rarely find ways to work with and through such challenges without taking the draconian step of family separation. Children lose the most.

Criminalizing addiction, especially when child welfare is involved, all but assures failure. Parents have a slim chance to recover, successfully complete a case plan in time, and ultimately regain custody. Addiction experts argue we need to take a different stance on addiction, recovery, and parenting, particularly for those parents who have been incarcerated. Dr. Richard D. Blondell, professor and vice chair of addiction medicine at the University of Buffalo, says that although addiction is treatable, there is no cure. "It's a chronic disorder. Once you get it, you have it. We have treatments that can keep it under control." He says that it can be thought of as a chronic disease like diabetes. With diabetes, we don't expect people to have perfect control their whole life. "An individual with a substance use disorder can respond to treatment and the disorder can get into remission, but reoccurrences are common." In the end, the children lose out because our criminal justice system is so concentrated on punishing the parent for their addiction, which can even facilitate a relapse.

Losing parental rights can come about in any number of ways. Parents may not be able to get a handle on their addiction or don't have the resources to make it to court. Regardless, once they have lost those rights, they are no longer able to visit or speak with their children, or even learn where their children end up. They will have no idea if their child has been placed in a stable, permanent adoptive home, or if their child is bouncing between temporary foster homes or is languishing in a group home. Under the current law, parents who lose their rights will only ever see their child again if the child chooses to seek out the parent after he or she turns eighteen. Losing custody of your children, even to family members, can be a devastating event. And it can contribute to relapse.

After custody of her children was transferred, Dawn's sense of loss settled in deeper. She took off on the back of a motorcycle with Walter with just a tent and her clothes. She lived a true gypsy life. Camping out in Tennessee, serving at a steakhouse, bartending, just hustling and using. "We just run rampant, just out like real live drug addiction," Dawn recalls. She figured her kids were safe. Meanwhile, Dawn was caught in a vicious cycle of status crimes like writing a cold check, driving without car tags, disorderly conduct, and failure to appear. "I always felt like the law's coming," Dawn says.

It was.

7

MORE HUMAN
Mississippi

In 2015, on a warm, sunny afternoon in late April, about twenty-five demonstrators gathered on the steps outside the federal courthouse in Jackson. A heavyset black woman with fire engine red streaks in her hair held a sign that read "Peace." A white woman with dirty blond hair, a bare face, and sunglasses wore a T-shirt with the line, "It's a loyalty thing, you wouldn't understand." The youngest of them all, a brown-skinned girl with a bow around her ponytail, donned a T-shirt that read, "Free My People," with prisoners' faces on it—her father's picture included. Her fist was raised midway in the air, and her sign read, "Family."

Among them was Ruth, coming from her night shift at work. She wore black sunglasses and a red Mississippi Advocates for Prisoners (MAP) T-shirt. Her sign read "Pro-Conjugal." These women are members of a tribe, a band of mothers and wives joined together in support of their imprisoned partners. They vehemently objected when a reporter referred to them as "prison wives." They are far more than that: they protest prison conditions, corruption, and most of all, the continued stripping of visitation rights. In February 2014, the Mississippi prison commissioner ended the last of their spousal visits—the state's prison conjugal visitation program—citing budget cuts, among other reasons. Ruth and the other members of MAP were fighting for a reversal of the commissioner's decision by illustrating how important the visits were to their families.

Inside the prison, William saw Ruth on the news and felt proud that she was protesting and fighting for their visitation access. One of his favorite memories is when he watched his boys, Kevin, Robert, and Naeem, haul fishing poles to the edge of the lake on the prison grounds, their snacks and gear nearby. Naeem, the youngest of the Anderson boys, was still learning how to fish. He knelt in front of the big lake as his father showed him how to tie a knot and then hook the bait. "Shhh," William warned gently. "You have to be very quiet. You don't want to scare the fish away." After that, Naeem was stealthy. Once he caught a fish, William showed him how to skin and cook it.

That was one of many moments the Anderson boys got a chance to experience time with their father during the Extended Family Visitation program, widely known in Mississippi as the Family House. It ran from 1974 to 2012, until it was cut. These visits went far beyond the usual hypersupervised, limited-contact day visits. They were the most intimate form of visitation and the country's most progressive family and spousal program. Family House, aimed to rehabilitate prisoners and strengthen their family ties, allowed unsupervised visits that lasted from three to five days and took place on the facility grounds, in small apartments.

Conjugal visits, which were thought to boost prison morale and maintain family ties, were an additional form of visitation. These visits were permitted only for married prisoners, once a week, and only for a single hour. In both instances, only minimum- or medium-security detainees who demonstrated good behavior were eligible to participate. Prisoners had to be tested for and be free of infectious diseases, and they couldn't have any sex-related convictions on their records.

These family visits, which happened four times a year, were a highlight for the Anderson family. On holidays, Ruth brought the ingredients to make a traditional Southern Thanksgiving or Christmas dinner—turkey, dressing, greens, macaroni and cheese—as if the family were all at home. Other times, William would fire up the grill, and load it with seasoned ribs, steak, and chicken that Ruth brought on the long visit. When they weren't focused on one-on-one time, they enjoyed sitting outside at a picnic table where they played a game of spades with other married couples.

As kids, their boys made new friends during the visits, played in the sandbox, and rocked on the seesaw. As teenagers, they shot hoops on the basketball courts until they could beat their dad. William talked to the boys about school, staying out of trouble, and the puzzling world of girls. They spent time in a separate room, just the boys and their dad. During these visits, the Andersons found a semblance of normalcy. "It made the boys feel closer to William," Ruth recalls. "It wasn't like they didn't know their father—they made memories every visit."[1]

THESE UNIQUE VISITATION PRACTICES, which started in 1974, have racist roots. It was in Parchman, no later than 1918, that the Mississippi State Penitentiary—twenty thousand acres of delta plantation that was then devoid of high walls and gun towers—became the birthplace of conjugal visits, which led the way to extended family visits. Started informally, these visits weren't originally intended to unite spouses or connect families, but rather were based on racial stereotypes.

Black men were thought to have superhuman strength and uncontrollable libidos. So conjugal visits were introduced to tame them and make them work harder at slaughtering hogs and picking cotton in the prison's farming operations. At the time, marriage wasn't a prerequisite, and prostitutes visited the prison on Sundays. A decade later, black men weren't the only prisoners getting these visits. Beginning in the 1930s, white men were also allowed conjugal visits, and by 1972, women were too.

In 1961, prisoner construction crews began building new conjugal-visiting facilities, and in 1963 the prison added marriage as an eligibility requirement. Back then, Mississippi state prison officials reasoned that "a man and his wife have the right to sexual intercourse, even though the man is in prison." Prison officials believed that allowing these visits helped assure prisoners that their families were well. "One visit in private is better than a hundred letters because he can judge for himself," said one corrections officer. A report reviewing the program noted that "with adequate facilities, careful selection, and appropriate counsel, it is possible that the conjugal visiting program in Mississippi could be developed into one of the most enlightened programs in modern corrections."[2]

It was.

Seeking both to mend families fractured by incarceration and to quell prison upheaval, several states followed Mississippi's lead in the coming decades. In 1968, California launched its Family Visiting Program at the California Correctional Institution at Tehachapi and soon expanded the program throughout the state. South Carolina introduced family visits around the same time. New York started its program in 1976, and Minnesota began its own in 1977. Similar ones followed in Washington, Connecticut, New Mexico, and Wyoming in the early 1980s.

This type of visitation revolutionized the way families maintained ties through the confines of imprisonment. As for the Andersons, these visits both helped strengthen their family and allowed them to expand their clan. Ruth and William had no plans for a third child, but fourteen years after William went to prison, they learned that Ruth was again expecting. "I was forty!" Ruth says with embarrassed laughter. When she found out she was pregnant, she didn't believe it. She'd already finished her years of changing diapers, sleepless nights, and watching cartoons on repeat. Her time going to school PTA meetings was closing with her second son, Robert, who was already in high school.

In denial, she took multiple home pregnancy tests. When they all came back positive, she headed to her doctor's office. Eventually, she took a blood test. After that test also indicated she was pregnant, she wanted another blood test. "I just couldn't believe it," she recalls. Finally, she came around and prepared for her unexpected baby. "I thought it was all good because I was established," Ruth says. "I didn't have to go on welfare." Ruth had been a licensed practical nurse for over a decade before becoming a registered nurse a few years before the unexpected pregnancy. She supported herself. "The government wasn't taking care of me. I had insurance. The government didn't even know Naeem existed," she says.

Naeem was born in the summer of 1995. Ruth's nephew drove her to the hospital when she went into labor. No one from the family was in the delivery room with her, but her eldest son, Kevin, stood in for William. He was by her side after the delivery. William knew when Naeem was due and called home after the expected due date and heard the news of his son's birth. At the time, William was at the prison in Parchman, and they were on a semimonthly visiting schedule. A week after her delivery, Ruth bundled Naeem in blankets and drove him to meet his father. She continued to take him on regular visits every two weeks. Shortly after, she took Naeem on his first family visit. He slept between Ruth and William in the bed they shared. "He was a little ole bitty baby," William recalls. "I used to hear people roll over on babies; I ain't never roll over on him." Naeem would be spoiled far beyond his older siblings.

Family visits allowed William to take an active and physical part in raising his sons. He was able to feed Naeem and rock him to sleep as an infant. Naeem's first memories of Family House are from visiting as a toddler. He would hop on his father's back to go for a walk or stand with him in front of a stately tree picking pecans. William, who's a big sports fan, often challenged Naeem to a game of basketball during their visits. Naeem is now just under six feet tall and slender, with wiry muscles. "I got better," Naeem brags. "At first, I couldn't dunk or beat him, but then I started beating him." William pushed him, playing hard against him, never just letting Naeem win. Naeem had to earn it; it took years, but finally he won.

Naeem also remembers being a noisy fisherman. "I ain't never know how—I was young," he says with a Southern drawl, while twisting his coiled locks of hair around his fingers. "My momma ain't never showed me how to skin one." Ruth interjects, laughing, "Naw, because I don't do that." Some things were a father's duty and William did many of those things during extended family visits.

When William reflects on the Family House, he sits in the memory. He admits that the most difficult part of each visit was saying goodbye. "It's a painful experience. They getting in the car, you getting in the van, they going home, you're not." One year, when he was a teenager, that pain became too much for Robert. "He stopped coming," William remembers. "You feel for your kids. You hate to see them go through it. But the time that you spend together is *very, very, very* important." Despite the pain of goodbyes, William never wanted to see the visits end.

As mentioned, Mississippi had piloted the program in the 1970s, and other states followed suit. When the other states started making cuts in the mid-1990s, as state corrections became more punitive, Mississippi held out for longer than most. But then, despite how much it meant to the prisoners and their families, Mississippi, too, started making cuts. In 2012, family visits were cut. Families were blindsided. Ruth never received an official notice that Family House had been eliminated. It meant a radical reshaping of her family's life. Two years later, prison officials also cut the conjugal visits.

The one-hour weekly visit—the last bit of privacy for these married couples—was cut just as coldly as the family visits had been. A memo taped to the visiting-room wall was the only announcement of the end to conjugal visits. Families had to protest. They knew the visits weren't a right, but they knew how consequential they were to maintaining family ties. They wanted the corrections officials and society to see them as whole, as just as worthy as others trying to keep their families intact, and not merely as the spouses of undeserving prisoners. Visitation has a significant impact on families affected by incarceration, but remains an aspect of corrections that is most easily severed and seen as extraneous.

William, who used to work for the prison superintendent, always stayed up on what was going on. He had heard that the visits might be cut. But families were still shocked when the rumors proved true. "They knew people would get pissed off about the conjugal visit," Ruth says sharply. Losing the one-on-one time was devastating for Ruth. "I don't feel like I'm alive," she says, her voice aching with sadness. "They shut down all these feelings."

For qualifying Mississippi families, extended and conjugal visits were normal, something they had always known. But the mid-1990s marked the elimination of several conjugal and extended family visiting programs across the county. The eliminations were in line with the punitive approach that took hold in corrections following the 1994 Violent Crime Control and Law Enforcement Act, which did away with programs and policies that benefited prisoners and their families.

With a ballooning state prison population, resources became scarce and corrections had to stretch their budgets. Keeping families together was no longer a priority. In 1994, South Carolina's conjugal visits were the first to go. "As our new era in corrections begins," read an annual corrections report, "the South Carolina Department of Corrections has taken note of the growing trends for tougher restrictions on inmates." When Wyoming closed its Family

Visiting Center in 1995, the prison warden said: "Times and conditions have changed since the program was first implemented. With the increasing population, greater security responsibilities, and limited budget, utilizing employees and other resources to maintain the family visiting program can no longer be justified."

Nearly two and a half decades after the first states began making cuts, Mississippi joined the list of states that ended families' access to these visits. Christopher Epps, then the Mississippi corrections commissioner, explained in a press release that he'd ended the family visitation and conjugal visit programs primarily because of budget cuts, citing costs like building maintenance and the time that staffers spent escorting prisoners to and from the visitation facility. He argued the benefits of the programs didn't outweigh the cost to the overall budget.

Ruth doesn't buy the cost explanation. "The prison didn't spend no money. We paid and brought all the utensils. That fee? It paid for the refrigerator and stove. I don't know what they're talking about costs," Ruth fumes. Despite the commissioner's claim of budget cuts, Mississippi never released details on the amount they saved by cutting the program.

Shortly after Mississippi ended its extended visiting program, the Offender Management Services (OMS) of the New Mexico Corrections Department ended their family visitation program as well. Like with the MDOC (Mississippi Department of Corrections) program, only two hundred of the prisoners were eligible, and prison officials said that number was too small to be worth the $120,000 annual cost. And yet, in 2014, the program accounted for less than 1 percent of the department's $293 million budget. And that $120,000 cost was offset by a fee to families of $50 per visit.

When asked about New Mexico's decision to end family visitation, Alex Tomlin, the corrections department's public affairs director, inadvertently described what was, for many, the beauty of the program: "The majority were not spousal visits—they were [visits] with children or parents." For example, she offered, "an offender and his children, they would play football in the front yard." Tomlin argued they would have kept the program if there was evidence that the program reduced recidivism. She wasn't alone in her thinking that the visits were legitimized only if they reduced recidivism. Most studies that look at the effects of visitation aren't focused on how or if it preserves family bonds, or what they mean for children, parents, and partners. Instead, they evaluate recidivism and reentry, and treat them as the most important components when determining the effects of a program.

There's no study using a strong research design that specifically links extended family visits with either reduced recidivism or stronger family bonds, but several studies have consistently linked regular visits with both. In 2011, the Minnesota Department of Corrections conducted an in-depth study that tracked over sixteen thousand offenders released from the state's prisons between 2003 and 2007. When other factors were controlled, the study showed that prisoners who received visits were 13 percent less likely to be convicted of a felony after their release, and were 25 percent less likely to have their probation or parole revoked. In 2016, another study found that visitation decreased recidivism by 26 percent.[3]

Some states have acknowledged these positive outcomes. The Washington State Department of Corrections, which continues to offer extended family visits, has said that they "support building sustainable relationships important to offender re-entry and to provide an incentive for those serving long-term sentences to engage in positive behavioral choices." As of 2019, only California, Connecticut, Washington, and New York continue to offer family visitation widely. South Dakota, Colorado, and Nebraska had a very limited visitation policy: they are only for female prisoners, and the focus is on those prisoners with young children.

With studies indicating such striking benefits, and with such a small financial savings at stake, what was really at work? The debate in Ruth's home state of Mississippi was telling. In addition to the budget claims, Commissioner Epps said, he also ended the visits because "even though we provide contraception, we have no idea how many women are getting pregnant only for the child to be raised by one parent." He was not alone in his thinking. Richard Bennett, a Republican state representative who for three straight years wrote bills seeking to ban conjugal visits before the corrections department finally decided to end them on its own in 2014, agreed. "It's unfair to have a child without a parent," Bennett contended. The same racist thinking about black sexuality that led to the start of these visits had become the reason for ending them. Ending the visits was a form of policing black sexuality for the men said to have uncontrollable libidos. And though not expressly stated, this racist thinking also categorized the women as the stereotypical "welfare queen" who had babies so as to bilk the system for government aid. They were not regarded as women who were capable of providing for their children.[4]

"Taxpayers are paying for it. I don't think it's right," said Bennett. When asked about the importance of preserving the family unit, Bennett softened. He said, "I would like to see a place for the family to come and see each other." But he had one caveat: he would insist that the couple "stay separate at night." After a long pause, he continued, "I would like to see the unit together without the conjugal part. I don't think it's appropriate for parents to be doing that with the children [present]." He suggested that states like New York and California continue to maintain family visits only because, as he put it, "They're probably more liberal than Mississippi."

Naeem, who was conceived during the visits that were under attack, rejects the logic of Bennett, Epps, and others. "God gave me this life," he says with a commanding gaze. "Some people in there may never get out, and they need another piece of them out here living." Naeem views his parents' four-decade-long union as a "blessing," despite the barriers imposed by his father's incarceration.

For William, the visits did exactly what prison isn't supposed to do. "It made him feel like he was almost at home." And the visits kept Ruth looking forward to the future. It allowed the Anderson boys to develop intimate relationships with their father. "It made [William] feel more human," says Ruth. He even got to meet his grandchildren. William sat outside, holding his granddaughter in his arms for the first time. He sat with Ruth outside and watched the stars.

AMIDST ALL THE DEBATE ABOUT children being born to single parents and recidivism rates, corrections departments and policymakers rarely consider the impact these visits have on children. Ann Adalist-Estrin, who directs the National Resource Center on Children and Families of the Incarcerated at Rutgers University, said extended visits are the most helpful developmentally for kids. They allow kids the opportunity to see their parents as real and human, and they remove the strain of making each visit perfect. "During regular visits, kids are monitored seriously," she explains. "They're in very uncomfortable visiting arrangements, with hard seats, limited time face to face, can't touch each other. It limits the child's ability to go through cadence."

Cadence refers to the series of group developmental stages that some therapists have dubbed "form, storm, norm, and perform." Initially, the child is elated to see his or her parent. But during longer visits, there's greater room for upheaval: kids feel comfortable broaching difficult topics involving sadness or anger, because there's more time to recover and return to normal. "In a short visit, if kids are beginning to 'form' and 'norm' the relationship, they will not do the 'storm' part, because they don't feel comfortable," Adalist-Estrin says. "They don't have the time to resolve it before they leave."

Naeem and his brothers certainly felt more comfortable in extended visits. For two of the Anderson boys, it was the only experience they had with their parents in a home setting. There were a few times Naeem was afraid to go on the family visits because he feared his father would reprimand him. "I remember being scared going on family visits when I know I messed up in school and I was getting a whupping, but he never whupped me." Naeem fought a lot in middle school. He says he was targeted for allegedly flirting with other boys' girlfriends. "That's a situation where you call your dad and he tell you what to do," he shares. At the time, he couldn't do that and wasn't sure how to handle it. "He in there, so what could he do in there and I'm out here?" Naeem remembers his dad's idle threats after he learned about the fights in school. "He get to hollering at me, talking about he's going to beat me. When I was younger, I was always scared of my daddy." When he went on the visits, though, his dad just sat and talked with him. Over the phone he had to scare him into good behavior, but in person, he could take his time and *be* with his son, show him the right way. Having the extended visits meant they could traverse the range of emotions and experiences as father and son, play basketball, fish together, and have a conversation about misbehaving in school. If necessary, William could reprimand Naeem. They were able to experience a wide spectrum.

As the youngest, Naeem was the last of the Anderson boys to stop going on the visits. Around the time he turned sixteen, his trips died down. They were getting boring for him; no teenager wants to be stuck with his parents for a week. A year later, the visits were cut. He still thinks they are important for younger children. "I feel like it would be good for the kids to go. Those few days do matter at the end of the day."

Naeem suspects that corrections officials have no idea what it's like to be incarcerated. Incarceration is hard enough, and he feels it's excessive to continue stripping the incarcerated of access to their families. "You're looking at walls. It's a hard pill to swallow. When they take the one thing away that matters, what do you do?" he asks. "They shouldn't take that away. Just because it's not them they take it away. Just because their life is good."

In 2014, just months after ending the conjugal visiting program, then Commissioner Epps, who oversaw MDOC for twelve years, resigned amid corruption charges. In court, he faced a forty-nine-count federal indictment that accused him of taking at least $1.4 million in bribes and kickbacks for steering more than $800 million worth of state prison contracts. In 2017, he was sentenced to nearly twenty years in federal prison and fined $100,000 "for running one of the largest and longest criminal conspiracies in the state's history." Epps represents a prime example of someone who didn't see the importance of maintaining family ties while behind bars, who couldn't see the implication of his policy implementation or the impact. But now he's one of them.[5]

Although Naeem had already stopped attending family visits, he knew the end of the program would impact his mother significantly. Naeem had to figure out how to be there for his mom while she processed this blow. She continued her protests with MAP. Although local media outlets covered the families who were fighting to regain visitation privileges, the group wasn't successful in getting the MDOC commissioner to reverse his decision. The families would have to find other ways to keep their loved ones close.

8

A WOMAN'S WORK
Florida

When Randall was arrested on the murder charge, Ayana was only a few months along in her pregnancy with Niyah. While he was in jail, they had a tough conversation. "So, what are you going to do?" she recalls him asking. "What am I going to do about what?" she replied. "Our baby," came his reply. "I'm not going to force anything on you," he told her. She assumed he was trying to give her a way out of proceeding with the pregnancy, a path that allowed her to start over. But as a practicing Christian from a religious family, Ayana said there were no alternatives. "We have always been 100 percent against abortions," she said. "I have to have this child." That was her answer. He too wanted the baby, although he wasn't sure how the future would play out. He'd been thinking of fatherhood before he reached puberty. He requested a speedy trial so that he could, hopefully, get home to his family.

After Niyah was born, Ayana avoided taking her to visit Randall in jail because she thought he was coming home. "I didn't want to expose my daughter to that," Ayana says, meaning the visits. When Ayana realized the trial might not go as planned, she agreed to take

Niyah to see her father for the first time. She was not even one year old at the time. Jails are meant to hold people awaiting trial or serving a sentence under a year. Visitation varies in terms of structure and availability. In some cases, the visits are noncontact, and a barrier of plexiglass is placed between the prisoner and visitor. These visits are generally very short. Now that Randall had been convicted of first-degree murder and received his sentence of life without the possibility of parole, he would be transferred to prison. There would be no telling how far the prison would be or how soon Niyah could meet her father. Randall had seen his daughter only in pictures, and Ayana wanted to give him the opportunity to see her in person. So she went to visit him in jail. It was not only Niyah's first experience with jail. "That was my first time ever seeing someone in jail or prison," Ayana says. "I wasn't exposed to that, and I'm an adult."

She'd always said that she and Randall were from different sides of the track. Opposites even. The sheltered girl from a financially stable, two-parent household with all the protections that came along with it had fallen for the latchkey kid from the other side of town. It took Randall a long time to get her attention, but it finally worked. Randall was playing on the lawn in front of the three-story apartment complex where he lived when he first saw Ayana. She was wearing a green cheerleader's uniform and he saw her go into the apartment on the first floor. He stopped playing and asked his friend who she was. It turns out she was his friend's cousin. Randall asked his friend to go tell her that he liked her. Reluctantly, the boy carried the message but didn't return with a reply. Years later Randall learned she didn't want to talk to him—she'd referred to him as "the big head boy." It would be over a year before he got to know her. He went to the same evening church service as Ayana's family, where he and Ayana participated in a youth night. Randall wasn't able to say much to Ayana that night because her mother was there and her mother was not a fan. She had no issue telling Randall that she did not like him and didn't trust him. Randall was scared of her, so he didn't make a move.

When he transferred middle schools, he came across Ayana again when they temporarily shared a class. She didn't remember him. He reintroduced himself, but she wouldn't talk to him until she confirmed he was really a friend of her cousin. Randall recalls being in high pursuit of her, but she was reserved, conservative even. She had never engaged boys romantically. She rejected him a lot until she finally let him kiss her in the stairway of the school. "I knew there was something different about Ayana," Randall says. "But I was surprised to find out how inexperienced and chaste she was." He was her first boyfriend. While courting Ayana, he found himself in a trilemma—he was dating two of her schoolmates. The three of them found out and forced him to choose among the three. He chose Ayana. From that point on, they were officially in a relationship.

They were together for the six years prior to Randall's imprisonment. While Ayana eventually came to know that the charming, sweet boy she loved also sold drugs, she was blindsided by his murder charge. It's been a decade since the charge, and Ayana still doesn't seem to know what happened. "I don't know. He got caught up in a situation. I can't really tell you the facts of what really happened because I really don't know."

Ayana took Randall's sentence hard. "She was heartbroken and crying a lot," Randall recalls. "And I no longer wanted to be the cause of her tears." About a year into his prison sentence he ended their relationship, telling her that he no longer wanted to be with her. Randall saw the relationship as irreparable, given his sentence, and didn't want to be a burden to her. He felt she deserved better. At the time, she was hurt and confused at his decision. It would take years before she realized that Randall had her best interest and future in mind when he made the decision. In order to really convince Ayana he wanted to end their relationship, he had to do something drastic. Show her coldness. He didn't want to stifle her growth; he wanted her to live her planned life without him. After the breakup, whenever he called, he kept the conversation short and mostly asked about their daughter, Niyah. Later, he admitted to Ayana that playing cold was hard for him. He was just trying to push her away, force her to move on. "Now, I look back and I appreciate him for that. Because I probably would have been still so hooked on to him, and I would have been putting my life on hold," Ayana says.

Randall and Ayana have been separated for close to a decade, but she continued to visit him for the sake of Niyah for a long time, until she just couldn't do it anymore. In the early days, even after they separated, she continued to participate in the Children of Inmates (COI) Bonding Visits with their daughter. Soon she found the visits too painful. She hasn't been in two years. She doesn't have the strength for it. "You have to be strong and you have to be strong for your child," she says. She still argues with Randall about bringing Niyah to see him outside of the Bonding Visits. If he had it his way, which he doesn't, Ayana would take Niyah to visit her dad every weekend.

Ayana works full-time as a representative in the groups sales department of a hotel chain. She has two days off per week, one of which she often gives up for overtime to earn more money. On Saturdays, the one day off she keeps sacred, she attends church and reserves it for a break. "That's the only time I have for myself," she says. It's also true that she just doesn't want to take Niyah on the visits. The experience is draining for her. "I can't deal with it. I don't like it. Even though there's no connection with me and him, leaving a prison, knowing that I have to take my child in the car and she probably sad, I always break down and cry. And I hate it. It's been ten years. I can't. I don't have the strength for it anymore. I don't want to go there."

Today, Ayana and Randall have a relationship that oscillates, which makes co-parenting, especially through incarceration, difficult. "We have our seasons when we're friends and not friends," Ayana says. Since Randall has been away so long and the young parents don't have a relationship in which they talk with any regularity, Randall doesn't have any real insight into how she lives her life or what is required for her to raise their daughter alone. Because of this, she feels isolated and unappreciated sometimes. She says Randall has a difficult time seeing how hard it is for her to raise Niyah alone.

COI does offer support groups and services to help incarcerated parents understand what their spouse and family members are going through. In Randall's case, he wants to see his daughter no matter what it takes. This desire has temporarily blinded him to Ayana's plight as a single mother. To a large degree, Ayana has operated as a one-woman show, with work and Niyah being her only priorities. She hasn't engaged COI to help her with anything more than the Bonding Visits. They offer community support groups, crisis intervention, parenting classes, and advocacy. If families are facing something that's outside of their immediate wheelhouse, COI provides referrals to their social services partners. If parents are open, they'll help them find after-school care, housing, food assistance, and health care. COI can also help them navigate through the juvenile justice system.

Many families impacted by incarceration feel lost and don't know all the resources that can be at their disposal. COI organizers have learned that many families they work with do not seek the available services because they are scared or intimidated by the paperwork and the interview process that come along with them. This is unfortunate because the program bridges the divide. Children have access to camp, counseling, and leadership programs. The program can even get personalized to meet the particular needs of a family. Recently, the organization learned that a caregiver of nine children went without working appliances for months, and so the children went hungry. They found the caregiver a refrigerator and stove. When they learned of a caregiver's death, COI staff provided grief counseling and basic necessities during the mourning period. They, meanwhile, worked with the incarcerated parent to identify and legally coordinate new living arrangements for the children so that they could avoid placement in the child welfare system.

Once, Ayana told Randall she was struggling to do it alone. He reminded her that his mother had managed. "Oh, my mom did it," she remembers him saying. "That's your mom. This is not what I signed up for," she retorted. The other recurring theme, she says, that renders him out of touch is when she complains about her work schedule; he argues that she works too much. "If I don't work, how am I going to provide for me and Niyah? Living is not free." The cost of raising Niyah, putting her through school and keeping a roof over her head, is hard to manage on Ayana's salary. Research has shown that more than half of fathers in state prison report being the primary breadwinner in their family prior to incarceration, so economic hardship becomes a reality for many families.

Even though Ayana struggles to raise a young daughter with an incarcerated father, from the outside she makes it look easy. Ayana has tasked herself with giving Niyah everything she possibly can. "She deserves it. She's a straight A student, she's an honor roll student." Giving her daughter the best can be consuming. "It's a lot physically, mentally, and emotionally to be there for her, but financially as well," she says.

Each day, Ayana pulls her cherry-red Mercedes-Benz into the parking lot of the private school Niyah attends. When Niyah was set to go to elementary school, Ayana found herself googling the best private schools in her neighborhood. She had tried public school and wanted better for her daughter, the best the community Miami Gardens had to offer. Of the two that turned up in her search, she selected a school that incorporated religion, an important educational component she felt was missing from too many schools. At the Seventh-Day Adventist school, Niyah would take a Bible course, attend chapel biweekly, and pray in the morning and at lunch. It was a school Ayana felt would reinforce the beliefs she practices at home, serve as her core, and provide a stellar education.

Every afternoon when she arrives, Ayana must go inside to check her daughter out of school. Niyah is there, wearing a white shirt and multicolored pleated uniform jumper, a matching crisscross tie, white socks up to her calves, and black shoes. The large welcome banner on the wall is a picture of Jesus, his arms spread wide to welcome the children who will be under His instruction as they follow God's plan. Niyah has no interest in cheerleading or dance like her mom did as a kid. Instead, she runs track, is in the band, and recently signed up for a robotics class. All are activities Ayana is happy to let her participate in, but they aren't free. The ten-year-old often signs herself up for extracurricular activities without a second thought. Recently, she handed Ayana an application. "Oh, Mom," she said, "sign this." Ayana had to remind her daughter the extracurricular activities weren't free. She pointed to a line on the application. "You see, this is money I have to send." It was a $30 application fee. Her participation in the band costs $45 a month. She's on an academic scholarship, so Ayana has to pay only a percentage of her tuition, but it adds up. If Niyah keeps a 90 percent grade point average, she'll be eligible for additional funding. Ayana has to pay for school uniforms too; the shirts cost $25 and the dresses are $50. The school does not offer breakfast, and lunch is available for purchase at $7 per day.

The benefit for Ayana is that Niyah is far away from the risk of trouble, and she believes Niyah veering onto an unexpected path is unlikely. For Ayana, sending Niyah to a private school was not up for negotiation, because her expectations of success are hardwired. Ayana is providing her daughter with what she deems normal and appropriate, meaning as close as possible to what she had while growing up. "My life wasn't hard," Ayana says. "I didn't come from a rough family. My family is very successful, educated black people, so I look up to them." Niyah, she says, is naturally exposed to do the right thing and is given a surplus of examples. "When you're surrounded by positive, it's very hard for you to look for negative," Ayana says. "It's not like it's just me fighting poverty," she admits. "You pull up to my family's house and you're like, wow, what do they do for a living?" She has the support of her parents and siblings when it comes to raising Niyah. She grew up with both parents in a house on the more developed side of Overtown. Her parents separated when she was a teenager. Her father owns a mobile car wash and her mother is a bus operator.

Ayana never envisioned a life in which she would be a single parent. Although she has gotten used to it, on occasion she thinks to herself how great Niyah's loss is. "It's so sad that this child doesn't have a dad," she says. They both have it hard, but even so, neither is permitted a pity party for long. She doesn't allow Niyah to use it as a handicap. "I've seen others where they're lighter on their kids or use it as an excuse. They use that as a crutch. Versus me, I still hold the same expectations for my daughter. I don't give her any slack that her father's not around. I know that it's probably a very hard and difficult situation 'cause sometimes it's very hard on me as well," she says. "Being that I have to do everything alone, myself. I didn't make this child alone, why do I have to do this alone?"

Ayana tries to give her daughter the kind of life that doesn't remind her she has only one present parent. So far, she has a solution to fill one aspect of the void her daughter might otherwise feel. This aspect has to do with money. Her financial priority is Niyah, then bills, and finally her needs. "I bust my behind giving her stuff because I don't want her looking at my nieces who have both their mom and father home, working parents, both in their life fully and Niyah be like, 'Oh, I wasn't able to get an iPod because my dad's not here.' No. I don't want her to feel that. I don't want her to feel an absent parent. He's absent and she feels it physically, and mentally, but I don't want her to feel it as in I can't get these things. I can't get these shoes because my dad is absent."

While Ayana actively tries to fill the monetary void, she often omits Randall from the picture. It's as if he's an extra in her mother and daughter film. She doesn't talk about Randall's absence with her daughter. Early on, when the girl was younger, Ayana didn't include him on Niyah's family tree for a school project. Ayana preferred to keep it simple, and she wanted to avoid questions, even though she said she had made peace with his confinement. Sure, in the beginning it was tough. Back then, Randall's incarceration was a sensitive topic. But over the years she has been forced to face her new reality as a single mom. She is not as sensitive about his imprisonment anymore. If someone asks her about Niyah's father, she tells them, "He's incarcerated with life." She doesn't feel the need to lie. "This is not something to be sensitive about," and she'll say, "It's been ten years already." Even if Ayana has reconciled the situation, Niyah is still sensitive about it because she's still unable to contend with where her father is. She has her own relationship with her father, whereas Ayana doesn't normally see cause to talk about him. Since Randall and Ayana separated, they live lives wholly independent of each other, participating in the most distant version of co-parenting, merely touching base when they need to arrange something for their daughter. Ayana's focus is on working, surviving, and taking care of her little girl. This leaves little time for her daughter to pepper her with questions about her father.

It's hard to tell if Niyah senses the on-again, off-again tension between her parents. It could be why she doesn't talk to her mother about her dad. She knows her father is in prison, but she has no idea why or how long he'll be there. Of all the adults in her life, Cynthia, her grandmother, is the one who engages her the most about Randall. Cynthia always wants to know if they've spoken, what they talked about, if she's excited about their visits. Once when Niyah refused to acknowledge where her father was, Cynthia pulled out her phone to let her granddaughter hear the caller ID that was attached to Randall's number. It was "Jailhouse Rock," a lighthearted testament to how much Cynthia loved her son, and how she had to face the reality of where he was.

Although Randall's imprisonment is a fact, Ayana doesn't always volunteer the information, especially at Niyah's school, where the community is so small and close-knit that students greet her with, "Hi, Niyah's mom." All the students know one another. "I don't mention her dad in school and when I do, like collages and stuff, I don't put pictures of him up. Because I don't want to open that world," she says. She isn't sure if that world consists of ridicule, compassion, or pity. Whatever that world is, she doesn't want to open the door to any of it.

Still, it comes up. Niyah's second grade teacher often inquired about Randall. One day, Niyah's maternal grandmother, Evelyn, satisfied her curiosity and showed the woman Randall's picture. She didn't think his incarceration needed to be a secret. Before then, no one had told the teacher that Randall was in prison. The teacher told Evelyn that her own father served a long prison sentence and that she still hadn't seen him. Evelyn shared this with Niyah, hoping to illustrate that parental incarceration happens to a lot of people.

But when Niyah recalls her grandmother telling her about her teacher's experience with family incarceration, she leaves out an important detail. "My grandma told me [my teacher's] dad was in the same place and now she's a grown up and she still hasn't seen him." Instead of saying that her teacher's father was also in prison, she uses a shorthand. Ask her what "the same place" is and she will lower her voice, shifting her tone to imitate someone substantially younger, and repeat, "In that *place*." She might say the prison's name, Dade, but she won't call it a prison. She also doesn't really know what he's in prison for. Niyah asked her dad before but says she has since forgotten what he told her.

WHERE YOU LIVE HAS A huge impact on the quality of education your child can receive. Currently, Ayana and her mother, Evelyn, live in Miami Gardens, a middle class black enclave. They live together as roommates, splitting the cost of bills down the middle. Evelyn helps her take care of Niyah. Recently, Ayana's sister and her two toddlers moved in. This stay is supposed to be temporary; they'll be looking for a new place soon. Ayana, too, is looking for a place of her own again. The option to move was prompted when the Miami Dade Housing Authority pulled, after a decade, Ayana's name from their waiting list. She had signed up for the housing assistance when she was pregnant with Niyah.

The Housing Choice Voucher Program, more commonly known as Section 8, is a federally funded program that would allow Ayana to receive a subsidy on a rental in the private housing market. The subsidy is paid directly to the landlord on behalf of the participant, and the renter pays the difference between the actual rent charged by the landlord and the amount subsidized by the program. A family generally pays 30 percent of their adjusted gross income in rent. To qualify, participant households either must not exceed the higher of the federal poverty level or they must earn less than or equal to 50 percent of area median income (AMI). For Ayana, that means she can't earn more than $31,500 a year. The amount of support someone receives is based on their income. For Ayana, she would receive a 15 percent subsidy to use on a one-bedroom place that rents for no more than $1,100 per month. She's a month into her eight-week time frame to find an apartment. If she can't find a suitable apartment in sixty days, she can request two extensions, totaling 120 days. The rental companies or landlords she's encountered so far require first and last months' rent and a security deposit, which for Ayana is $3,300 dollars.

Because Ayana is not living below the poverty line, she has a hard time qualifying for any government assistance. She once tried to apply for the Supplemental Nutrition Assistance Program (SNAP), which helps people with limited income buy food. "They offered me seven bucks [monthly] of food stamps and you know Niyah takes lunch to school every day." The monthly assistance would have been

the same amount required for Niyah's lunch every day if she purchased it at school. "I'm like, even if you guys give me food stamps
enough for Niyah, that's fine," she says, perplexed. "I can't even fix
the taco meal with seven dollars." Ayana feels like most assistance
programs are designed for people living in extreme poverty, not for
the working class or working poor. "They want you to not have a
job," she posits. "The system is just really messed up."

Ayana is right that recipients must be living below the federal
poverty line to be eligible for many resources. States differ in how
they define income and household assets, which in turn determine a
family's eligibility for SNAP. However, gross monthly income generally must be at or below 130 percent of the federal poverty line.
States can set the gross income thresholds to be a SNAP recipient,
but the federal government sets the net income requirements. The
federal government expects a family to contribute 30 percent of their
income to food costs, and after net income is calculated, the SNAP
program will make up the difference between that 30 percent and
what they believe a family should be receiving. The bottom line is
this: The less you make, the more you qualify for. But there's a catch:
SNAP now requires most unemployed working-age adults receiving
benefits to register for work and accept almost any job they are offered. For Ayana, working overtime means she can provide more financially for her daughter, but it also means she is disqualified from
most subsidies.

The housing voucher program has called her in to update her
employment information multiple times over the last ten years. One
time her employer made a mistake on her check and failed to pay her
for all the hours she worked during a pay period. As a result, she was
told she was $200 away from not qualifying. "It's to the point that
you get so frustrated. The only reason I haven't said 'forget it' and
I'm taking it as a blessing is because I have Niyah and it will help."
Even if the assistance was just over $160 a month, it was something.

All the apartments that Ayana has viewed through the program have wait lists that range from four to seven years. This is because she is looking in desirable, low-poverty neighborhoods. Research shows a strong positive physical and mental health effect on families when they move to areas of low-poverty concentration. Families that use their vouchers to live in these neighborhoods and stay for extended periods of time have an increased likelihood of finding jobs and have higher incomes, and their children have higher scores in school and are more likely to enroll in college.

Ayana is trying desperately to find an apartment in one of these areas. Instead, the only availability she has found is in Overtown and Liberty City, both neighborhoods that remain high-poverty. A pamphlet provided by the Housing Choice Voucher Program doesn't even mention these neighborhoods in their profile, and Ayana refuses to move there. "Why do you want to take your kids and raise your kids in those environments?" she asks. A realtor showed her a few rentals that were above the allowed budget, and even those were subpar. "One place I saw made me sick. I couldn't even go back to work for my overtime. Niyah was with me, and the rent, it was like they wanted $1,300. It was disgusting."

Ayana wants to use her voucher but will move only if she's able to secure a safe and nurturing environment for her daughter. They've been on their own before. Ayana had her own apartment in North Miami Beach when Niyah was one year old. It was gated and had security cameras throughout. She felt safe. Then she started to find notes on her car windshield. One read, "Hey Queen, we see you and the baby are alone. You need a guy," Ayana recalls. Being watched shook her. She continued a routine of work and home. When she had to do laundry or go grocery shopping, she made sure she did it before turning in for the evening. She feared going in and out of the complex. Once she was out all day with Niyah visiting Randall three hours away, when he was in Okeechobee, Florida.

When she returned that night, her apartment had been broken into, robbed, and trashed. She was told the cameras were broken.

Another evening while Niyah was away at her grandmother's home, and Ayana was in the apartment working on her laptop doing classwork and listening to music, she heard a commotion. She ran to the peephole in her door to get a glimpse of what was happening. She saw a male neighbor who lived across the hall. Ayana had seen the man chastise his wife before for wearing outfits he deemed "too sexy." She often heard the couple arguing loudly. Earlier that same day, Ayana had seen the woman walking into her apartment. She was wearing a slightly revealing blouse, heels, and jeans. Ayana soon heard the man yelling at the woman. "Where were you? You weren't answering your phone. You liar. Cheater." Shortly after, she heard the woman running down the hallway screaming, then the sound of banging on her door. It was the woman in a pool of blood begging Ayana to call the police. She had been stabbed. She passed out in front of Ayana's door.

Ayana was too afraid to open the door. She called 9-1-1. When the operator asked her to open the door to see if the woman had a pulse, she refused. "Are you crazy? I'm here alone." Ayana screamed and cried while the operator tried to get her to calm down, to no avail. When the ambulance arrived, the woman didn't have a pulse. They used a defibrillator to shock her back to life. The police handcuffed the guy and then brought him to Ayana's door and asked her to identify him. She was in shock. That night the police escorted Ayana to her car with her bags, and she went to her mom's place. She stayed with her mother for a few days.

When she returned to pay the rent at her apartment, she asked the employee in the building manager's office if the woman survived. They had no idea what she was talking about. "I didn't feel safe." Her mother suggested Ayana and her two siblings get an apartment together. They did. Her sisters, who were also mothers and were still with their romantic partners, eventually moved out to live with their partners. Then it was just Ayana and Niyah. Ayana couldn't afford the rent alone, so her mother moved in to help. She feels safe in the house where she lives now, but she hopes to find another affordable place where she doesn't feel the need to watch her back.

AYANA IS DOING EVERYTHING she can to put Niyah first and give her opportunities. But sometimes she jokes with Randall about what her life would look like if he got out. How she would be child-free. Ayana says she would take off and let Randall be a single dad. "I tell him, if they were to say 'You can be free tomorrow,' I would have Niyah there with the bag at the gate waiting for you and I would be dust. Entirely,'" she says seriously. "He'll say, 'Where you going?' I'll say, 'To live my life.'" She laughs. "He be like, 'Well, when you gon come back?' I say, 'Ten years.'" Since he hasn't been the disciplinarian, she assumes Niyah would prefer to live with her dad if she got the opportunity. "People will be asking, 'Where's your daughter?' I don't know. With her dad. I'm living my life." She pretends that she'll take an extended vacation.

"I'm going to come back when I feel like it. I'll call in and check on her," she tells him. But Randall knows what her daughter means to her. He replies to Ayana, "Oh, you . . . saying that now. You big crybaby, as soon as she leaving." Randall is right, the two are inseparable. When Niyah leaves for the weekend with her grandmother, Ayana misses her. "I'm like, 'Oh my God, I miss my child so much.'"

9

LABELED A FELON

Kentucky

Dawn played gypsy for a couple of years with Walter. She popped into Kentucky from time to time and visited her children on occasion. While she was in Tennessee, she learned that Taylor, who was sixteen at the time, was pregnant. Taylor recalls her mom being upset, but then reminded Dawn she couldn't say anything. Over the phone Dawn expressed idle threats. "I'm going to come up to Kentucky and whup you," Taylor recalls her mother saying. "Well, at least I'll get to see you if you come up here, you know, to do whatever you say you're going to do, so . . ." she told her estranged mother. By the time Dawn moved back to Kentucky, Taylor had already given birth to her son. She took her son to see her mother sometimes, but Taylor would be eighteen and moved out of her grandmother's home before Dawn got sober.

In October 2014, Dawn went to jail. A year earlier she sold two pills to an undercover informant. As a result, she was caught up with a sealed indictment, a charge that is hidden from the public until unsealed, and became wanted for trafficking in controlled substance in the first degree. When she saw her picture in the local newspaper, she knew she had to turn herself in. She was staying in Walter's mom's basement at the time and didn't want to have the police looking for her there. What's more, she was tired of running. She purchased white T-shirts, socks, and multiple changes of underwear—things she knew she could keep in county jail—and put them on. When she turned herself in, she was sentenced to two years.

In jail, Dawn finally met sobriety. She was housed with another woman battling a substance addiction who was known around town for sex work. "I got thrown in the holding cell with her, and she was so sick, just throwing up and diarrhea in this holding cell where they give you a little one-ply thing of toilet paper, nothing to clean up the mess, and there's a metal toilet with your sink hooked to the back," Dawn says. She held the woman's hair and helped her, and she didn't feel any symptoms of drug withdrawal of her own. "I didn't have one symptom of withdrawal. That's when I knew right then, 'Dawn you will never do this again,'" she says. It was in the jail cell that Dawn had her moment of realization. "I knew I was never going to touch it again. I knew I was done. I never wanted to be that person. I never wanted to be out there lying and leaving my kids and hurting my mom, but that sickness was so bad that I had to have it and it didn't matter at what cost."

Taylor, who lived close to the jail, put money on her mom's commissary account. Some was her own, some was money Dawn had given her to hold before she turned herself in. Soon Dawn gained trusty status for good behavior and started working at the commissary store in the jail. After she spent four months in jail, she was given the option to finish her sentence at the jail or go to court-ordered drug treatment at the Healing Place (THP). She chose treatment.

Dawn, her mom, Jo, and her daughter Annabel all prepared for the two-hour drive to Louisville and her stay at the treatment center. "Yeah, I drove like a maniac getting her up there," Jo says. "Well, they told us she had to go from there straight on up there." Dawn had about four hours. The two women ran inside department stores getting towels and personal hygiene items. There wasn't any time to go to a nice sit-down restaurant, so they went to a McDonald's drive-thru. "She was scared," Jo remembers.

The Healing Place is located in the Park Hill area of Louisville, on a street lined with warehouses and tall, abandoned buildings. It's just a turn away from the Park Hills Housing Project, feared for its drug dealing, prostitution, murders, and general violence. Jo saw that Dawn was nervous and gave her a pep talk instead of telling her how scared she was of the neighborhood and the center. "It'd be okay. You got this, you're a likable person, everybody really likes you," Jo told her. "You'll be fine." For Jo, being in a big city was a big change compared to what she was used to in Mount Sterling, her rural, quiet, and small hometown. At home, Jo feels like she knows everybody and she feels safe. In Louisville, she says, they have "hardcore thugs"; whereas in her hometown the most she would encounter are "little old drug addicts." She's not afraid of them.

Jo's exposure to crime is limited because she lives in a small, rural town where she knows the majority of the people in her community. Since drug addiction has ravaged her town, she's used to someone acting out while high on drugs. In those instances, she's sure she could win a fight. "I'm a big woman, so I can pick you up and break you," she says of a drug user who might harass her. Coming to a big city and leaving her daughter there was scary for her, and her fear was amplified by the low-income, high-crime neighborhood. "We don't have little scary areas like that." There have not been many large-scale studies that evaluate the neighborhoods that house treatment centers. One study examined roughly twenty-three thousand clients and five hundred treatment centers in Los Angeles County. It found that clients were exposed to "markedly higher levels of disadvantage, violence, or drug activity where they attend treatment than where they live."

Dawn admitted to her mom that she wanted to run. Since she was court ordered to be there, she would have had a warrant out for her arrest if she didn't go in. "You ain't darting, you're going right in there," Jo told her daughter. She walked Dawn in as far as she could. As she recalls, "They'll only let you go to that front part, and then took her back." She was glad Annabel was with her, so she would not have to drive back by herself. But watching her daughter walk away wasn't as easy as she tried to make it out to be. "It was hard, it hurts," Jo says. "I didn't want her to see. But then at the same time I'm telling myself, 'This is a good thing.' This is where she needs to be. I told Dawn, 'I would rather you be here than lost in the prison system.' It's easier to throw them in an old jail, and then turn them loose and they don't have help," she says. Jo believed this was Dawn's last hope. It had to be okay. Seeing one out of her three children get clean was something to be proud of. Dawn's brothers, both addicted to drugs as well, were nowhere close to surrendering to sobriety.

RECOVERY IN LOUISVILLE at the Healing Place was unlike anything Dawn had ever experienced before. There were small treatment centers in Mount Sterling, mostly ones that offered services that lasted no longer than seven days. Dawn had been a couple of times, but she admitted she wasn't serious about her sobriety at the time. She also knew a week wasn't enough to kick an addiction as severe as hers, or any drug habit for that matter. She wasn't even out of the fog after a week. The lack of centers, she believes, stems from a denial of the severity of the problem. "People just didn't want to talk about it so much down there," Dawn says. The level of recovery and mental health support in Kentucky's rural areas lagged behind that in the urban areas. Officials believe Kentucky's rural areas are harder hit because of the high level of poverty, low graduation rates, meager job opportunities, and a sense of inevitability about drug abuse.

Even at the Healing Place it would be a long road for Dawn. The long-term residential program consisted of four phases, and Dawn would live on campus for six to nine months and be immersed in a communal, educational process that would be guided by Peer Mentors, women who had recently completed the program. She would have to complete the twelve steps of Alcoholics Anonymous (AA) and a curriculum on the disease of addiction and recovery.

When they first arrive, women in recovery at THP have to go through the first phase of treatment, a nonmedical detox, meaning they can't use any type of prescription drug to ease their withdrawal symptoms. In medical detox at other centers, women detoxing from opioids are given a prescription medication such as Suboxone, a partial opiate that works to block pain receptors, which prevents the women from feeling the withdrawal symptoms. The detox at THP lasts between five to seven days, depending on where a woman is in her recovery. Withdrawal symptoms vary in severity and usually include hot and cold sweats, muscle aches and pains, goose bumps, abdominal cramping, nausea, vomiting, and diarrhea. Since Dawn went through detox in jail, she wouldn't have to go through the full detox in THP.

The second phase is the motivational track, called Off the Streets, in which women start the Safe Haven portion of the program. They cannot leave the campus for two weeks unless it is for court dates or medical appointments. They attend about eighty classes in which the facilitator pulls something from the four-hundred-plus pages of the Alcoholics Anonymous book and turns it into a class discussion. They also attend twelve-step meetings. This second phase lasts usually from one to three months, and it is meant to move the women away from a street mentality and help them learn about their addiction.

Phase three is the recovery stage. This is when the women learn how to apply the twelve steps of Alcoholics Anonymous and Narcotics Anonymous. The women participate in a rotation of cooking, housekeeping, laundry, maintenance, security, and office work to emphasize structure, responsibility, and accountability. They have community meetings three times a week. The women focus on interpersonal skills, and they provide accountability for others in the program through role modeling and giving support to others. The recovery phase lasts three to six months.

Phase four is continuing care. Once the women complete the recovery program they address issues of employment, education, vocational training, housing, and more. They work on relapse prevention exercises, participate in an alumni community, and attend AA meetings. The women then begin to reestablish ties with their families and build clean and sober lifestyles for themselves.

Every morning during the motivational track, Dawn, along with close to ninety other women, gathered all of her belongings—shoes, clothes, books, everything. They packed them up in bags and backpacks and then carried them on a one-mile trek. The women were "trudging," walking with purpose, to get better, to get clean. They had to trudge every day; people in the neighborhood recognized them as women in recovery even though they looked like they were off to a hiking trip. At the end of their walk they arrived at St. Stephen Church, where they took classes to learn about the disease of addiction.

Each day while trudging, the women passed factories. Walking in the snow one day, wearing donated Timberland boots that she would never have worn in her old life, Dawn stopped in one of the factories. "Hey, you hiring, what's going on?" Dawn asked in her usual bubbly tone. She introduced herself to a woman working at the factory, which produced paper boxes. Dawn told her she'd be back in a couple weeks. She was laying bricks for her future job search. Later in the program she would be able to look for a job.

When Dawn reached the twelfth step of the program, she went back to care for women in detox. The idea is for the women who have completed the program to go back and remember where they started. "So you go back, and those girls that's laying there sick in those detox beds, you're helping them, holding their hair, run their bath water. You're remembering like you don't want this again," Dawn explains.

Reaching the last step of the program meant Dawn could start to build a life outside of THP. She moved to the opposite side of the building, where she paid $37 dollars a week for housing. Women got help there with finding a job, saving money, and planning for the next step. Dawn went back to the factory where she had met the woman earlier in her recovery. She was hired full-time, putting boxes together, earning minimum wage at $7.25 an hour. Dawn had seen women face so many challenges looking for a job that she was happy to get any opportunity. "They give me a chance off the street, it was better than nothing," Dawn says. Each morning she got a little paper-bag lunch, from donations given to the Healing Place, and headed down the road to work. She worked from 7:00 a.m. to 4:00 p.m. A week later, she got another job at a second factory, where she worked part-time. She ended many of the evenings at 11:00 p.m. Dawn needed to save up money to afford a place to live, buy a car, and start paying off her more than $6,000 in back child support to her ex-husband Ethan.

WHILE DAWN WAS INCARCERATED and in treatment, her children remained with family members and Ethan. She was earning minimum wage when she started back in the workforce; shelling out $300 each month in child support was a huge financial burden for her. Kentucky is one of eleven states—along with Montana, South Dakota, Kansas, Oklahoma, Arkansas, Tennessee, Virginia, Georgia, South Carolina, and Delaware—where child support orders cannot be reduced or suspended due to incarceration. Child support obligation continues for incarcerated parents, like Dawn, meaning they accumulate high levels of debt that they need to pay when they are released. In Kentucky, when parents owing child support are released from jail or prison, they must contact the local child support office handling their case to update their address, employment information, and make payment arrangements. Kentucky Child Support policy prohibits local child support offices from filing actions to review or change a support obligation of a parent because of incarceration. In the event that a parent files a motion with the court on their own to request a change to their support obligation, the local child support office will contest the modification and request the court deny the modification. They would argue that reduction in income because of incarceration is voluntary.

For many parents, the challenges of finding a job during reentry further reduce their ability to pay off the debt when they are released. On average, an incarcerated parent with a child support order leaves prison with nearly $20,000 in child support debt, double the amount from when they entered. Child support policies vary from state to state, but at least thirty-six states consider incarceration to be involuntary unemployment, unlike Kentucky, thus parents are allowed to request a modification to their order.

By the time Dawn completed her recovery program, she had reduced her child support debt to $4,800. She continued working her two jobs, saved up $1,200, and used it to purchase a little black Saturn. The next step was to move out of THP. With the help of the Coalition for the Homeless in Louisville, she got an apartment in Beecher Terrace, a notorious property operated by the Louisville Metro Housing Authority. She was determined, though, to take steps to finally get to where she wanted to be no matter where she had to start. She paid $300 per month in rent and stayed there for five months. Then she moved to another apartment, where she paid $525 per month. Getting the second apartment required her, admittedly, to return to some of her old ways. "The only reason I was able to get that is because I had to swindle that system. I went to a rental company that was in Indiana that was only going to run a background check in Indiana, but they owned a property here. So that way I was able to get a place. You know, housing, it's once you check that box it's over, like who wants a drug dealer in their community, you know, because that's what you get labeled as like people didn't get to see like the new things you're doing," Dawn says. "It's hard to start over."

Later, when she got the job at a local restaurant and eventually worked her way up to a manager position, she was thankful and determined to do the work. She would do whatever was required to maintain her sobriety and get back. "I can bartend, I can serve, I can work sauté, I can work the kitchen, I scrub floors. I'll be in the dish tank. I tell my employees I wouldn't ask you to do one thing that I won't do right beside you toe to toe."

The next and most vital step of Dawn's recovery was rebuilding her relationship with her children.

10

TIME
Mississippi

Extended family visits were crucial in allowing William to be a part of raising his boys. But once the boys considered themselves to be too old to be cooped up with their parents for five days, Ruth and William used their visitation time to strengthen their bond, cooking, talking, and sitting outside enjoying the breeze and the night's sky. These moments supplemented the calls, letters, and regular visits that had helped sustain their four-decade-long marriage. After the extended visitation program ended, the couple upped the phone calls, made Saturday visits a second religion, and buried themselves in work to avoid feeling the cold, glacial pace of William's prison sentence. As they both neared retirement age, they also hoped William would be finally coming home. They hoped to spend the last leg of the journey together.

For both Ruth and William, working helped the time sail by instead of inch by. The income Ruth earned from decades of hard work would go toward their retirement, if they were ever able to share time together outside. She worked a twelve-hour nightshift and took overtime whenever it was offered. After so many years

Ruth had become hardened to the blows that incarceration inevitably landed on her family. From the start, she took each one and kept pushing. "I always been a fighter," she says. When William went to prison, she didn't have much time to mourn. She had to survive. She's been working nonstop ever since.

During the early part of their marriage, Ruth had already completed a year of nursing education, and she had a licensed practical nurse, or LPN, certificate. But an entry-level nurse's salary wasn't enough to raise her boys. "I didn't have a husband," she reflects. "I didn't have but one income. I had to take care of my children. It's a financial burden to lose your spouse. It's part of your income." She decided to return to school. She went to Mississippi College and received a bachelor of science in nursing, or BSN, degree. She started working as a registered nurse.

A few years after William's imprisonment, his cousin, who was eighteen at the time, moved in to help Ruth with the boys. By then, Kevin was a preteen and Robert was a young boy. Meanwhile, William was also working in prison.

William got his GED and became a certified janitorial and orderly clerk. He also completed graduate-level courses in the early part of his imprisonment. Over the years, he's worked around nurses, doctors, staff wardens, and fellow prisoners and for prison superintendents. "I've been working the whole thirty-seven years I been here," William says proudly. Many years he worked seven days a week, missing work only on the days he took off to spend with his family during extended family visits.

At his first prison, Parchman, William never had to work under the hot sun in the acres of cotton fields or cut grass. Instead, he got a job as a bookbinder. The private sector sent books to the prison to be redone. There, he chained covers, fixed pages, sewed them together; later, when the bindery became the print shop, he printed names on T-shirts, made business cards, and created banners.

Soon, he transitioned to janitorial work, buffing floors, cleaning bathrooms, and dusting. He later worked for the prison hospital. He was there for fifteen years, then he worked in the dental clinic. He was there for seven years. He also worked several years as a laboratory apprentice in a doctor's office. He even worked for several wardens over the years. He cleaned their bathrooms and offices, and "kept the floors shining like glass." Those jobs, William says, are long gone now.

William learned new skills while working the various jobs through the years, but he was never paid. "He didn't get a dime," Ruth says. William was clear that he wouldn't get a nominal salary or be allowed to receive good time because of the length of his sentence. Those were luxuries afforded to other prisoners, mostly men in other states and with lesser sentences. He knew it wasn't a part of his deal. "I just work for the privileges," he says. William wears green and white horizontal-stripe pants, which signifies that he's A-custody, which is minimum custody, rendering him a trusty. Prisoners in B-custody, which is medium custody, wear black and white horizontal-stripe pants. Those in maximum security wear red and white horizontal-stripe pants and yellow jumpsuits. "They give you a little more freedom than the others," William says about his trusty status. A person sentenced after 1994 is not eligible for trusty status. This change followed the punitive movement after the 1994 crime bill. One of the privileges for A-custody offenders used to be going to the family visits. Today, being minimum-custody level simply means William gets a weekly visit, while the others get semimonthly or monthly visits. And he's eligible for jobs, such as mowing the lawn. This allows him to venture outside the perimeter of the electric fence without the threat of being shot down by prison guards.

In 2019, William worked in the prison library, serving as librarian to his fellow prisoners. He enjoyed making his own hours and helping men find books that resonated with them. He delighted in getting an unexpected arrival of hundreds of new books. William wiped them clean, put them in alphabetical order, recorded the titles, and then filed them away. Anything positive to keep him busy, to keep him pushing until his next hearing and hopeful release, was welcome.

William's decades of prison labor are made real when Ruth gets their Social Security earnings statements, which seem to come more frequently as they reach retirement age. At sixty-three years old she was saddened when she saw what she had earned over the years and what awaited her in retirement, mostly because it forced her to compare it to what William had, which was zero. In 2020, when William turns sixty-six, he won't have enough credits to receive Social Security retirement benefits because he's been in prison. "I can see how much he made in, like, 1979 for the whole year. He only made $2,200," Ruth says, her hands folded in her lap. The amount William earned for the year back then is the same amount she earns in two weeks. She finds it strange to see William's work history stop. "Mine go on and on, it shows how much I done made over the years. Especially as I got older, I made more." She is silent for a moment, the significance of the empty slots sitting with her. "His is blank from '82, '83, '84. It's just blank, blank, blank, blank, blank," she says with a melancholy tone. "His stop at 1981. That's been a long time ago. He doesn't have enough credits to get Social Security because he only worked in prison. All those years he worked at Parchman, he wasn't on payroll," Ruth says.

"That is a long vacancy," she says, pausing to think about it. "That kinda saddens me. And brings me into reality." When looking at her Social Security statement, Ruth has a visual timeline of her more than four decades of work history and her contributions into the Social Security fund. She's worked to contribute to her retirement, to her spouse's retirement, and to her children if they become eligible. William's statement is a testament to the nearly four decades he's worked in prison, work for which he was never paid.

In order to be eligible for Social Security benefits in retirement, a person has to have worked and paid Social Security taxes for at least ten years. Even if William had worked long enough to receive credits, he wouldn't be eligible. Under the 2009 No Social Security Benefits for Prisoners Act, prisoners cannot collect their Social Security benefits while incarcerated no matter how many years they've worked or how much they've paid into the fund. If someone works for forty years, then commits a crime and gets a life sentence, they will not get their benefits. If a prisoner is released, only then are they eligible. Still, they can't receive retroactive payments. These benefits, which they earned, would be particularly helpful to the financial health of their families while they are behind bars.

Some prison labor goes without pay. With only a few rare exceptions, prisoners working inside prisons in Alabama, Arkansas, Florida, Georgia, and Texas are not paid. Most incarcerated workers earn pennies per hour. If they work a regular, nonindustry job inside the prison, such as cooking in the kitchen, doing laundry, or delivering mail, on average they earn between $0.14 and $0.63 an hour. A smaller portion of the prison population work in correctional industry jobs.

These are jobs in state-owned businesses, producing goods and services—such as eyeglasses, furniture, and janitorial supplies—which are then sold to outside customers. They earn nearly twice as much, with an average of $0.33 to $1.41 per hour. An even smaller sliver of the prison population, about 6 percent, earn the prevailing local wage if they work for private businesses that are contracted with states through the Prison Industry Enhancement Certification Program (PIECP). In the program, state and local certified departments of corrections are exempt from normal restrictions on the sale of prisoner-made goods in interstate commerce. Created by Congress in 1979, PIECP lifts existing restrictions on prisons, permitting them to sell these goods to the federal government in amounts above the $10,000 maximum that is generally enforced.[1]

Prison labor started with convict leasing and has gone through several iterations over the years. In the beginning, it was seen as part of the punishment. In 1865, the passage of the Thirteenth Amendment of the US Constitution, which made slavery and involuntary servitude unconstitutional in the United States "except as punishment for crime," led to the widespread use of the convict-lease system in the South. Convict lease started slowing down in some states as early as the 1900s due to social and economic pressures, though some persisted until the 1920s. Chain gangs, groups of prisoners chained together doing menial labor under excruciating conditions, then replaced the convict-lease system in the early 1900s. They were finally outlawed in the 1950s.

The culture that accepts that prisoners should be put to work has persisted into the twenty-first century. The 1970s War on Drugs contributed to the exploitation of prisoners as a labor source. Modern proponents of prison labor argue that the work is rehabilitative. It gives prisoners job skills, teaches them a work ethic, and prevents prisoner idleness. Opponents argue that it's exploitive, because many prisoners aren't paid and the ones who are paid don't receive a living wage, don't have labor protections, and don't have bargaining power or in many cases a choice to work or not.

In 2018, Mississippi legislators wrote a bill that would make Mississippi prison industries pay employed prisoners the federal minimum wage, arguing prisoners should be guaranteed basic workers' rights. They insisted that prisoners ought to be given a wage that allows them an opportunity to provide for their families, make restitution or other fee payments, and become rehabilitated by learning the legal way to work and have a source of income. The bill died in committee in 2018.

Mississippi is not alone. Prisons appear to be paying prisoners *less* today than they did two decades ago. With some exceptions, most prisoners, once cleared by prison medical staff, are required to work. They can face punishment—solitary confinement, loss of earned good time, and revocation of visitation—for refusing to take a work assignment. However, many prisons don't have enough jobs to satisfy the large quantity of prisoners, so many are left with nothing to do even though they desperately want to work.

In Mississippi, the most coveted job for trusties like William is working in the Governor's Mansion doing maintenance and landscaping. It has become a Mississippi tradition for governors to release trusties who worked at the mansion. In 2011, by the end of his second term, Governor Haley Barbour, a Republican, had granted just over two hundred pardons, including seventeen for people convicted of murder.[2] Five of his outgoing pardons were for people who had worked as trusties in the Governor's Mansion. Barbour, who later came under fire for his pardons, defended his choice, saying the prisoners he pardoned were rehabilitated and wouldn't have gotten a second chance if it hadn't been for him. He also explained why he hired people convicted of murder to work in the mansion. "The experts say that those are the people who are least likely to commit another crime and that they are the ones who will serve the best," said Barbour. "I have found that to be the case." He said he was so confident the five men he released, who worked as trusties during his second term, wouldn't harm anyone that he would let them play with his grandchildren. In 2012, Governor Phil Bryant, a Republican, ended the half-century-old program of prisoners working in the Governor's Mansion. He also said he would look into narrowing the guidelines that allow governors the power to singlehandedly issue pardons.

Over the years, William has applied for a Governor's Mansion job a few times—taking the exam, undergoing the psychological evaluation, and going for an interview. At one point he had to turn down an interview because of his knee injury. He didn't think he could perform the tasks. Workers were on their feet most of the day. Later, while working for the prison superintendent, he highly recommended William reapply. In 2010, after he had the long-awaited procedure on his knee, he applied again. He didn't get the job.

RUTH TRIES NOT TO REFLECT on or internalize what it means to lose a partner to lifelong incarceration, but as they both near retirement and she reflects on their decades of work, reality makes her ache. She believes something greater must be in store for her family. The end of extended family visits must mean that her husband is coming home soon.

Naeem is particularly concerned about how his mother will do going forward without that lifeline. Naeem wants his father to come home, but not for him. As he explains, "I've been dealing with it for twenty years. I needed him more as a child. Now, I can do stuff for myself. I want him to be here for my mom." Naeem grew up feeling more like an only child since his brothers are significantly older than him. As a youngster, he found brotherhood in some friends who lived a few blocks away. But at home, he feels like his own person. "I've been the man, no brothers, no dad, just me. One person," he says. Naeem wants his mother to feel safe, and he doesn't want to have to worry about how she is doing. If his father was released and came home, he would feel secure that she is protected. "I don't want to wonder if she's okay, I want to know she's okay."

Feeling like he doesn't need his father at twenty years old might have to do with the fact that he's distanced himself from the reality that his dad has been in prison his entire life. "I never have a chance to talk about it," Naeem says. "My momma always told me just don't go talking about your daddy in jail. She didn't want to feel shame. So I couldn't say anything." Ruth nods her head in confirmation. "I didn't go asking them how they felt about it," she says. "We didn't talk about it. I think because we didn't want to cry. We knew we had somebody missing, part of the family." Ruth subscribes to the motto "never let 'em see you sweat." "I wanted to be strong and move on," she says. Not move on from her husband or building her family, but move on from the conviction that shaped her life. "I'm that kind of person. That's not good, but they kind of took the same thing." None of the Anderson boys lets their father's confinement keep them down. Naeem, like his mother, kept moving, fearful that if he stopped to look at and feel the reality, the pain would be too much to bear.

As a kid, Naeem told friends that his father was a truck driver or in the army. He began telling the truth about his father's confinement when he was in the eighth grade, first to friends, then to teachers. Still, he never let them see his pain or what he yearned for. "Some of them have built a relationship with me. I built relationships with them," he says, his voice lowering. He imagines they took pity on him, but he doesn't want sympathy or special treatment. "It's the truth," he says nonchalantly. "If I don't feel bad for myself, you shouldn't feel bad."

At twenty years old, he no longer feels like a kid aching for his father. He once wished his father could participate in his school's WATCH D.O.G.S (Dads of Great Students) program for fathers and their children. The initiative allowed fathers (and grandfathers, uncles, and other male adults) to volunteer at their child's school. If William were home, he could have read to Naeem's class, played sports with them during recess, or monitored the school's entrance. Whatever he did, he would have been present for Naeem and visible to his teachers and classmates.

Naeem was the teenager who wrote handwritten letters to the parole board, pleading for his father's release so he wouldn't have to continue lying about where his father really was. In one letter to the parole board, he credited his dad for being a good father from behind bars:

My father has been a father to me in prison. He calls me once a week and we visit at the prison. When I get in trouble at school, he told me to tell the teacher when I am having a problem. He told me to tell the teacher when I need help with my work. I got in a fight this year in school and got suspended. My dad talk to me about not letting my anger control me. Every year he sends me a Christmas present from prison. He sends books to me and sometimes they are about sports.

I respect my father because he is a strong black man. He does not let anybody break his spirit. He won't run in the street if he is paroled. Me and my mom will help him until he can get on his feet. A lot of people want him to be here and do good. Other people love my dad too.

He has been in prison all the days of my life. I hope you will let my dad come home. I'm proud of him I miss him and need him.

The parole board ignored his pleas. And now, he considers himself grown. He feels he had to be.

In fact, Naeem has been relatively independent for the last four years. When he turned sixteen, he started working and establishing his own independence. He feels that he finally achieved it "when I stopped asking my mom for money or rides." He learned to save and bought his first used car. It got him to and from work. He even met a girl, Brooke, and they became serious. He feels he is growing into a young man.

Proclaiming to be an adult doesn't mean Naeem thinks he knows everything. He often leans on his father, finding wisdom and refuge in his experience and advice. Although he stopped going on family visits as a teenager, he visits William twice a month and continues to speak with him via phone, building on the bond they created during those extended visits. "We have talked about safe sex, girlfriends, staying in school, and becoming a man," William says. The conversations that William had with his son years ago in the Family House program continued and deepened over the last few years.

Ruth and William both recall Naeem having several girlfriends. "He brought a few of them around here to meet me," Ruth says, "but this last one met the mark, and Naeem said he was going to introduce her to William. That was a big deal for him." An admitted flirt, Naeem talked to several girls, but in his junior year of high

school, when he met Brooke, everything changed. It led to his first
serious relationship.

In true millennial fashion, Naeem saw Brooke on Instagram
and liked a few of her pictures. When she checked out his profile and liked a couple pictures back, Naeem figured "that might
mean she like what she see." Later, they ran into each other at the
mall. He was heading out, she was coming in. Small talk ensued and
they went their separate ways. Naeem didn't send her a direct message on Instagram immediately. He has pride. "Well, you know you
can't just be too thirsty, you can't write soon when you get in the car.
You got to wait until like a day later," he says. Eventually, he sent
a message and the conversation started. In the coming weeks, they
started dating. Naeem took her to movies and treated Brooke to
Chili's, her favorite restaurant. Sometimes they went to Longhorn,
his favorite spot for grub.

After spending eight or so months together, they started solidi-
fying their relationship—they began spending entire days together,
talking about their lives, sharing their secrets. Naeem shared aloud
what he'd tried to hide for years, how he longed for his father. When
Brooke was a child, her mother went to prison for killing her father.
Her mother came home from prison when she was sixteen, but they
shared a loss that bound them at the core. "She ain't have no father
and I ain't have no father," Naeem says. "So we talked about that.
About our problems. How we wish we had our fathers there." Their
bond strengthened over the common loss. They spent the holidays
with each other's families and started looking toward a future together. On some weekends, it was just the two of them on a highway
to some other city. New Orleans was one of their favorite places to
go. They loved dancing on Bourbon Street.

When the couple hit the two-year mark, it meant something significant to Naeem. "One year is kind of iffy, it's still loose," he posits.
"That's pretty serious when it gets to two years." He decided it was
time for a grand gesture. "It was only right for her to meet my dad."

Naeem had already let Brooke speak to his dad on the phone, but he took a big step when he gave her an application to fill out so she could be approved to visit. William could add visitors only twice a year. "He'd never brought a girl to meet me," William says. "I'd been telling them how to get along over the phone for a while, but that visit was real important." It was more than a phone call, more than a letter or a picture. "You could see that she cared a lot about him," William recalls. "Naeem wanted to play Mr. Tough Guy in front of me, but I knew she was the one for him." During their visit, he says the two talked about money. "The young lady said, 'Naeem, your money is our money, and my money is our money. We split everything fifty-fifty.'" William told his son that if they decided on a long-term partnership, then that was indeed the way it should go. "She's good for him," William says happily. "I'm not going to choose who he's going to love, but I'll guide him to make smart choices." Naeem trusted his father, so he took his advice. He started spending even more time with Brooke.

RUTH SITS IN A BLACK CHAIR, its decades of wear bound up by mounds of silver heavy-duty duct tape. Grace, her hair stylist of thirty years, places a towel over Ruth's shoulders and wraps her hair in large purple rollers. Every surface aside from the floor in Skip's Barbershop and Hair Salon is home to something. Countertops and sinks are filled with various items and products: rollers, paper towels, books, brushes, hair dye, combs, and more. On the wall, "No credit, don't ask" is painted in red capital letters. On another sign, a red "no" symbol sits over an image of a handgun, reminding customers that no guns are allowed. Newspaper articles, comic strips, posters, and calendars cover the walls. Many date back decades and are about slavery, civil rights, neighborhood shootings, and mass incarceration. One poster shows black men with shackles around their necks telling onlookers that slavery isn't over. Other posters ask viewers to support black prison abolition, honor Martin Luther King Jr., end racism, and support union justice.

Some walls host photographs of Skip's clients throughout the years. Among them are photos of a younger Ruth and Naeem. Ruth and Skip have known each other for over forty years. From across the room, Skip asks Ruth how William is doing. Soon, Skip falls into an old memory.

"You remember that bike he used to let me have?" he calls to Ruth.

"Uh-huh," she says, laughing.

"When I didn't have a car, he let me use that to find a job and go to work when I was doing construction. The name of that bike was Cadillac," he says, nodding his head. "It ran smooth."

Grace laughs loudly along with the joke.

"William would tell me, 'Bring that bike back Skip when you get ready. Don't worry about that bike,'" Skip recalls. "'Cause he know I was tryna get myself together."

Ruth sits silently, smiling, nodding in agreement with Skip.

"He always had a good heart," Skip says, looking away from the women. "One of my best friends. . . . He should have been home long time ago. I don't know why they got him in there so long. As long as he been gone he done paid his dues."

He asks the question that he's been asking for years. Skip wrote a letter of support for William's last parole hearing. The handwritten letter asked the parole board, "How much longer can a man endure?" He talked about the pain both families endured. He told the board that he was sure God had forgiven William for whatever he was charged with. Ruth just sits and listens to Skip reminisce about his old friend. Grace removes the rollers from her hair. She's asked herself the same question countless times but never got a sufficient answer.

Each month the Mississippi Parole Board gets a list of prisoners who are eligible for parole. When deciding to grant or deny a person parole, the board is supposed to include a number of factors, specifically: "severity of offense, number of offenses committed, psychological and/or psychiatric history, disciplinary action while incarcerated, community support or opposition, amount of time served, prior misdemeanor or felony conviction(s), police and/or juvenile record, history of drug or alcohol abuse, history of violence, crimes committed while incarcerated, escape history, participation in rehabilitative programs, arrangements for employment and/or residence, and whether the offender served in the United States Armed Forces and received an honorable discharge."

William first went up for parole in 1995, fifteen years after his conviction. He was denied parole and received a five year set-off, which meant he couldn't go before the board again for another five years. The reasons for denial were the serious nature of the offense, number of offenses committed, prior felony conviction, community opposition, and insufficient time served. Additionally, the board didn't believe he would be a law-abiding citizen if paroled. In the five years before his next hearing, he would continue to work on his rehabilitation by taking classes, working, and serving his sentence. He went up again in 2000 and was set-off for another five years. In 2006, he was denied parole and told to wait three years. When he went up in 2009, he started to see a serious reduction in the set-off time, which implied the board thought he was nearing suitability for parole. By seeing him once a year instead of once every five years, it appeared they were more interested in seeing him and evaluating his rehabilitation. From 2009 to 2012 he went yearly and was denied and set-off for one year each time. The parole denial reasons that remain consistent for William are the serious nature of the offense, community opposition, insufficient time served, and the belief that he won't be a law-abiding citizen. William has served thirty-nine years, has taken all classes possible, and has been a model prisoner. He's even received letters of support from prison staff. He continues to have family support and job offers, but he has not been paroled. In 2013, he was denied and set-off for three additional years. There was no reason provided for the set-off going from one year to three years.

William always had a lot of support when he went before the parole board. Ruth's church congregation often formed a line of support that reached a block long. On occasion, the pastor had sat in on the hearing with her. William was always denied. "He met the criteria," Ruth says. "But [one board member said] the governor wasn't letting people with life sentences go." Ruth and William say a parole board member told them that the victim's family opposition was strong and they couldn't get all the votes needed. The board considered that largely in their decision. Once, Sally Fran Ross, a retired Methodist preacher and friend of the Andersons, said she went to the victim's family to try to make contact between them and William—to explore restorative justice—but was coldly denied. People like William, convicted of capital murder, need four votes from parole board members in order to be granted parole, while those convicted of other crimes need only three. "We couldn't get all the votes" has become a familiar phrase to the lawyer who represents William.

National data on the number of people who receive parole doesn't exist. Parole boards largely operate behind closed doors and don't have to release their records. There have been legal actions to force clarity. For example, in 2008, two rulings from the Supreme Court of California eased the historically stringent parole requirements for prisoners in that state. The rulings prohibited prison officials, and in turn parole boards, from using the severity of the applicant's underlying crimes as the sole reason to deny parole. It also mandated that prisoners' records while incarcerated and their volunteer work must count heavily in assessing their parole. Such considerations are not the case in other states. Participation rules also vary. In California, for example, family members of the prisoner can't attend the parole hearing, but the victim's family can. In Mississippi, both families can attend.

The California rulings have meant thousands of lifers have received a new lease on life. In the six years between the 2008 rulings and 2014, the parole board granted parole to nearly three thousand lifers. In the three decades prior to the rulings, only 1,800 lifers were granted parole. William talks to people all over the country who have seen different experiences with parole for lifers. He often hears: "Guys down here get out on good behavior." Mississippi is different, he contends. "You could be a monk and not get out," he says melancholily. "One thing I found out about Mississippi, it's not that caring state."

William is right. Everything varies so much from state to state that it's too hard to paint the picture with a broad brush. A common thread that links parole board decisions is the influence of politics. Investigations into parole boards have revealed that most boards are deeply cautious about releasing prisoners. There have been some highly publicized cases of prisoners being released on parole who then go on to commit a crime. Board members fear that the decision to release the wrong person could come back to ruin their career, so they release only a sliver of those eligible and almost never release those who have committed violent offenses, even if they don't pose a threat to society. According to an investigation by the Marshall Project, the reason boards are so sensitive to politics is tied to the number of politicians who are board members. They found that at least eighteen states have at least one former elected official on the board. In forty-four states, the board is appointed by the governor. It's a lucrative job that can be given as a gift to former aides and political allies. Even if the parole board decides to grant parole, governors have the power to veto the decision. A Stanford University study found that of lifer paroles between 1990 and 2010, a person convicted of murder had only a 6 percent chance of leaving prison alive because governors are given the power to veto board decisions.

The *Model Penal Code,* an influential text written by legal scholars to assist state legislatures, declares parole boards to be "failed institutions." Recidivism rates drop steadily with age, and older prisoners who have committed serious crimes and have served the longest terms are the least likely to commit new crimes upon release. Though people age out of crime and the average annual cost per prisoner doubles at age fifty-five and continues to climb thereafter, most states refuse to release lifers.

For the last decade, William has had a lawyer representing him pro bono in front of the board. "They talked so well, I thought I was gonna be free. They covered everything," William says of his last hearing. Still he was denied. William doesn't understand the denials; he wants a reason. "What is the cause of that? There has got to be a purpose," he says. "The nature of the crime is not going to change. The victim's family isn't going to change. That can't be the only reason. Race plays a part; they would never say that. But we know that. It always will, which is wrong. Mississippi is always going to be behind the rest of the states."

William goes up for parole again in the summer of 2020.

11

THE MEANING OF LIFE
Florida

In 2008, Randall was frozen with shock when the judge sentenced him to life without parole (LWOP). He knew exactly what it meant—that he had been sentenced to die in prison. "Most people thought it was twenty-five years, that I was sentenced to twenty-five to life," he recalls. His family and friends thought he could serve twenty-five years and still get out with some life left to live when he turned forty-five years old. "That maybe come from miseducation or not being educated," he says with a nervous chuckle. His family and friends, like many people, recall the time when offenders served a portion of a life sentence. His mother hadn't been involved with the prison system before Randall, but she's heard of people getting out after ten or fifteen years despite receiving a life sentence. "Life was something else back in the day," his mother recalled. She's right; those convicted of murder in 1981 served a median sentence of five years. During the punitive era of the 1990s life came to mean a literal lifetime. Still, a life sentence largely depends on in what state a person is convicted. However, LWOP is another matter. Today, in Florida, adults sentenced to LWOP are expected to remain in prison for the rest of their lives. For a long time, no one sentenced to LWOP had ever been released on parole in the United States. That has started to change for some people sentenced to LWOP for crimes they committed as juveniles (known as JLWOP). Recent Supreme Court rulings have banned LWOP sentencing for most juveniles. So, some people sentenced to die in prison for committing crimes as a youth are now eligible for parole hearings or resentencing. However, being granted a parole hearing does not mean they'll be released.[1]

In the US, when a person is convicted of a crime and sentenced to a life term, they must remain in prison either for the rest of their natural life or until paroled. Life sentences are broken down into two categories: life with parole (LWP) and life without parole (LWOP). One sentence is determinate and the other is indeterminate. In determinate sentencing, a judge sentences the offender to a specific time period, which is usually set by the legislature. With indeterminate sentencing, the offender's sentence is a range of years, rather than a specific period of time. An indeterminate life sentence could be "fifteen years to life," which means that after the minimum sentence passes, the state parole board will hold hearings to determine if, during that range, the convicted person will be paroled. A determinate life sentence means the offender is sentenced to a definite length, such as life without parole, which can't be changed by a parole board or other agency.

Although all states and the federal government allow prison sentences that are so long that prisoners are expected to die behind bars, certain government officials can offer a convicted person clemency in the form of a pardon or commutation. A pardon is executive forgiveness of a crime, whereas a commutation is an executive lowering of the punishment but not an erasure of the conviction. Clemency for murder while serving a LWOP sentence is incredibly rare. Randall cannot expect either a pardon or commutation.

As RANDALL SAT in the courtroom, on trial for murder, he replayed the last five years of his life, thinking about how things changed after that first evening shift of drug dealing while his mom worked late. That's the thing with the drug game, once you enter, there is no real way to dictate what happens next. Randall was accused of fatally shooting a rival drug dealer over a dispute about drug territory and theft. In the beginning, the prosecutor wanted to avoid a trial. According to Beresford Landers, Randall's attorney for the case, they didn't have a witness, or a solid case for that matter. The prosecution offered Randall a ten-year sentence as a plea bargain, which he declined as he maintained his innocence. His attorney didn't prepare enough for the trial because he didn't think there would be one; he would go on to classify the case and trial as the worst in his career. The judge still remembers it and it reminds him how horribly he performed. Before he knew it, the attorney was sitting in front of a judge being pummeled by two prosecutors.

Randall wore a suit during the trial, which he'd gotten from the court chambers. As he looked around the courtroom and saw his family and a handful of friends, he felt grateful for the support. But at the same time, he feared how some of his support system appeared to the jury. One of his friends was a towering six feet four inches and had jet-black skin and dreadlocks. Randall feared that stereotypes about people who look like his friend would cast a negative shadow on his case.

Randall, having never been on trial, wasn't sure how much he could be involved in the court proceedings but found himself wanting to speak up and interject on numerous occasions. He felt he wasn't being adequately represented. It was going horribly, and at one point later in the trial Randall asked to take a role in his own defense.

When Randall started defending himself, Cynthia found herself making signs to help him during cross examination. "When he got stuck, when the man was asking questions, I was making signs,"

Cynthia says. Randall tried to avoid looking at his mother. Seeing her crying would have broken him down, and the few skills he tried to use to defend himself would disappear if he allowed himself to internalize her pain. Soon, Cynthia's efforts were thwarted. "They put me out the courtroom. They told me I couldn't do that. They caught me doing that. I didn't mean to do it. He got stuck. He was looking at me." They said, "Oh, you got to go." Cynthia says she had to leave and could not return until her son was sentenced.

The crime in question was a shooting that occurred outside, after nightfall. There was no weapon or DNA evidence linking Randall to the murder, but the testimony of a sixteen-year-old eye witness led to his conviction. Randall denied any association with the crime, but the defense's argument of mistaken identity was shot down. The results were devastating for both sides. "They were both young, young, young, black kids," says Landers. "The way I look at it, we lost two black guys in society," Landers says as he reflects on the case. "One to death and one to the prison system." Landers now refuses to go to trial when LWOP is on the table if convicted. "After that case, whenever I hear a possibility of life in prison [without parole] I don't even go for it. I say no, no, no, no. They can plead this case out, we're gonna plead this case out for something, whatever they give you. Whenever I hear that, whenever I hear the terminology now, if you go to trial and lose, you're facing life in prison, and you're gonna get life in prison. I don't even waste my time. I don't go unless they're offering life and you have nothing to lose."

After the conviction, Randall filed an appeal asking for a rehearing. The public defender on appeal argued that the trial court failed to conduct an adequate Faretta hearing—a pretrial hearing to determine if a defendant seeking to represent themselves at trial is voluntarily waiving his or her right to counsel—when Randall said he wanted to represent himself. The court found that Randall didn't require a formal Faretta hearing because he didn't make an unequivocal request for self-representation. Unfortunately for Randall, he didn't know how specific he needed to be or what his rights were exactly. Upon appeal, the State argued that the trial court's inquiry can be only as specific as a defendant's complaint, and since Randall only expressed general dissatisfaction with his attorney, he wasn't due a Faretta hearing. He would have had to make a formal allegation of incompetence, insist on firing his attorney, and request to represent himself. His request for a rehearing was denied.

RANDALL HAD JOINED the unprecedented number of people being sentenced to die behind bars. The number of people serving a life sentence has reached an all-time high. Nearly 162,000 people are serving a life sentence—one of every nine people in prison. In the early 1970s, LWOP use was rare, reserved for the last resort, but now it has seemingly replaced the death penalty. Opponents argue that states have merely traded one form of the death penalty for another, as those sentenced to LWOP are expected to die in prison. Some scholars argue that LWOP is as "ethically fraught" as the death penalty. When Connecticut ended its use of the death penalty, their LWOP provision required prisoners to be in solitary confinement twenty-two hours each day, and they were never allowed contact visits. It's an existence that scholars argue raises the question of whether being sentenced to death is any different.[2]

In 1972, the US Supreme Court ruling in *Furman v. Georgia* struck down capital punishment statutes. An increase in the use of LWOP sentencing followed. Before *Furman v. Georgia*, only seven states had LWOP statutes, and they were rarely used. Then several states enacted and strengthened their statutes regarding life sentences, especially pertaining to LWOP. Illinois, Alabama, and Louisiana all passed LWOP statutes in direct response to *Furman v. Georgia*. From 1971 to 1990, twenty-six states enacted LWOP statutes. From 1991 to 2012, seventeen states enacted LWOP statues.

Since 1984, the number of prisoners serving life sentences has more than quadrupled. The LWOP population increase has dramatically outpaced the changes to the LWP population. In 2016, nearly 162,000 people were serving traditional life sentences, but the number increases to 206,268 if we include virtual life sentences. One in seven prisoners behind bars has a sentence of life with parole (LWP), life without parole (LWOP), or what's been called a virtual life term of fifty years or more. The increase in the LWOP population is critical and means more and more families will deal with the collateral consequences of mass incarceration for significantly longer. Moreover, it is disproportionately handed down. No other state uses LWOP more than Florida (16.7 percent). Following Florida in LWOP sentencing are Pennsylvania (10.1 percent), California (9.6 percent), and Louisiana (9.1 percent). Nearly half (48.3 percent) of people serving life and virtual life sentences are African American, equal to one in five black prisoners overall.[3]

With increasingly long sentences, families are faced with decades of emotional and economic hardships. Children are growing up having never experienced life with their incarcerated parent beyond prison walls.

AT TWENTY YEARS OLD, Randall wondered what he was supposed to do with his life and his sentence. Was there a way forward? What would be the purpose of existing? The message he got from his sentence was, "You have no reason to live. You will never be free again," he said. "I would think that I have just made a person dangerous, by taking all hope away from them. So, now, it's only right that I put you in a cage and keep you from everybody and keep you because you have nothing to live for."

There was no hope beyond the appeal process, which he pursued and was denied. In prison, he has seen men grasping for their own version of hope, some turning to religion, others opting for gang affiliations, and others using drugs to numb their existence. But a lot of men just give up. Randall would have an unfortunate orchestra seat to such scenes. He would witness a fellow prisoner slit his own throat, blood pooling on the floor as he bled out. It would be hours before the lifeless body would be discovered and moved.

In the beginning, giving up seemed like the easy solution, one that didn't allow Randall to take responsibility for his decisions or to be as present as possible for his family. He would not give up, although he has wanted to. "I could have. Easily. I have felt like that one time when I wanted to end my life." Eventually, he realized he wanted to be around for *his world*—his daughter and the other people who wanted him to find a way to survive. Though he was away, he felt like he had to persist for others, for the people who loved him. His mother, his sisters, his best friend. "I had to stay strong for them." That meant adjusting to prison life.

He decided to capture hope and redemption and bottle it. But that realization wasn't immediate. The first year behind bars was the hardest. He had started thinking about fatherhood when he was a preteen. His obsession with fatherhood and parenting came from his father being absent and from a lack of meaningful connection with his mom, or any adult figure. Being incarcerated at the time of his daughter's birth took a significant emotional toll on him. Randall wasn't in a cell alone or with a roommate when he heard of Niyah's birth. Instead he was with several dozen men in an open room the size of a small auditorium with double bunks lining the walls. He called his family minutes after his daughter was born. He didn't speak with Ayana, but her sister let him know he was a father. He hung up the phone, tried choking back his tears, but couldn't. He wept uncontrollably as the other men looked on. He laid on the top bunk with his face crammed into a pillow. The combination of joy, disappointment, fear, and embarrassment soaked into the pillow. The men watching him imagined someone had died. Nothing else, they thought, could bring a man to such intense weeping. Once the guys learned he had a little girl, they understood and shared their experiences with fatherhood with him. He knew he couldn't be there for his daughter in the way he wanted, that he, too, would be unable to offer his child a life. His sentence rendered him absent, as far away as his father had been. He was overwhelmed. But the men who had more experience navigating fatherhood from lockup comforted him and made him feel less alone.

Niyah's birth made his absence painfully real. She was premature, her continued life barely a reality. Ayana was alone. "I felt like a failure. I felt like I failed. She was my purpose for living. Even before she got here." This hopelessness, for a while, left him aimless. He was broken and had no true knowledge about how to serve a life sentence behind bars, so adjusting to prison was tough: someone telling you when to eat, speak, and sleep. He faced abuses of power, in which officers would arbitrarily lock him up, make him do push-ups for their amusement, or assign him to extra cleaning duties. Anything they wanted. There was no time to process the change or adopt the proper attitude.

At the time, he didn't want to. He continued behavior that had become second nature in his street life. In spring of 2009, as he prepared for a visit with his daughter, his actions crept up on him. Prior to getting approved for the visit, he had to take a urinalysis test. His test results came back positive, evidence he'd smoked marijuana. He wasn't able to visit his daughter. He was also punished by being placed in solitary confinement for sixty days. It was the first time he was placed in solitary, and over the years solitary would take its toll on him.

First, Randall went to administrative confinement, which is the temporary removal from the general prison population. There he could keep his radio, a few books, and photos of his daughter. From there, he had a disciplinary hearing, which is an administrative proceeding to determine if there is sufficient evidence to find a prisoner guilty of a rule violation. He could plead guilty, not guilty, or no contest. Prisoners are allowed to give a verbal statement in addition to the optional written statement they can make prior to the investigation process. Randall says the prisoners call the process kangaroo court, because it is nothing more than a mock court where the principles of law and justice don't exist. Once a prisoner is found guilty, he is moved to disciplinary confinement, a form of punishment in which prisoners are confined for specified periods of time to a small cell away from other prisoners. There, Randall would not be able to have any belongings. It's the ultimate punishment.

Solitary confinement—also referred to as isolation, the hole, the SHU (special housing unit), and disciplinary segregation—is confinement behind a solid steel door for twenty-two to twenty-four hours a day. The conditions vary in prisons and from state to state, but they all have many of the same systematic policies and conditions. The average prison cell in isolation is between six-by-eight feet and nine-by-ten feet. Individuals remain in the cramped cells with a toilet, cot, and sink. They receive their meals through a slot in the door. Depending on the prison, individuals are let out for zero to two hours a day to take a shower or to go into a walled-in pen outdoors. Depending on the institution, they might or might not have access to phone calls or visits.

Prisoners can be placed in the hole for minor offenses like talking back to a prison guard, or for something more serious, like fighting another prisoner or being caught with contraband. The time in confinement can last from a few days to months or even years. Albert Woodfox notoriously spent forty-three years in solitary confinement in a Louisiana prison. People of color continue to be disproportionately represented in isolation units. Studies have reported that long-term solitary confinement can have harmful psychological effects, such as "visual and auditory hallucinations, hypersensitivity to noise and touch, insomnia and paranoia, uncontrollable feelings of rage and fear, distortions of time and perception, and increased risk of suicide and post-traumatic stress disorder (PTSD)."[4]

IN 1890, THE SUPREME COURT ruled that solitary confinement led to mental deterioration and did not rehabilitate prisoners. It was largely discontinued, only to be re-implemented in the 1980s and 1990s as part of the War on Drugs. The number of people in solitary confinement went from sixty thousand in 1995 to over eighty thousand in 2005. Today, there are over eighty thousand adults in solitary confinement in America's prisons. The number increases to one hundred thousand if county jails, immigrant detention centers, and youth centers are included.[5]

Through the years, Randall would encounter men who couldn't handle the confines of solitary. One prisoner swallowed a battery, another tried to take the tube from an asthma pump and swallow it. Tormented by the absence of touch, some acted out just to be removed from their cell. To be touched. People who get roommates are considered lucky, the ones left in a cell alone aren't. "What are you going to do in a cell by yourself?" Randall asks. "I'm talking about days on end. You go to banging on the wall, you go to talking to the ant. You go to talking to the guy next door to you or across the hall from you." They just want a change of scenery. In some instances, forcing their own removal is a way for prisoners to retaliate against a guard's mistreatment when the prisoners don't get items they are supposed to be provided with. "I have seen guys that didn't get fed. They miss you on your meal. You might not have any toilet paper; your toilet might not be working in your cell. You might not have toothpaste, a toothbrush, a sheet," Randall says. "Sometime there might be a lack of it, they might not have enough toilet paper or enough toothbrushes. They may mistake you for someone trying to waste their time because you in confinement. If you tell 'em you didn't get yo tray, they might not take you serious. Or they might not care," he says.

By swallowing a battery, the prisoner can disrupt the guard's day or routine, forcing him to do paperwork. It is the man's way of saying, "You don't want to pay me no attention? I'm going to make you pay me some attention," Randall explains. Many prisoners don't want to make a fuss because they risk getting even poorer treatment or more time. Randall has watched fellow prisoners be stripped of their basic necessities in winter. "An officer took all of their mats, sheets, blankets, jackets. I had all of those things he took from them and I was still freezing. So I was feeling for those guys."

After a Florida prisoner is in disciplinary confinement for thirty days, he's allowed one hour of recreational time per week. "Now you're let out your cell, and you're placed in a cage," Randall says. "The only benefit to that is you feel a breeze. You can't work out and get a full workout because you're being placed back in your cell, where you're not allowed to shower."

Over the years, Randall has sometimes been placed in double-cell confinement, solitary with another prisoner. Instead of one bed, there are bunkbeds attached to the wall. Having a roommate meant he would not meet the fate of most men who end up starved for another human voice. Randall spent time talking to his roommate; he learned signed language.

Of that first time he was alone in solitary, Randall says: "If you don't have anything inside of yourself to cling to, as an anchor—it's a really hard place to be." Alone in his empty room, he "picked up the Bible as a broken person and I discovered God." He became a student of the Bible. Fascinated by it, he began to understand some of the spiritual and practical interpretations. "I started to build myself and my identity around what it meant to be Christ-like."

As he sat in solitary confinement, he realized there were levels to confinement. It could get worse. Still, he was forced to slow down. He was alone with his thoughts, his actions, his past, and his future. His purpose became clearer. "Me knowing that I had smoked marijuana and jeopardized my visit with my daughter who was coming to see me after being in prison, I felt like the most wretched person in the world."

He realized if he continued behaving that way, the consequences would travel far beyond the bars that confined him and seep into his daughter's life. "I'm not only hurting myself; I'm hurting her." She became his fiercest motivation to change his outlook. Falling into Christianity meant he surrounded himself with men who helped him stay out of trouble and find focus to navigate a system equipped to swallow him whole. Over the next decade, Niyah would be his reason for pushing. "Just my daughter," he says. "That's my world."

Ayana agrees that Niyah has been Randall's motivation. She has seen a marked change in him. "If he was to walk out of prison right now, he would be a totally different person," she says. "Because I think that my daughter has changed him. I don't think he would have had hope to get out or to continue to fight. He would have just been fighting and carrying on."

His relationship with his mother has also grown stronger during the course of his incarceration. In addition to the quarterly visits, they speak on the phone regularly. Even now, a decade later, he writes her letters. "Stay strong for me and I'm gon stay strong for you," he writes her. On occasion, she'll write back. "I take so long to write back he be done wrote again," she says. When he fusses at her, asking for her to write him, she'll say, "I ain't no young chicken to sit down and write letters." She's found a solution, though. She'll purchase a greeting card from the drugstore that captures what she feels. "I sign it and say, 'There go your letter.'"

NIYAH DESCRIBES HER RELATIONSHIP with her father as good and views his absence as a constant in her life. "Since I was here, he hasn't been out, so it's kind of normal." She doesn't have any experience to compare their relationship to, so she doesn't know if she would feel differently if she had met her father outside of prison and then seen him taken away. "I don't know if I would be crying . . . babies don't really know their dad until they're like toddlers and stuff," she says. "So I probably would have just been, you know, regular."

The father and daughter build on their relationship by writing each other letters and speaking on the phone. These activities help close the divide between an incarcerated parent and child. "The relationship is great because I get to talk to him and we have this app called imo and I get to video call him," Niyah says. Lately, he has been speaking with her almost every day. He often asks her about her day, her classes at school, plans for the weekend, and he even helps her deal with challenges as they arise. He knows what she had for lunch, if she's looking for someone to take her for ice cream, or if she's at home bored. They're able to maintain this level of communication because he has access to a cell phone.

Most prisoners have only a few legal options to call their friends or family members. They can call collect or use a prepaid account that family members have deposited money into. They cannot select their calling provider; specialized phone companies win monopoly contracts with prisons. They have no rate restrictions and often charge families exorbitant amounts per call.

The procedure to approve a phone number varies by state. Some states allow prisoners to call any number, while others have strict limitations on the number of people, and who, a prisoner can call. In Florida, in order to get a phone number approved, the incarcerated person must submit the telephone number, name, and address for verification and activation before the number can be added to their approved call list. They are allowed a maximum of ten numbers and can make amendments to the list every six months. Anyone who wants to be added to the prisoner's list must submit a copy of their phone contract for approval.

Nationally, families spend $1.3 billion annually to receive telephone calls from their incarcerated loved ones. This national cost is likely slightly larger, because not all phone companies in correctional facilities are overseen by state regulators and therefore are not required to submit information. The Prison Policy Initiative reported that hundreds of counties charge around $15 to $18 for a fifteen-minute in-state phone call, and at least three charged $24.95. The prison phone industry is dominated by a handful of private companies. Two of them, Global Tel Link Corporation and Securus Technologies, own

70 percent of the market. They set rates and fees significantly higher than regular commercial providers. Relatively few calls come close to the $0.11-per-minute or $1.65-per-fifteen-minute cap that the Federal Communications Commission (FCC) had wanted to impose.[6]

The FCC tried to bring the costs of collect calls down so that families impacted by incarceration could afford to stay in touch. The latest rules would have required companies to cap charges at $0.25 per minute for instate and out-of-state calls. But in 2017, after Donald Trump was elected president, the FCC chose not to defend the regulation in a federal appeals court case. The court then struck down the cap for instate calls, which account for more than 92 percent of all prisoner calls, though the cap on interstate calls was left. Families of the incarcerated have no choice but to use these services, giving these companies much to brag about. In 2014, Global Tel Link touted that they reached a record high of 215 million prison calls, totaling three billion minutes. One Christmas Day, Securus completed the most calls in its history—celebrating a milestone that meant exploiting families.[7]

These costly rates are driven up by the hundreds of millions of dollars in concession fees, known as commissions or kickbacks, paid by the phone companies to state and local prison systems in exchange for exclusive contracts. According to a *New York Times* article, in 2013, jails and prisons and state, county, and local governments received $460 million in kickbacks. These high fees drive up the cost of phone calls because the companies say they must try to recover their investment. The fees are legal and are reportedly used to cover various expenses within prisons as well as outside of them. Facilities have become increasingly reliant on the revenue from these companies.[8]

A 2011 comprehensive study by *Prison Legal News* (*PLN*) found that the commission is based on a percentage of the gross revenue generated by prisoners' phone calls. *PLN* calculated the national figure for kickbacks to be 42 percent. A recent report by the Prison

Policy Initiative shows many states receive double that commission. The higher a kickback, it seems, the more likely a company is to win the contract. In Baldwin County, Alabama, ICSolutions agreed to pay 84.1 percent of profits back to the county.[9]

Despite paying out the fees, these companies are valuable, especially the two key players. According to a *New York Times* article, since 2009, Global Tel Link and Securus Technologies have been sold twice to private equity firms. "Global Tel Link, which controls 50 percent of the market for correctional institutions, was sold for $1 billion in 2011 to American Securities, a New York–based firm. Securus, which has about 20 percent of the market, was most recently sold in 2013 to Abry Partners, based in Boston, for $640 million."[10]

Florida ranked thirty-second in the nation for the affordability of a fifteen-minute call at $2.10 per call. Still, it's too costly for many families. Prisoners are increasingly aware of the enormous rates that the for-profit prison phone industry charges, and they have found ways to push back by circumventing prison rules. "Cell phones are not taboo in Florida," Randall says about access to cells in prison. It's a common form of prison contraband. Cell phones and accessories can be expensive inside and remain in high demand, but the penalties for being caught with one are severe. Still, for many prisoners the costs and risks are worth it. Randall is nearing two years on the same cell phone. Access to a mobile phone has been a part of his journey for a long time. Cell phones inside facilities have proliferated across the country over the years. A 2017 report said that some 38,179 cell phones and accessories had been found and confiscated in Florida prisons over the previous four years. The most common way to smuggle phones into prisons is through prison guards. Phones can cost prisoners up to $1,000 per device. One guard raked in $150,000 in a single year by smuggling in phones and selling them to prisoners.[11]

Over the years, Randall has gotten the money for the cell phone from family and friends. They understand the risk, but they also believe it's worth it. Cynthia sees the phone as a literal lifeline for her family and her son. "That phone is keeping my son alive and keeping me alive," she says. "That's what's making his time so easy. Just that. 'Cause he can call me. Sometimes he text me, he say, 'I love you.' I say, 'I love you.' Sometimes he say, 'I miss you.' And we send little pictures," she says. "Listen, for the guys serving life, it means a lot."

One father incarcerated in a Florida prison used a cell phone to speak with his fifteen-year-old son. When he was caught, his visitation privileges were suspended for two years. His wife and son suffered beyond what he imagined. When his wife wanted to speak to her husband, she was afraid of the idea of him calling from a cell phone. She would tell him to wait until she could borrow the money so that she could pay for an approved call. She wasn't sure how she would come up with the money, and her husband, serving a fifteen-year sentence, knew it. His wife admits, "I don't have it. A lot of the families are low income like myself, and just don't have the money." She realizes it's hard not to speak to her husband for weeks, but she doesn't believe the risk of using a cell phone is worth it anymore. She's learned a strategy: "You have to learn to space out the calls, but then the calls, they're short," she says. "What I used to do with my son is, I'll talk for fifteen minutes and then he'll talk maybe ten." But sometimes there's a situation that the father and son need to discuss, or that she'll want to talk through with her husband. In those moments, she says, "Sometimes it'll be three calls, four calls because you can't get it in right, you know, and then if you're on the call and they call for count, that money is gone. He has to hang us up." When the visits were cut because her husband was caught with the cell phone, she saw a difference in her son. "When we go on the trips and come back, he's different for a few days. He does better in school. He does better at home with me 'cause it's hard." Once the visits were gone, she started seeing her son's positive behavior dissolve.

Men who are caught with a cell phone inside a Florida prison can face punishment more severe than losing their visitation rights. The highest penalty is a third-degree felony, which could add up to five years on an offender's prison sentence. While many prisoners use the cell phones to communicate with their families for free, unmonitored mobiles behind bars can pose a security risk. Without any surveillance, corrections officers fear, prisoners can use the phones to make drug deals, orchestrate murders, plan escapes, intimidate witnesses, and more.

Randall says he uses the phone to stay connected to his family, watch movies, and read books on the banned books list, like Michelle Alexander's *The New Jim Crow*. He said using the cell phone is also an act of political resistance, a concession for the myriad mistreatments they experience as prisoners. "Florida [prison guards] are very laxed. I get a chance to talk on the phone, a lot—that represents how relaxed they are in Florida," he says. "The benefit in it for us is they think we so stupid and so unharmful, that we be able to get away with things like talking on a cell phone. And sometimes we compromise and we settle for that. We settle for having them leave us alone than having them mess with us, or meet some demands that we may have."

Randall says the guards know about the cell phones but pretend they don't. "They're starting to not even document the phones that they're finding because it looks bad on them." Contraband like cell phones help numb the effects of prison, especially when organizing isn't in place. "If you have access to drugs or a cell phone," Randall argues, "it will keep your mind off greater issues." It isn't the best way to go about serving time, but for some offenders it is an easier and safer alternative to being roused out of a slumber. "If we have an officer who was clearly being abusive or oppressive, we would say [to one another], 'Hey man, forget about that because we have this cell phone.'" For Randall and others, it is a trade-off that has to be carefully evaluated. Even if some prisoners have legitimate complaints to file against corrections officers for their abuse of power, they fear retaliation and disruption to the relaxed vibe Randall mentioned.

Officers could simply decide to crack down on things they didn't regulate before. For example, an officer might take a prisoner's extra sheet that he hung for privacy while using the toilet. Engaging in the smallest type of resistance and provoking the guards doesn't always seem worth it to some prisoners, especially if they have contraband. In the end, it generally has to be a collective decision to fight back or keep quiet.

In recent years, prisoners in other states have gone on hunger strikes to protest mistreatment. Prisoners have taken other actions, like in 2018 when they staged a nationwide prison labor strike and put out a list of ten national demands. In other actions, prisoners have gotten media involved or encouraged activists and families and friends to protest. But Randall doesn't feel that Florida prisoners have real access to resistance. They don't have anyone to disrupt the political status quo. "You have Angela Davis in California. We don't have hell-raisers down here in Florida," Randall says.

He wants to partake in some robust form of organizing, and he wants to support actions that hold corrections officers accountable, actions that tell the free world about their conditions of confinement. But he had not heard "an inkling" about the nationwide prison strike that started on August 21, 2018. The strike was in part a response to the deadliest prison riot in twenty-five years, which had taken place at Lee Correctional Institution in South Carolina earlier in the year. Seven prisoners had been killed. The prisoners were protesting prison labor, which they called "prison slavery," and they had a list of ten demands. Among their demands, they called for the Prison Litigation Reform Act (PLRA) to be rescinded, an act that makes it significantly more difficult for incarcerated persons to file civil rights lawsuits based on the conditions of their confinement. PLRA prevents incarcerated people from filing suits that allege mental or emotional harm and includes a strict exhaustion clause that says prisoners must seek all avenues of administrative remedies internally before attempting to file a lawsuit, among other things.

They also demanded that prisoners and formerly convicted persons get their voting rights back. The protest continued until September 9, which was the forty-seventh anniversary of the historic Attica prison uprising. This is the kind of movement Randall wants to be a part of.

12

THE KIDS
Kentucky

A fter she completed the drug treatment program, Dawn went
back to court to petition for visitation of her youngest child,
Wesley, who was living with his father, Ethan. After drug tests and
home inspections, she was granted visitation rights. Every other
Friday night she drives two hours to pick up Wesley in Bath County,
then she drives back home that same night. On Sunday she makes
the trip to return him to Ethan. On alternate weekends, she makes a
Sunday trip to visit her four daughters, who all live in different parts
of Eastern Kentucky. The visits are an important development, but
Dawn has a long road ahead of her as she works to reestablish the
mother-child bond.

Dawn met and became close friends with a lot of women in the
recovery program who were also working to beat their substance
addiction. Like Dawn, many of the women are mothers from rural
Kentucky who lost custody of their children at some point during
their addiction and incarceration and were court ordered to treatment in Louisville. Some of the women had their children placed
with family members just like Dawn, and they, too, have some form

of visitation. Other mothers have lost their children to the state child welfare system, and those children remain in foster care. Being from rural counties that are up to five hours away from Louisville, communities the women say aren't conducive to recovery and don't offer opportunities anything like the ones in Louisville, means they live miles away from their children. Choosing to continue their sobriety and rebuild their lives in Louisville, away from their children, has made regaining custody even more difficult for them.

All the mothers are racing against a clock when it comes to regaining custody of their children. They all had some form of a child protection case opened during their addiction and incarceration. Taking time away to seek sobriety meant a longer separation from their children. The problem is, once children are in state care, parents have limited time to complete their case plans and prove they are suitable parents that should be reunited with their children.

According to data from the US Bureau of Justice Statistics, two-thirds of incarcerated mothers were the sole custodial parent of one or more children before their incarceration. Mothers represent one of the fastest growing demographics in prison and are increasingly facing sentences so long that they are incompatible with the timelines established by the Adoption and Safe Families Act (ASFA). Signed by President Bill Clinton in 1997, ASFA requires state foster care agencies to begin the termination of parental rights (TPR) whenever a child has lived in foster care for fifteen of the most recent twenty-two months, with very limited exceptions. Since then, some states have decided to terminate rights even faster. ASFA was passed to offer permanence to children who might otherwise be bouncing between foster care placements and group homes. Even so, this act has made it extremely difficult for incarcerated parents to maintain rights to their own children.

Five years after ASFA's implementation, there was a 250 percent increase in the TPR for incarcerated parents. Incarcerated parents across the country face a higher likelihood of losing their parental rights because of their incarceration as compared to other parents, even those parents with child welfare cases in which they're accused of serious abuse. The Marshall Project analyzed nearly three million US Department of Health and Human Services child welfare cases, finding that in one out of eight cases, incarcerated parents lost their parental rights, regardless of the seriousness of their crime. According to the data, between 2006 and 2016 at least thirty-two thousand incarcerated parents had their children permanently removed without being accused of physical or sexual abuse, though many of the separations were tied in part to factors related to poverty. At least five thousand of those cases involved parents who appeared to have had their parental rights severed due to their incarceration alone.[1]

A problem for incarcerated parents with children in foster care is that the two systems, though both run by the state, have completely distinct missions and rarely communicate well with each other. The focus of criminal justice policymakers is sentencing and punishment, whereas child welfare officials are focused on safety and permanence for children. An almost total lack of meaningful coordination between these systems contributes to the heightened risk of permanent separation between an incarcerated mother and her children. The women in recovery at the Healing Place are caught on the wrong side of the timeline in various ways as they try to rebuild relationships with their children. The most glaring issue with the timeline is that women are confined to the program and are often unable to travel to make visits to their children.

AS BAD AS RELINQUISHING CUSTODY to family members might have been for Dawn, custody issues are far worse for many other parents. Jo, Dawn's mother, was Dawn's safety net, but as Dawn later learned, many mothers who get involved in the web of Child Protective Services have a nearly impossible time getting their kids back. This is especially true if the child is in foster care while Mom is locked up.

Christina Walker, another woman at the Healing Place, did not have family members who were able to take in her children during her battle with drug addiction and her incarceration. Her ten-year-old daughter, Da'Kayda, and three-year-old son, Rivez, have been in foster care for close to two years now. They have been in the same home the whole time, and the foster parents want to permanently adopt them.

Christina says she was prescribed opioids to manage her scoliosis, but eventually started abusing them as a method of self-medicating while she was in an abusive relationship. Her partner had served seventeen years in prison, and a portion of that sentence was for nearly killing two women. "I didn't know that until, like, a year and a half in. I was already in too deep," she said referring to her daughter's father. "He was like a drug to me. He was worse than any other drug that I've ever done and that's reality," Christina says somberly.

One Sunday in 2016, Christina was pulled over by police. She was arrested when the officers discovered she had a warrant for a previous failure to appear in court. The warrant was in Allen County, twenty-five miles east of where Christina lived. In the past, if she was arrested, she would be transferred to the county of offense within a day, and then released. This time she wasn't immediately transferred and released. Her children were left in the care of her boyfriend. She called him from booking and asked him to take them to her brother's home until she was released.

Her brother had watched her kids in the past, so she assumed they would be safe there until she could straighten out her warrant. After a few days, she still hadn't been transferred to the local jail. Meanwhile, she was served with papers from child welfare services alleging her daughter had been the victim of mistreatment while in the custody of her brother. While in school, Christina's daughter had told school officials her mother was in jail and her uncle's girlfriend had whipped her and verbally abused her.

Christina was released from jail eighteen days later, and her children remained in foster care. "I still had a job, a house, a car. I worked at a college and they didn't give me my kids back," she recalls. "That's when my life fell apart." Christina was still using opioids. She said she felt hopeless and spiraled deeper into her addiction. "I had went from having my kids every single day of their life and them being in the home with me to not getting to see them at all," Christina says. "When they didn't give my kids back, there was no point for me to do anything different," she says. Four months after her children were removed, she faced three new indictments for felony charges.

Shortly after her children were removed, Christina also got devastating news about Da'Kayda. "My little girl tried to kill herself. She was eight years old. She was in this mental hospital for, like, two weeks, but they wouldn't allow me to even go there to see her," she says. "I know she was scared. I was scared, so I can imagine how her little mind feels."

From the outside, Christina admits, her daughter's life looked great at home with her. She lived in a six-bedroom, three-bath home on five acres of land and had everything money could buy. But inside, Christina says, "it was chaos." Da'Kayda saw a lot of domestic violence between her parents. Christina admitted that in her addiction she was verbally abusive to her daughter, replicating the treatment she received from her boyfriend. "She saw a lot of violence. I feel like she feels guilty because she went and said something, you know, and that's probably why she tried to harm herself," she says, her blue eyes welling up.

Christina has no insight into her daughter's current state because she's not allowed to visit her. She is allowed to write her letters. She writes her and gives the missives to her social worker, who then passes them on to the girl's social worker. Christina, however, questions whether her daughter actually receives the letters she writes. "She's written me back one time and that just doesn't seem like my daughter," the mother says. "I know my daughter."

With the help of a state-appointed attorney, Christina was eventually granted visitation rights to see her son once a week for one hour. His foster home, however, was a two-hour drive away from Christina, and she was still in treatment at the time. "It's a hundred twenty miles one way and we're not allowed to have a car or drive while we're in the Healing Place. So they knew that it would basically be impossible for me to have visitation with my son if they didn't bring him to me," she says. Her lawyer made the request, but the foster parents refused. Christina couldn't understand it. "Our house is very well equipped. We have a kid's playroom. We have two playgrounds. We have everything that a kid needs there, and there's no reason why my son shouldn't have been able to come. But they wouldn't do that for me. They tried to make it nearly impossible for me to see my son."

The only way she could have visitation with him was by going to the Department of Community Services, where she and her son were left in a room alone but monitored via camera and audio. Every Tuesday, someone volunteers to drive Christina the 240-mile round trip to see her son for one hour. When she arrives, she's not allowed to identify herself as the boy's mother for fear it will confuse him. He has been in the care of a lesbian couple for nearly two years and refers to them both as "Mommy."

Christina has spent the last twenty months incarcerated and in a court-ordered residential drug treatment program. As a result, she is at substantial risk for permanent termination of her parental rights due to the ASFA timeline. She, like hundreds of formerly incarcerated parents across the country, is struggling with the challenges of reentry while fighting to preserve her parental rights against the tight ASFA timeline. Christina recently received a petition from child welfare services to terminate her parental rights.

As Christina fights to maintain custody of her children, she is told her daughter doesn't want to see her or speak with her. If it's true that her daughter has refused to see her, she believes it's a defense mechanism, a way for her to detach. She believes her daughter might have anxiety about her safety since she watched so much domestic abuse. "Her fear isn't that I'll overdose, her fear for me is that her dad is going to kill me," Christina says. "So, if she still has anxiety from that, how do you ever let her know that I'm doing something different?" Christina doesn't believe letters can show her daughter that she's making positive changes, that she's on a new path. "I feel like it's cruel to her."

During Christina's most recent court hearing to terminate her parental rights, the child's father didn't show up, so the judge postponed the court date for six months. Christina has used the time to continue her journey of recovery and reentry by getting a job and apartment of her own, with the hope that she will get back custody of her children. "The people that have my children, they're great people and they've done great things for my kids. I'm not downplaying that or ungrateful for that at all. However, they want *my* kids," she says. "I don't even want to take my kids completely from them. I just want to share my kids with them." Christina realizes that the wider the support system she has, the better. She wants her children to be surrounded by people who love and support them. "But they don't want to share my kids," she says. "They want them all for themselves and it's not fair."

Activists and formerly incarcerated parents impacted by ASFA have sought and won reforms to ASFA guidelines in a handful of states. New York, California, Colorado, Washington, and Illinois have passed bills giving foster care agencies more flexibility when it comes to filing TPRs against incarcerated parents. Nebraska and New Mexico originally included exceptions for parental incarceration in their legislation. Massachusetts and Tennessee have bills pending, and Connecticut is exploring the option. Families in states without exceptions are especially vulnerable to separations, and some states with exceptions aren't enforcing them.

EVEN AFTER MOTHERS GET SOBER and they aren't dealing directly with their state's foster care system, they still face nearly insurmountable challenges when trying to maintain a relationship with their children. And even when the children are with family or the family of the ex, it's still hard for mothers to get to see them.

Melissa was incarcerated on two trafficking charges; when she was arrested, she was in the possession of two oxycodone pills. She also got a complicity charge because she was in the same room as her then-boyfriend when he trafficked drugs. As a result, she received a ten-year sentence. She went to prison and served about 20 percent of her time, a little over a year and a few months.

Before going to jail, she had an open Child Protective Services case due to her substance use disorder. The open case changed to a neglect case because she was away from her kids for an extended period of time due to incarceration. While she was in prison, child welfare services closed her case and granted custody of her children to the paternal grandparents. Once Melissa was released from prison, she was court ordered to a residential substance abuse treatment program, where she remained for seventeen months.

For the nearly two years Melissa was in treatment, her ex-partner's parents, who had taken in her children, wouldn't allow her to speak with them. It was a painful experience that Melissa never wants to go through again. "I would rather go back to prison than never be able to talk to my children again until they're eighteen," she says. Not having the freedom to communicate with her kids when she likes is terrifying.

When she came home from prison, she wanted to fight for the custody of her oldest son, but she couldn't afford to hire an attorney. The other costs and struggles associated with reentry were simply too high. She couldn't find housing, so she eventually roomed with two other women. She didn't have a car, so she had to use public transportation three hours a day to commute to work.

She chose to stay in Louisville for the employment opportunities. "I couldn't have got a job there," Melissa says about her hometown in Martin County. "Even the people there without records can't get jobs." She wouldn't have anywhere to live either. Martin County, the same county where Lyndon B. Johnson started the War on Poverty, is one of the most impoverished places in the country. Economic opportunities there are miniscule. *U.S. News & World Report* rated it the worst-performing white-majority county in the nation. "So I stayed in Louisville to try to build a life and thought maybe one day I can get my kids back and provide for them."

She has not been able to regain custody of her children. But she is approaching her seventh year clean and sober, and she has developed a relationship with them. She gets to see her children, but it's at the whim of her ex-partner's parents, so she is careful. Once a month she takes the 3.5-hour drive back home to Martin County to see them. Her youngest son was only five months old when she went to prison, so he doesn't understand that she is his mother. Her older son, who's now in the eighth grade, gets to stay with her during the summer and for some holidays.

Though she isn't a full-time mom, she knows her situation could have been worse. Her children would have gone into foster care if their paternal grandparents hadn't stepped in. Melissa's work is directly related to her past experiences in the criminal justice system and the aftereffects of her conviction. After working at the Healing Place, Melissa moved on to work as an advocate at a local nonprofit criminal justice reform organization.

CAREGIVERS WHO TAKE IN THEIR kin can apply for legal status. Some become what is known as a resource parent—a foster parent or kinship caregiver—a designation that comes with significant financial and social support but requires families to first surrender custody of the child to the state. Later, as the state seeks a permanent home for the child, it will usually ask a grandparent who has gained resource parent status to adopt. Doing so involves the wrenching decision to permanently sever parental rights, making the mother a legal stranger to her own child. Caregivers who don't want to be involved in the child welfare system take care of children as legal guardians, which preserves the mother's parental rights. As legal guardians, caregivers gain legal standing. This gives them full decision-making power on behalf of the child they care for. They can seek medical care, enroll the child in school, and even register for benefits if the child is eligible. They maintain control over day-to-day parenting decisions that would otherwise be forfeited in the child welfare system.

A relative caregiver who becomes a kinship caregiver through their state's child welfare system gains a status that triggers a stipend to help them cover the costs of raising the child. Kinship caregivers, however, run significant risks through their loss of autonomy, since they are essentially contracted by the state to provide the child a temporary home until the department of human services (DHS) can find permanent placement for the child. With slight variations from state to state, to be certified as a kinship caregiver, applicants must pass a medical exam, get child abuse and criminal history clearances, and participate in training programs and parent preparation activities. A DHS social worker then conducts a full inspection of the home, describing the family's strengths and noting any problems, including potential safety hazards. DHS then follows up by interviewing references outside the family. If a prospective caregiver is approved, a social worker is assigned to the family and begins a series of at least once-a-month visits. Many caregivers consider these requirements intimidating, invasive, and constrictive, limiting the way they raise their kin. They describe the visits as feeling more like surveillance. With a few perceived wrong turns, a child can be removed. Because of these factors, many caregivers opt to go it alone.[2]

When Jo took in three of her four granddaughters, she didn't go through Kentucky's child welfare system. Instead she decided to become a legal guardian through family court. She got legal standing, with full decision-making power on behalf of the granddaughters in her care, and Dawn maintained her parental rights. When Jo gained custody of Dawn's girls, she qualified for Kentucky's Kinship Care program, which pays grandparents or other relatives caring for children removed from their homes because of abuse or neglect. But Jo didn't apply for it. Dawn's sister, who took in Dawn's youngest daughter, did apply. She got in under the wire: in 2013, the program stopped accepting new applicants due to funding cuts.

Jo isn't alone in assuming the role of parent without receiving financial support from the state. Across the country, in 2018, for every child in foster care with relatives, there were nineteen being raised by grandparents or other extended family, informally, outside the foster care system. Jo did receive state support to get the girls health insurance, but she did the rest on her own. She has worked as a private nurse for most of her adult life. "I always saved," she says. "I'm good about saving. Always saved enough that if my job ended I had enough to do me for three months. So I know I can find a job in three months, because it's not beneath me to go to the factory because I did that, until a patient comes up," Jo says.

Even though Dawn is standing firmly in her sobriety, she thinks it is best to leave her children where they have been for the previous years. She is trying to rebuild the severed relationships with her children. Some of the rebuilding will be easier than the rest. She faces the biggest challenge trying to reconcile with her sixteen-year-old daughter, Willow. Willow had witnessed her mother deep in her addiction, and unlike her older sisters, she had never seen any other side of her mother. "She was a little younger, and I think that it done more damage to her than it really did the rest of them," Jo says. Willow, who lives with her grandmother, started exhibiting signs that felt too familiar to Dawn.

"She started doing the same rebelling stuff that I seen in me as a teenager. The acting out with guys. The smoking. The stealing. In and out of the court system," Dawn says. The teen got caught for shoplifting. She had stolen a pair of shoes. Her grandmother thinks she's looking for acceptance and has tried to steer her back onto a better path. Once, when Jo got a call from Willow's school saying she had been absent for three days, she found out Willow was hanging out at someone's apartment. The grandmother devised a plan to bring the teen home. "I go down to get her and all I done was grab for her. Bust her butt. I called the law," Jo says. Jo was doing what she thought was necessary to get her granddaughter out of the apartment and home. Afterward she was shocked by a knock on her door from social services. "She told them 'Yeah, she grabbed me and pushed me down.'" Jo denied the allegations of abuse. She couldn't help but compare the incident to when she herself was growing up. In her experience, parents had freedom to reprimand their children. "I wish it had been when I was growing up because she wouldn't be doing this right now. I mean, she's in a house, I'm gonna yank her out. Yeah, I did it. I did take her arm and I did pull her out of that house. If I hadn't, you'd have been out here and said I wasn't taken care of my kids," Jo says. The social worker made Willow remove her makeup to prove she had been hit in the face as she alleged. She hadn't.

Willow was sent to Appalachian Challenge Academy, a military base. The courses there are aimed at correcting sixteen-to-eighteen-year-old high school dropouts. The program focuses on life skills, education, and self-discipline. That didn't work out for Willow. "I think she's blaming everything on her mother," Jo says. "She went through a time period of self-mutilating herself." Jo has looked for many solutions, but nothing has been effective. Dawn has tried to present herself as a cautionary tale to her daughter, but they don't have the type of relationship in which Willow will listen to Dawn. "I've tried to go back and talk with her and do stuff but she's not hearing it," Dawn says. "She's so angry at me that I know I have to just keep sitting still. Just showing her I'm still gonna be here when all this pans out. Wherever you wash up, Mama's going to be there."

Willow was later court ordered to Job Corps, a federal program with state chapters for sixteen-to-twenty-four-year-olds who are trying to get on a career path. The program offers job skills, training, education, and counseling. "Just before she went to Job Corps she tried to commit suicide. They had to break my bathroom door in," Jo says. Jo took her to the hospital and expected that Willow would be placed on an automatic seventy-two-hour hold for suicide watch, but they sent her home. If Willow doesn't complete the Job Corps program, she will be sent to a Kentucky juvenile detention center.

Jo has urged her granddaughter to make amends with her mother with the hopes she'll get past the anger and hurt. "I've tried to talk to her, like, you know, 'You need to really forgive your mom so you can move on, it's nothing to do with your mother, I want you to feel good about yourself.' So, she's had a lot of resentment on that part." Jo is hopeful that the latest program will be a turning point for the teenager. "She's doing a whole lot better." Willow gets to come home on the weekends, and Jo can take the thirty-minute drive to see her whenever she wants. Willow is also taking business courses as part of the program, and by the time she is done she will have a high school diploma and a trade and will have earned $1,000. Her older sister Annabel is not as hopeful. "I think she's just like my mom."

When Dawn got clean, Taylor was eighteen and Annabel, who still lived with her grandmother, was seventeen. Dawn had free rein to visit them when she liked, so they agreed it didn't make sense for Dawn to go to court to try to regain legal custody. She managed to go back to Mount Sterling to watch them both graduate high school. They were both preparing for college and had started building their lives as young adults. A few years later, the relationships have improved. Taylor, now twenty-one, is engaged and has two children and a small farm in Mount Sterling. Annabel, now twenty, is a dental assistant and still lives with her grandmother for now. She refers to her mom as Dawn and says she isn't sure if the relationship can be salvaged. "The relationship will just never be there. I love her and I'm proud of her," Annabel says about her mother. Pointing at her grandma, she says, "She's my mom and that's just what it is."

Taylor, too, is proud of her mom, but she still doesn't see or talk to her as often as she would like. Her children don't know her as well as they do their paternal grandmother or maternal great-grandmother. "I think that she thinks she has to stay in Louisville to stay sober—because she's brought that up especially in the first part of her recovery—and I could see that, because our town's really small and that's all that's around here," Taylor says. "Anywhere you look you're going to see someone that you know, that you may have used to party with or something like that," she says. But Taylor thinks it's an excuse, a crutch. "I think she's in a stronger mind-set now to where she could move closer. I just think maybe she's afraid to . . . I feel like she's still missing out a lot."

As Taylor sees it, Dawn's main focus now is building her relationship with her youngest child, Wesley. "I see her when she's coming to get Wesley. She doesn't come specifically for any of her other kids, and if she is down here, we don't see her very long." Taylor admits it makes her a little jealous. Even though she's older now and has children of her own, she would still like her mother to try to be there for all her kids.

Dawn's daughter Hannah still lives with Dawn's sister, Robin. They have a good relationship and Dawn plans to let Hannah continue living with her aunt. After years of making the long drives to visit her son, Dawn has arranged for Wesley to come live with her.

One winter evening in 2018, Wesley, who is twelve years old, called his mom to remind her of the news. "I'm gonna get to come live with you," Wesley told his mom. "I'm probably gonna stay like two or three years." She smiled into the phone. "Okay, okay. You can stay as long as you want to," she told him.

"My next journey is having my son live with me," Dawn says.

13

THE DEVIL IN HELL
Mississippi

It was a normal shift for Ruth one night in December when she received an unexpected call from her neighbor. "I just wanted to call you and tell you it's a bunch of police at your house," he told her. "Police?" Ruth asked, her voice tinged with shock. "What police doing there, what done happened?" she asked. Nothing seemed off in the neighborhood and the officers hadn't come to the neighbor's home. He didn't know. "I thought about Kevin, really," Ruth recalls. Kevin, her oldest son, had served time and been in legal trouble before and was a self-professed hothead. It was plausible they were looking for him for something, but he didn't live with her. He had since turned the garage at his house into an auto body shop and was running a successful business. He had stayed out of trouble for the last four years.

She phoned her middle son, Robert, who was staying with her at the time. Robert sat inside the house nervously. He told his mom it was the second time in the last few days that the police had come by. They were looking for Naeem. Ruth was surprised. There had to be a mistake. "Looking for Naeem? Looking for Naeem for what?" she asked him, perplexed. He didn't have the answers either.

Naeem lived at home with his mom, so Ruth tried to recall the previous days that she saw him. She worked a twelve-hour night shift, so she left home in the evening and returned to the house early in the morning. Many of the mornings when she got home Naeem would still be asleep. She had noticed that Naeem wasn't there a couple of mornings, but at the time she didn't think too much about it. He'd recently been laid off from his seasonal job at Walmart, so she thought perhaps he was going out early in the morning to look for a job. She remembered seeing him on at least one occasion with his toothbrush and toothpaste in hand, but still, it wasn't cause for concern. Maybe he was staying the night at a friend's house or spending the night in a hotel with his girlfriend. He was twenty, so she gave him flexibility.

It was on the third night that she received the call from her neighbor, heard the news from Robert, and reflected on the last few days. She couldn't think that Naeem was in some sort of trouble and was keeping it from her. That night, she called Naeem but wasn't able to reach him. On the next night, around two o'clock in the morning, she received a call from Kevin. "I got Naeem with me because these people, they looking for him," he breathed into the phone. "'I done hid his car,'" Ruth recalls him saying.

"What?" Ruth asked loudly into the phone, confused and panicked by Kevin's admission. She had no idea what was going on, but she knew that Kevin trying to hide Naeem's car was a bad idea. "Kevin you don't need to be trying to hide . . ." He protested before his mom could complete her sentence. "I ain't gonna let them get my brother," he told his mother. Ruth was tense and didn't want her coworkers to know what was happening. She had a quieter back-and-forth conversation with Kevin on the phone. Finally, realizing she wouldn't be able to get through to him via phone or get the full details, she told him, "I'm leaving work right now. Where Naeem at?" Kevin hadn't told his family where he lived, so Ruth couldn't just drive directly to his home. He had Naeem in the car with him, he explained, and they could meet somewhere. Kevin wouldn't meet at his mother's house because it was too risky, so they met in a shopping center parking lot in Jackson.

"What is going on?" Ruth asked Naeem as soon as she saw him. He told his mother that he'd robbed a Ruby Tuesday restaurant in Rankin County. Ruth felt the weight of the news pour down on her, heavy like concrete. She didn't have all the facts but it was enough to incite fear. "Why did you do that to yourself?" she asked her son as tears streamed down her face.

MISSISSIPPI HAS A HARSHER VERSION of racism compared to more progressive states, one that compounded Ruth's general fear for Naeem's life and involvement in the criminal justice system. This sounded like something that Naeem's boyish charm and natural kindness couldn't get him out of. Ruth was simultaneously sad, afraid, and disappointed. He had committed a crime; he was on the run; and he did it in a county his parents had long since told him to stay away from. William had warned that young black boys from Hinds County should stay out of Rankin County. Rankin County had a median household income of $61,605, a 9.3 percent poverty rate, and a population that was 76.5 percent white and 20.6 percent black. Hinds County, where Naeem lived, had a median household income of $41,011, a 20.2 percent poverty rate, and a population that was 72.5 percent black and 25.6 percent white.

The Andersons talked explicitly about racism with their kids and grandchildren because it was often quite visible in Mississippi. "We tried to tell the kids about certain areas in Mississippi and how they feel about young black men," William says. "Mississippi is known for this racist mentality, it's still here," Ruth admits. She'd grown used to it. "I was born and raised here. We a racist state." Mississippi is the state where, in 1955, Emmett Till, then fourteen years old, was accused of grabbing and whistling at a white woman. He was brutally murdered, his disfigured body found in the Tallahatchie River. His mother's choice to have an open-casket funeral spurred conversations about equality and anti-lynching legislation, and became a tipping point in the fight for civil rights in America. More than seven decades later, in 2018, Cindy Hyde-Smith, a white Republican senator, was elected despite making racist comments. A video surfaced in which the senator, who faced a runoff against an African American Democrat, joked about attending a lynching. "If he invited me to a public hanging, I'd be on the front row," Hyde-Smith said during a campaign stop in Tupelo, Mississippi.[1]

Ruth was afraid to hear what her son did. Naeem knew better than to go to Rankin County to hang out, much less do something against the law. In general, he grew up thinking most white people in his home state looked at young black boys differently. Sometimes it was apparent, and sometimes it was less so. He used to ride along with his mother to a grocery store in Rankin County. That was where "all the good stuff was at." He didn't notice shoppers or workers looking at him strangely while he was with his mom. Ruth had a commanding presence; it was impossible to tell her that she didn't belong somewhere. But whenever she dropped him off at the Northpark Mall in Ridgeland, a predominately white neighborhood, he was profiled. He and his friends were perceived as being ghetto kids and were immediately seen as a threat. Often, they were forced to disband, because five in a group was considered to be a pack. They were often kicked out of the mall.

As for the robbery, the police report said a tall, slender male, wearing all black, entered the Ruby Tuesday from the kitchen door in the back. He then headed to the office, where the manager was counting money. The man put a gun to the back of the manager's head, tossed a backpack on the desk, and directed the manager to put the cash in the bag. The manager thought it was a coworker playing around with him, so he reached behind his head without looking and swatted at the gun. "Stop playing," the manager said to the man, thinking it was all a prank. The man then reached over the manager's shoulder, grabbed the money out of the cash drawer, and ran off. On the way out, the man slipped on the wet floor and dropped the gun, which broke into pieces. An employee chased after the man, throwing a big rock at the man's gray sedan as he sped away.

When the police arrived on the scene, they found a few $20 bills in the parking lot and the rock the employee had thrown. Inside, employees collected the parts of the gun. It was a BB gun, its broken handle revealing the metal air canister inside the hand grip.

Eventually, police viewed the restaurant's camera footage and learned that the man hadn't acted alone. It showed Naeem's best friend, Jared, an employee at the restaurant, go to the office, get the manager's key, and proceed to unlock the door to let the would-be robber in. After opening the door, he motioned for the man to come in. Jared stepped forward and then the man ran past him and went straight to the office. After directing the man, Jared got on a phone call with his girlfriend, and he remained on the call during the robbery. From the footage, he was the only identifiable suspect.

During the police interrogation, Jared cracked under pressure and identified Naeem as the man in black. That's when the police started their search for Naeem, going to his mother's house and the house of his girlfriend, Brooke. Jared denied that he was an accomplice and placed the full blame on Naeem. Police retrieved the boys' cell phone records, which showed that the two had talked before and after the robbery.

After Ruth read the police report, she was floored. It didn't sound real. It was instead something out of an awful movie, one filled with a comedy of errors with serious consequences. Jared was eighteen and Naeem was twenty. They were best friends. They had clung to each other since childhood. For Naeem, Jared was like a brother. They even lived by a code of solidarity and had adopted a "one swing, we all swing" mantra, which landed them in plenty of fights together in school. Most recently, they worked at Walmart together until Naeem lost his position. Jared still had that job and also worked at Ruby Tuesday.

"I had a little money but Christmas was coming up and my car note was due," Naeem said later. "So I was kind of desperate, and he came up with the idea that we would rob Ruby Tuesday." Since Jared worked there and stayed until closing, he knew the routine. They thought "it was going to be easy." They would use a fake gun. No one would get hurt or get caught, and they'd make off with some quick cash to push them through the holidays. It would be done in five minutes.

RUTH HAD TO RETURN TO WORK. Kevin took Naeem back home with him. "You can't keep him," Ruth told her emotional son before she left. "You cannot hide him. You can't do that." Ruth's spirit was unsettled for the remainder of her shift. When she returned home in the morning, she had to come up with a plan. William called her and she told him what was going on. They cried on the phone together. She didn't want to turn her son in, but she knew she had to. William suggested she reach out to her nephew Corey, who was a corrections officer in the same jurisdiction where Naeem committed the crime. Corey was levelheaded and would be able to figure something out.

When Ruth finally got a hold of Corey, he could hear in her voice that she was upset. He agreed to help. Corey made his way over to Kevin's house, but Kevin still refused to give his brother up. Unlike Naeem, Kevin had grown up in the street, and so his first instinct was to try to protect his younger brother in the only way he knew how—even if it was too late or meant more trouble. Naeem was the only Anderson son without a criminal record, something Kevin was proud of him for and thought he should take advantage of. He wanted him to do anything constructive as long as he didn't end up behind bars. "I've been telling him 'Boy as many times that I've been to jail. And

Dad? You ain't learned nothing?'" He too was blindsided by Naeem's situation. He knew it was too late to scold his little brother, but he felt partially responsible, like he had failed him. "I feel like I could have done better as a brother," he says. So there he was, in his own way, trying to make it right. If he let Naeem turn himself in, he could be devoured. The alternative, in his eyes, was to run.

Corey pleaded with his cousin. "Kevin, now we don't want him to get hurt." As a corrections officer, Corey knew the risk of being on the run. Ruth cried and explained the severity of the situation to Naeem, who had started to realize just how bad things were. Ruth could see his fear. "He was just scared," Ruth recalls. "When I looked at him, he was scared. And then when I started hollering and crying that made him cry." Through the tears, she kept asking the same question, "Why did you do this to yourself?" She knew that he didn't fully comprehend the consequences. "You just don't know," Ruth pleaded. "This is trouble."

In Ruth's view, the crime was stupid. Based on what she knew about Naeem and Jared, it just showed how immature they were. It was quite silly even. But black boys and black men aren't allowed to make dumb mistakes. Instead, they are systematically prosecuted to the fullest extent of the law. More to that, many don't make it safely to court, jail, or prison. "If the police had came, it wouldn't have been like you're young and stupid. You'd have been dead," Ruth says. "I mean, you trying to run away?" She couldn't believe it. It was good that he made it out alive. Now she had to figure out how to get him to the police station. Ruth knew just how bad things were and could get if Naeem didn't turn himself in, and quickly. "I know sometimes they don't come to a good end when they looking for you," Ruth says. "I've seen them have shoot-outs with people." Naeem didn't have a gun, but that wouldn't matter.

In 2016, black males between the ages of fifteen and thirty-four were nine times more likely than other Americans to be killed by law enforcement. That same year, 253 black men were killed by police.

At least thirty-nine of those men were unarmed. Unjustified police violence against black people was painfully visible. The Andersons knew it. They didn't want to see Naeem become a casualty.[2]

Finally, Ruth and Corey managed to convince Naeem to go to the precinct. Ruth, her sister, and her two nephews headed over in separate cars. Naeem rode in the car with Corey so that Corey could prepare him for the process of turning himself in. Corey would speak directly to officers he knew on the force so that the police would handle the arrest with consideration.

Kevin didn't go.

NAEEM BEING INVOLVED IN SUCH a crime was senseless to Ruth and William. It was the furthest they had ever seen him drift. Ruth replays the details out loud. "You done slip down and can't even rob a place? It's stupid." She reasons that Naeem couldn't have realized how serious the offense was. "He must have thought in a twisted way that it was gonna be like stealing or something. It was childish. It was immature." This was more than some dumb plan gone wrong. It was dangerous. "I just wouldn't have ever thought," Ruth says, pausing to think of what possessed her son. "That was the devil in Hell."

Every time Ruth and William had asked Naeem how things were going, he said they were good. He never let them know he was having financial difficulties. He'd had jobs, lost jobs, and got new ones. He was resourceful. He was independent. He also kept things bottled up, preferring to illustrate his capacity to survive alone. When he explained his reasoning for committing the crime—he didn't have any money, he couldn't pay his car note—they couldn't believe it.

Ruth never asked Naeem to pay bills for the house, although William teased her about it. He said she should let Naeem pay the water bill, to teach him responsibility. "William thought I was a wuss. Too lenient," Ruth says. Naeem had illustrated that he was responsible without paying a household bill. Ruth let him keep his money for himself so that he could manage his personal bills. She didn't need his financial contribution. Ruth raised Naeem during a time when she was financially secure and could offer him anything within reason, though he didn't ask for anything as he got older. She enjoyed seeing the new sneakers lined up in his bedroom, him paying the insurance on his car, paying his cell phone bill, or taking weekend trips with Brooke. She was proud of him. He earned around $1,400 a month when he worked at the warehouse, and he managed to handle his own bills and whatever else he needed to deal with.

One day, the car Naeem had bought on his own stopped running. He worked in Madison County, which was at least thirty minutes away by car. There was no public transportation route, so Ruth started dropping him off at work in the afternoon. It was inconvenient because she had to wake up earlier than she would for her night shift in order to drive him across town. Normally she would sleep through the afternoon so that she could be alert for her shift. She decided he needed a reliable car, so they went to the dealership. He paid for the down payment on the car, but Ruth cosigned. If he fell behind on payments, it could impact his mother's credit.

Ruth admits to being tough on him about the car note. "I think because I preached about it so much." But if she knew he couldn't keep up with the car note, she would have easily helped. It was around $300 a month. "I signed for the car. I'm not gonna let my credit go bad." She reasons that he didn't want to get behind because he feared it would disappoint her. When Naeem decided to drop out of high school, he went to work right away and determined to never ask his mother for financial help. He was proud of his independence and relieving his mother of financial duties. "He never asked me for any money. He was the type didn't want to ask." He refused to be a burden to his mother. "Mom, you ain't gotta buy me nothing," he would say. "I'm gonna take care of myself."

Ruth never imagined he would go this far. "He wanted to be his own man, I guess, show me that he could do things and I think that he got lost in that." She keeps recalling what she said to him about the car note. "I help you get this car, but you're gonna pay it," she said. "I said it in a firm way and I think he took that to heart." If he had believed his mom would let his car get repossessed, Ruth thinks, he had a lot of growing up to do. "It hurt me to my heart," Ruth confesses. "I thought he was more mature than that. It floored me."

Ruth told her son that needing money wasn't a good excuse to commit a crime. Jobs would come and go. But he couldn't see far enough into the future to understand that. "When you fill out an application, you may not hear from them, but all of a sudden everybody calls you. You couldn't see, you couldn't see that far? That show that you were immature. I thought you were more mature than that," she says.

It was painful for Naeem to watch his mom—always tough, impenetrable, the pillar—soaking in tears. He did not want to continue causing her pain. "I already know my momma stressed out, she crying," he says. That's when he knew he had to turn himself in. The matriarch, a statue of perseverance, finally letting her boys see she could be shaken moved them. Naeem also needed to do some reflecting on why after all these years he'd "adapted to his environment," which, he says, was robbing. He says he needs to get his thinking on track and figure out what his next move will be.

Ruth didn't take immediate action after Naeem's arrest. She had to strategize. "I was trying to think. I knew I had to come up with some money. I wasn't going with a court-appointed lawyer," she says. Ruth needed a lawyer who would be present, responsive, and fight for her son. She had to choose right. She asked a close friend, and she also asked the lawyer who represented William pro bono for his board hearings. Finally, she decided on a lawyer, a white woman. Ruth believed the county was racist and hoped a white lawyer would garner favor. It took a month before Ruth could raise the money to afford the $5,000 retainer. She wasn't able to cash Naeem's income tax return check to help, so she asked a friend.

THE JUDGE SET NAEEM'S BAIL AT $250,000. This meant that, in order for Naeem to be released from jail until his next court date, he would need to give the court this amount. The court would hold his payment, or a pledge of property worth that amount, until he returned to court and was sentenced. He would then get the money back. Bail practices vary from state to state. The amount of bail is supposed to depend on the crime, but it is also at the judge's discretion. When determining the amount of bail to request, a judge is supposed to consider the seriousness of the charged crime; whether or not the defendant has a past criminal record; whether or not the defendant is employed; and if the defendant has close ties to family and the community, is a flight risk, or is a danger to others. Setting bail at $250,000 for a failed robbery in which no one got hurt, the weapon was fake, and the defendant had no criminal record is extremely high.

When defendants can't afford to bail out of jail, they must sit behind bars. On any given day, 60 percent of the US jail population consists of people who are being held but haven't been convicted of a crime. Bail is often set so high that most defendants don't have the money to bail themselves out. Studies have consistently found that courts set bail significantly higher for black defendants than they do for white defendants.[3]

Defendants who can't afford to pay their bail can seek help from a bail agent, who will post bail for them by writing a bond for the full bail amount. Generally, the bail agent requests a fee from the defendant, which starts out at 10 percent of the bail amount, but can often be significantly higher. For the remainder of the bail amount, the bail agent will ask the defendant to supply collateral, such as a house or car. If the defendant does not have enough collateral, the agent might seek out relatives and friends to assist in covering the cost of bail. Whether defendants are found innocent or guilty, the court returns bail money to them once they appear in court. But bail bond agents do not return the money collected from the defendant.

Many of the contracts from bail agents include exploitive terms that defendants are forced to agree to if they want to get out of jail. There are more than twenty-five thousand bail bond companies operating in the US, but only about ten insurers underwrite the bulk of the $14 billion in bonds issued yearly. The big insurance corporations behind the bail bond industry have made laws, regulations, and practices that protect their profits. They have a long-standing relationship with the American Legislative Exchange Council (ALEC), a conservative corporate lobbying group that drafts a number of anti-reform laws, to successfully write and pass their own custom laws in state legislatures nationwide, thus blocking reforms.[4]

The industry that rakes in between $1.4 billion and $2.4 billion in profit annually has trapped thousands of families in debt across the country. Over a five-year period, Maryland families, who were overwhelmingly black, spent $250 million dollars in bail bond payments. At least $75 million of the nonrefundable bail bond payments were for cases that were resolved with no wrongdoing found. In 2015 alone, fewer than five thousand families in New Orleans paid $4.7 million in nonrefundable bond premiums. Illinois, Kentucky, Oregon, and Wisconsin are the only states that do not allow for-profit bail.[5]

Ruth didn't have the $250,000 to bail Naeem out. When she sought the help of a bail agent, she needed to come up with a nonrefundable 10 percent fee of $25,000 and collateral to cover the rest of the $250,000 bail. She didn't have the money. She'd have to put up her house, which wasn't paid off at the time. The company offered to let Ruth put $7,000 down and arrange a payment plan until she reached the $25,000. When she asked Naeem's lawyer to try and get it reduced, she said it was unlikely. "'They're most likely not going to reduce his bond because they don't like people from

Jackson coming over there and stealing things,'" Ruth recalls her lawyer saying. Later, when Naeem waived his rights to a preliminary hearing because he planned to plead guilty, his bail was reduced to $100,000, which meant he'd have to come up with $10,000. It was still too much.

Across the country, courts are setting defendants' bail so high that people who are poor or who do not have the money to pay it are sitting in jail for long periods of time before seeing a judge or being sentenced. Their lives are disrupted each day they're in jail. They risk losing their job, housing, and even custody of their children, which then perpetuates cycles of inequality. Naeem is one of them, and he knows it. "Rankin County, they can give you unreasonable bonds. They gon hide you," he says.

RUTH SITS ON THE SMALL stool and waits. A thick blue box sticks out from the wall like an old TV. Naeem shows up on a grainy screen, but there is no antennae for Ruth to adjust the view. There are no contact visits in the jail. The black plastic receiver rests on her ear; she asks her son how he is doing. He sounds upbeat, though even if he weren't, he'd hide it from his mother. He stands in a room with a handful of other young men who watch him have his video visit. He's no longer wearing the yellow jumpsuit from his court hearing; instead he wears a black-and-white-striped top and bottom.

Since Ruth can't afford Naeem's bail, she opts for the most financially feasible way to connect with her son. She speaks to him on the phone, via remote video from a laptop, or she goes to the jail to have a video visit with him. When she drives the twenty-five minutes to the jail, the video visit is free. If she wants to have a video chat with him without making the commute to the jail, it costs $6 for fifteen minutes—yet another inflated cost she will have to bear for a few minutes of contact with her son. Between juggling her work schedule, seeing William, and registering for a time slot to visit Naeem, she's found the costly video visits to be the most viable option. She wishes the courts would hurry so that he can be sentenced and hopefully released; if not, she knows he will serve his time in a prison that allows in-person visits where she can hug him, see his eyes up close. In the meantime, she has to take what she can get—the grainy screen at the jail or a view from her phone.

14

SOON

Florida

Randall was asleep when a few men in his unit rushed to his bed to wake him up and let him know his daughter was on the phone and desperately needed to speak with him. For Randall, having access to the cell phone meant he could talk to his daughter whenever she wanted, even if that meant waking him up in the middle of the night. Niyah's rigorous search for her father was unusual. He'd recently returned to the hiding place for his phone and discovered that it was gone. Someone had a fight and had a weapon, so the corrections officers did a contraband sweep, meaning they turn over the prison looking for contraband. Randall was sad and depressed about losing what he considered a lifeline. But he knew the game. Just like that, a phone could disappear. Since his cell phone was gone, she couldn't call him directly. When he got to the phone, Niyah was on the other end frantic and crying.

She needed to tell her father what happened. She had left her Beats headphones on the couch with her little cousin. They were her most prized possession, and her mother had warned her to take care of them, telling her, "Make sure your Beats don't break." But when she returned to her headphones after leaving them unattended, she discovered they were broken. She texted her mom to give her a heads up that "something happened to my stuff." Ayana knew that it had to be her headphones and told her that she was going to get in trouble.

Niyah tried to solve the problem. She called her aunt and both grandmothers, and tried all the numbers her dad had called her from in the past. Finally, she reached Randall. "That's nothing to cry about," he told her. He explained that it was a material object that she shouldn't be attached to. "You're crying like somebody died." Talking to her father made her feel better and she stopped crying. She admitted to him that she was sad about her broken headphones, but she was also afraid she'd get a whooping from her mother. "Then he texted my mom and said don't hit me and she didn't hit me," Niyah says. Her father, despite the distance, rescued her.

Ayana is happy that Niyah has a close relationship with her father and is glad he's involved, though she doesn't appreciate when he intervenes in how she disciplines her daughter. She worries that Niyah doesn't always understand how expensive the things she wants are, and she wants her to learn that "everything is earned. I don't give her anything just to give it to her. She earns it." She's not always sure whether Randall is backing her up when she tries to impart these lessons.

Ayana admits that she's shocked at how Randall and Niyah have managed to forge something so strong despite his imprisonment. "It amazes me," she says. "When she met him, it was behind bars. She don't know him at *all* outside of prison." Ayana grew up with her father, so she can't understand the type of loss that her daughter might be experiencing. "It would be hard to get close to someone who's really not here. He's here, but how often do you see him? You've never slept next to him. He's never fed you. Spanked you. Screamed at you. You don't get in trouble from him," Ayana muses. She notes that Randall isn't able to fully explore the various roles of parenthood because of the time constraint during visits. "'Cause every time he sees you, he wants it to be a good time. So, it's like, do I really know this person?"

Niyah has not pondered all the questions that plague Ayana's adult mind. Ann Adalist-Estrin, a child and family therapist and director of the National Resource Center on Children and Families of the Incarcerated, has some ideas about why. Attachment between children and incarcerated parents can be simpler than what Ayana perceives. Niyah has had a pretty consistent relationship with her dad via phone, video, letters, and visits since she was born. A child's needs get defined based on the context they're in, Adalist-Estrin says. As long as the child feels nurtured and protected by the parent, then the attachment won't be compromised. Niyah's needs are being met when she speaks to her father on the phone or when they play games during visits, and when he saves her from a whooping from her mom. "The predictability of that kind of contact is very helpful for attachment," confirms Adalist-Estrin.

As far as Ayana can tell, Niyah doesn't talk about Randall's incarceration or let it affect her. She has normalized his absence. Instead of focusing on him being away, she often talks about what life will be like when her dad comes home and where he'll live. "When my dad come home, he's gonna be at Grandma Cynthia house or you gonna let him come with us?" she often asks her mom. "No," Ayana will reply. "He can go with his girlfriend."

When asked about her plans if her father comes home, Niyah has a few things on her list. "Well, first to my mom's house with me where I live," she says. She then changes her mind and switches up the order. "I'll come here, then my house, then Chili's," she says, nodding her head confidently. "Oh, you gonna come here first?" Cynthia calls from the kitchen. "Because I'm the mama, all right, I'm the big dog!" Niyah smiles at her grandmother's animation. "I have a Nintendo; I'll show him that, and I'll show him interesting things that I have." Her mom plays *Mario Kart* with her, but she'll play the game with her dad when he comes home. They'll eat close by at Chili's. For adventure she has a few ideas. "Might go to this place called Xtreme Action Park. And my dad knows about it too. It has bowling, skating, a trampoline, go-karts."

Ayana worries that Niyah is too focused on Randall coming home and has noticed that her daughter still refers to prison as school, a story they agreed to tell her when she was younger. After several years of going to visit her dad in prison, she still doesn't say the word. Randall has told his daughter where he is and showed her the inside of his prison cell when they had a video chat. Niyah simply commented on how messy his bed was. "Even when I talk to her and I say 'prison,' she don't want to say it," Ayana says. "She say 'school.'" Niyah knows he's not at school, but she finds a way to make sense of the idea. "He's at school, well they told me he has a teacher, so, that's school." He has been enrolled in classes over the years, so she has a point.

Even if Niyah's family had wanted to tell her the truth about Randall's incarceration from the beginning, they didn't know how. Ayana didn't have a therapist she could call; she was barely surviving the reality herself. Randall didn't know what to tell her either. There's no uniform support for incarcerated parents when it comes to the big "how" of telling their children. Some incarcerated parents are lucky enough to be in parenting programs that might offer some support or access to material, but that varies by state and facility. Many parents are faced with telling their children a simple lie, for instance that the incarcerated parent is away at school or in the army. Adalist-Estrin says parents should tell children versions of the truth from the beginning, and then offer a more fully developed explanation of that truth as kids get older and grow developmentally. That way parents eliminate the big reveal of where the parent really is. It's also easier for kids to adjust.

Ayana is growing more concerned with Niyah's perception as she gets older. She doesn't want to see her daughter hurt in the long run. When she hears about Niyah's plans for when her dad comes home, she worries. She thinks it's time that Niyah gets a better grasp of how long he'll be away. If she learns too late, she thinks, Niyah could have resentment. "I hope that she keeps that same gracious spirit. She's a happy kid." Ayana fears that Niyah could change if she doesn't eventually reunite with him or learn of his sentence. "If he don't come home sooner or later or get the time back . . ." she trails off. She's read articles about and met people who didn't have their fathers in their life, and as a result they harbor pain and resentment for years. "They're bitter. They're angry. I don't want that to happen to her," she says. She thinks Randall can prevent possible heartbreak by being open with Niyah, now that's she's old enough to understand. She wants their relationship to continue building and thinks it's time for Randall to have an in-depth conversation with their daughter about his incarceration.

Now that Niyah is being told the truth about her father being in prison and not school, she has to reframe the narrative she's known since she was a toddler and grapple with how she feels about it. Before children reach age seven there isn't a lot of shame or stigma, says Adalist-Estrin, so in the child's mind they're really just visiting a parent in a prison or a jail. The location is relatively benign. Mommy can explain why Daddy is away in pretty simple terms: Daddy did something that the law wouldn't allow and so being behind bars is a form of adult punishment. But once children reach the age of seven or eight, the age of social emotions, they begin having an ever-evolving sense of comparing themselves with others and their norms. They start thinking about how other people see their situation. They experience shame and stigma, even though they've developed a strong attachment to this person as someone in jail or prison.

Over the last few years, Niyah has come to an awareness that having a dad in prison is something that people will judge and consider shameful. In Niyah's case, she developed an attachment to her dad as

someone in school, and then, at the same time that shame and stigma
are kicking in, the people in her life are changing the story. It's hard
for Niyah to deal with it. A child who is left to negotiate the after-
math of the lie, Adalist-Estrin explains, wonders not only why the
lie was told, but what it means. Between the ages of nine and eleven,
where Niyah is, children make meaning of everything. It's an age
of semantics and of trying to understand the moral underpinning of
everything, says Adalist-Estrin. A child like Niyah will reflect quietly
on questions like "Where is he?" and "What does that really mean?"

Ayana thinks Niyah is old enough to know the truth but isn't
ready. "She don't want to admit to the truth." Niyah understands
that if you do a crime you go to jail or prison, so she will have to contend with her father having committed a crime. When asked what
should happen to someone if they do something bad, she doesn't
pause. "They should go to jail if they break the law," Niyah says.
She doesn't have a real grasp on sentencing. When asked how long
people should have to stay in jail or prison if they break the law, she
has an answer. "Let's say, they set someone on fire, they should stay
forever. But if they, let's say, if they don't have on their seat belt,
they should probably stay for a month . . ." In the same breath, when
asked what she thinks should happen for kids whose parents are
away, she says the families should be reunited. "They should let 'em
out and make them go home to their parents and their children,"
she says, lowering her eyes as if she believes what she says is wrong.
"And even the ones who don't have children too."

Ayana thinks it's time for Niyah to know, but she wants to respect Randall and let him be the one to go into the details. And she
isn't sure that Randall is ready to tell his daughter the truth. "I think
he's scared because he thinks she's going to judge him," Ayana says.
"I think that he needs to face reality and even if he does come home,
you know, it'll be a blessing and we have to be hopeful, but I'm at the
point where I think he needs to break it down to her. He needs to
let her know the case. She needs to know what he did. Let her know

what he's charged with," Ayana says. "He needs to let her know because it'll ruin her when she having hope looking for a date that they're going to release him when he knows that he doesn't have a date right now. So stop telling our child two years, a year . . ."

Failing to give Niyah a definitive date is getting more difficult for Randall. "She always want to know when I'm coming home. That's the number one question," Randall says. His reply has always been "soon." That answer doesn't work as well anymore; she calls her father out on it. "She like, 'You always saying soon.'"

Telling your daughter that you've been sentenced to spend your entire life in prison isn't easy, and Adalist-Estrin doesn't suggest telling a young child the parent is never coming home. "The issue though is that the adults don't want to feel the feelings about it, and they don't want to deal with the kids' disappointment and the kids' questions," Adalist-Estrin says. Although it's important to talk to children about the truth, Adalist-Estrin has found that even really seasoned people who have been doing advocacy work for years admit. that explaining the realities of a long sentence is always really hard.

Lately, Niyah's questions have been more frequent and more detailed. She has asked what Randall did and when he's coming home. Instead of "soon" he told her that he was caught up in street life and involved with the wrong people, and that he'll be able to get out when he can afford a good attorney. She asked how much the attorney costs, and he said tens of thousands of dollars. That will hold her for a little while longer.

IN EARLY 2019, RANDALL AND NIYAH had to face a new, more difficult hurdle in their relationship: Randall was suddenly transferred to Graceville Correctional Facility, nearly six hundred miles away and an 8.5-hour drive from where Niyah lives. There is no comprehensive data on how prison transfers are made, how many people are transferred, or why. Often, prisoners are transferred without warning and are unable to warn their family in advance.

But Randall has a theory about why he was moved. Before the transfer, he was put in solitary confinement again. He says a sergeant with whom he'd had a long-standing contentious relationship demanded that Randall do push-ups. He refused, was sprayed with mace, and then put in segregation. His sister sent a letter to prison officials asking what happened and demanded his release from solitary confinement. In the meantime, Randall was back in the worst part of prison. It was tough: "on top of what prison already is and the food that they serve you, how they care for your hygiene, coupled with confinement," Randall says.

He says guards often "lack the know-how to deal with people who are in a secluded state, being punished." While Randall was in solitary confinement, his family continued calling in protest of what they said was unjust confinement.

After being released from confinement, Randall was transferred to Graceville Correctional Facility. His new facility is a private prison, or for-profit prison, in which people are confined by a third party that is contracted by the local, state, or federal government.

Private prisons agree to hold those prisoners for a certain amount of time in their facilities. The government contracts to pay a certain amount of money per day per prisoner housed at the private institution. Between 2000 and 2016, the number of people held in Florida's private prisons jumped 211 percent (from 3,912 to 12,176). No other state has added more private prisoners than Florida. The Graceville facility is owned by the GEO Group, one of the largest private prison corporations in America. The company is headquartered in Boca Raton, Florida. Regardless of the number of prisoners held at Graceville prison, the GEO Group is guaranteed payment for 90 percent occupancy, which amounts to at least 1,696 prisoners. The company is paid close to $67,000 per day to hold prisoners at Graceville.

In order to lower operating costs and increase profits, it has been found, operators of private facilities may cut corners. They often

hire fewer employees and pay and train them less than their counterparts at government-run facilities. This leads to higher employee
turnover and decreased security. Private prisons are less safe, less
secure, and more costly than government-run facilities. There have
been widespread medical negligence and safety violations at private
prisons, leading to dozens of prisoner deaths.

In 2017, the GEO Group recorded revenues of $2.26 billion,
up almost 4 percent from the previous year, and $146.2 million in
profit. The GEO Group operates 133 correctional, detention, and
community reentry facilities, which amount to ninety-six thousand
beds. The company is also one of the country's largest providers of
halfway houses.[1]

The GEO Group has also been a huge supporter of President
Donald Trump, donating $250,000 to his inaugural fund. As well,
they moved their annual leadership conference to a Trump resort.
They also donated hundreds of thousands of dollars to a pro-Trump
super PAC during the 2016 election. The company has profited
handsomely from the Trump presidency. President Trump reversed
former president Barack Obama's decision to phase out federal private prisons, which has done more than just keep them in business.
A share of the GEO Group sold for just under $16 before Trump's
election, then jumped up after his election, and then climbed again
during the immigration crisis. A share was $23.41 in 2018.

In 2018, the GEO Group backed the First Step Act, a nonparti-
san bill that shortened some federal drug sentences and focused on
programs to help reduce recidivism upon release from prison. The
GEO Group has said they backed the bill because they are "part of
the solution and not part of the problem." The bill became law and
is seen as an effort to chip away at sentencing disparities, effectively
reducing the prison population. This means fewer filled prison beds
for private facilities. But the company stands to profit nonetheless.
In recent years the GEO Group has ferociously expanded into the
post-prison rehabilitation sector. This is one of the fastest growing

pieces in their company's portfolios. In 2017, they bought one of the country's largest providers of halfway houses, Community Education Centers, for $360 million. Both prison and post-prison rehabilitation are big business opportunities for the GEO Group.

WHEN CYNTHIA FIRST SPOKE to Randall, he said he liked the new facility because it had air conditioning, cable TV, and better food. But after the excitement of better amenities wore off, Randall realized he could not stay at the Graceville prison for long. He is behind the door more and can't get as much access to the law library to study. He sees himself filing grievances and agitating the system. In addition, it will be the first time in eight years that he won't get the quarterly visits from Niyah. His new facility is not contracted with Children of Inmates (COI), and the 8.5-hour drive makes it too far for regular visits. Without the access to a cell phone or money to afford regular collect calls, Randall must live on memories of his daughter.

He holds on to their last visit, which was the best yet because the father and daughter were able to spend some time alone. Niyah went with a chaperone instead of a family member. It was also a complicated visit. Niyah arrived in a bad mood. She had a certificate to give her father from a course he'd completed. When she handed it to him unceremoniously, he was taken aback. Randall thought his daughter should be proud of his accomplishment, but to her it was just a reminder of him being away. "I wish it was a certificate for you to come home," she told him, pouting.

They worked on division math problems during the visit, in which they both became frustrated. The young father used a sharp tone when telling his daughter that she wasn't paying attention. Niyah burst into tears. There wasn't much time to work on the problems, and he couldn't teach her how to do division in such a short time, especially when she wanted to spend the few hours just playing games and laughing with her dad. Randall was trying to be a full dad with the hours he had. He spent what felt like forever, which was really just a few hours, feeling sorry and trying to comfort her. By the time lunch arrived he had tried every trick he had to get her to cheer up and take a few bites. She finally did. He was afraid she would never forgive him. As the visit neared its close, Niyah recovered from her father's reprimands. She started showing him the latest dances she'd choreographed—five different routines in all—and asked her father to join in. He did. It was all he could do to get her to smile and leave in a good mood.

The family is now tasked with making the transition work. "I'm finna put the collect on my phone," Cynthia says. "But my godson gon pay my phone bill. That's his best friend." She'll look to her children to arrange for Niyah to visit her dad. "We gon get her to see him. We gon work it out. I got kids; they know how to pitch in the money to get a rental or they got new cars," Cynthia says. "We'll get up there. She gonna start missing him."

Nine months have passed and Niyah still hasn't seen her dad.

15

IT'S A CURSE
Mississippi

R uth sits on the creaky wooden bench. One hand taps her thigh, the other holds her sunglasses and driver's license. She opted for no makeup and wears a black-and-gray dress with a pair of low-heeled leather sandals. Ruth is focused on hearing her son's name. She looks straight ahead at the judge, an old white man with gray hair and small glasses. He wears a white shirt and red tie under his black robe. Behind him, the words "Rankin County, Mississippi" are encased in gold letters and circle an eagle.

The judge peers into the audience, a confetti of defendants and the people who love them. All are seeking some version of his mercy. A white man in blue jeans wears a dirty brown shag that falls past his shoulders, his eyes drooping, his decades-old multicolored tattoos creeping up his red arms. His blue baseball cap sits on his rocking knee. A black woman wears small stud earrings and a colorful nurse's top. Her hair is brushed into a neat bun and tied down with a blue-and-white scarf. She maintains a nervous smile. An overweight man wears a crisp white shirt with a gray pinstripe suit that matches his sleek hair. Wearing square black-framed glasses, he quickly flips through transcripts.

Everyone is invisible to Ruth.

The judge calls names and fumbles through the ones he can't pronounce. "Here, Your Honor" come the responses one by one. When he calls a name three times and doesn't get an answer, someone is in trouble. "Issue a bench warrant," he says. A mom stands up, pleads that her daughter is coming. He ignores her.

After most of the morning has crept by, Ruth's anxiety grows and her impatience becomes more visible. Her eyes close to a squint as they roam the crowded courtroom. She has not heard Naeem's name called and even worse, she hasn't seen his lawyer yet. She hopes she is present, tucked in a corner of the courtroom. She looks at her watch and continues sitting. She folds her arms across her chest as both legs rock with a slow fury. Her face is solemn. She prays that Naeem's attorney won't be a no-show again.

After Ruth paid her the fee to represent Naeem, she vanished. Months have passed since Ruth hired her, and she has stopped responding to Ruth's messages. The lawyer has been to visit Naeem only twice over the seventeen months he has sat in jail. The only advice she offered was for him to plead guilty and seek a deal. In exchange for pleading guilty, he would get a plea bargain that would reduce his charges so he could receive a lesser sentence. Taking the case to trial meant he would have to face the maximum penalty for his crime, which in Mississippi is life in prison. His parents were not willing to go to trial. They were afraid of the unpredictability of jury sentencing and the impact of race. So he pled guilty.

His attorney and the prosecutor had reached an agreement, which reduced Naeem's charge from armed robbery to simple robbery. The reduced charge carries a sentence of zero to fifteen years in prison and a fine of $0 to $10,000. With the plea bargain, the final sentence will be up to the judge. Naeem doesn't have any prior convictions, no one had been harmed during the course of the robbery, the weapon wasn't real, and he was young. His lawyer could ask the judge to use his discretion and show leniency.

The problem is Naeem's lawyer has disappeared. After striking a deal with the district attorney, the attorney avoided dozens of Ruth's calls, emails, and texts. The only occasion that she did pick up her call was when Ruth called her from a different number. Nearly a year after Naeem's arrest, they still did not have the discovery—evidence of the crime from the district attorney. She was a no-show for multiple court hearings. Ruth wanted her money back, so she could use it toward hiring an attorney who would actually help her son. She'd met with another attorney who offered her more advice for free than the current lawyer had for the fee. Ruth tried reporting her behavior to the Mississippi Bar Association, and they instructed her to ask the lawyer for a refund directly. It was simply another request to the lawyer that went unanswered. Contacting Naeem's attorney had become pointless for Ruth because she never replied to her messages.

Since the lawyer continued to be a no-show for Naeem's sentencing hearing, his court date kept being pushed back. So he sat in jail during the drawn-out process. Pleading guilty reduced Naeem's bail from $250,000 to $100,000, but Ruth still couldn't afford it. "Don't let my son sit in jail all this time. . . . That is not right," Ruth says. "She didn't try to get it any lower. I can't come up with a hundred thousand . . ." Ruth is tormented by not knowing what will happen to her son. She can't believe an attorney could behave in such a way. "She ain't nothing but a witch. Low-down and dirty." Ruth says the sheer disregard makes her feel like she will step out of character.

The night before this court hearing, Ruth called the lawyer to see if she would be in attendance. After more than a year of ignoring her and Naeem, she replied to Ruth's most recent call by sending a text saying she'd be in court this time. Her track record is awful, but Ruth is hopeful since she at least sent a text. After the morning passes, Ruth feels queasy at the possibility of having to push the sentencing date back even further. Before court, Ruth had said, "I want to get some good news and be done with her." By the time the judge takes recess for lunch, the lawyer still hasn't appeared.

During the break, the courtroom mimics the wheeling and dealing of a used car dealership: men in gray or navy blue suits and a woman with a clipboard are whispering in corners, all negotiating. The lawyer does eventually arrive, but only to tell Ruth that she has asked another lawyer to stand in for her. Naeem's new attorney is Aafram Sellers, an African American man in his early forties sporting a bald head, goatee, and blue suit. Aafram has a private practice and works as a public defender. He informs Ruth that her lawyer is no longer practicing law and that her license has been suspended. In 2019, the Mississippi Bar Association listed her status as "suspended-non-payment."

Aafram spends more time talking to Ruth about Naeem that day than the previous lawyer had during the course of seventeen months. But still, there isn't much time to prepare. He learns more about the story and assures Ruth he will talk to Naeem and do his best on the case. He tells her he is going to ask the judge for a continuance. This will allow him to catch up on the case so that he can effectively present Naeem and the facts of the case. They spend about thirty minutes strategizing. He tells Ruth that it will be imperative for them to gather letters of support for Naeem. Aafram is capable, and Ruth feels better. Finally, her son appears to be in hands of someone who will fight for him.

When Naeem comes into the courtroom, he wears a bright-yellow jumpsuit and a white T-shirt underneath. The words "Rankin County Jail" are printed on the back of the jumpsuit, a chain is around his waist, and he wears handcuffs. His hair is cut low. He doesn't smile. He is visibly tired, eager to learn his fate, glad to see his mother. Ruth twirls her thumbs around each other.

Kevin isn't attending the court hearing, but he is trying to reach his mom by phone to find out, finally, what the sentence will be. Will his little brother be coming home after all? With seventeen months already served, perhaps the sentence he receives will result in release.

Aafram asks for and receives the continuance. The judge pushes back the sentencing date a few months to allow him to prepare. They will have to wait with the hope that, when they return, Naeem will get a favorable sentence.

"GOD IS STILL ON THE THRONE," Ruth declares as she waits for court to resume. Finally, after a total of twenty months, Naeem will get a sentence and possibly come home. Aafram Sellers has proven to be a present attorney over the last three months since he's taken over Naeem's case. He promised to fight for him, and he illustrated his commitment by meeting with Ruth regularly and updating her on the progress of the case. Sellers meanwhile went back and forth in sessions with Judge William Chapman before the hearing.

When Naeem is finally called in to be sentenced that afternoon, Sellers approaches the bench several times to make a case for his client. He wants all factors considered, and he lays out the facts and presents Naeem as a multidimensional young man with a good core. He'd strayed for sure, but he is deserving of real rehabilitation and a chance. Naeem had never been in trouble as an adult before, so he doesn't have a criminal history; this robbery is his first offense. He hadn't used a weapon that could harm anyone. He'd worked most of his young life. An honest, hardworking mother raised him, and he grew up going to see his father in prison, who tried diligently to be as present as possible despite his incarceration.

Sellers presents letters to the judge from Naeem's support system. His pastor wrote a letter that says he's never seen Naeem exhibit any aggressive behavior. He acknowledges that he has made a serious mistake in committing the crime, which he is already paying for, but says that there is much good in him. He advocates for a second chance, in which he believes Naeem will prove to be a productive man and valuable citizen. Ruth wrote that her son deeply regrets the crime he committed and the pain he caused the staff at the restaurant. She recounts the first time she visited him in jail, how they both cried, how when he finally spoke, he said, "I'm sorry, Mama." In his eyes, she tells the judge, she saw how ashamed he was of his behavior. She even talks about the trouble he got into as a juvenile when he and friends broke into a house, how he'd become responsible after high school. She is dumbfounded that he didn't think he could ask her for help, heartbroken by his desperate actions, and most of all terrified that he didn't fully understand the consequences. The crime is out of character, a huge departure from the responsible, hardworking young adult she knows. She asks for leniency.

Sally Fran, the retired United Methodist pastor, also wrote a letter of support, though it is more nuanced. She and Ruth had met while leaving an extended family visit. They became friends and co-led Double Time, a family support group for people with incarcerated loved ones. Sally Fran wrote about how Naeem participated in family activities and summer camp as a young person. She wrote that Naeem's choice is not demonstrative of his core character, which has been modeled by his parents. She acknowledges that he'd struggled in junior high and high school, falling behind and getting into fights, and getting expelled on more than one occasion. But she wants him to have a chance to return to his earlier core values, which have been nurtured by both of his parents. She ends by writing, "The judicial system has the chance to break the cycle of incarceration by making the 'correctional' system be true to the name."

Sellers has talked to the judge about Naeem's father's incarceration. "This young man has the same fate of his father going to prison. He's never met his father outside of prison, that's a sad, sad commentary on this kid's life. For what is a bad decision, he's clearly not a bad kid," he told the judge in a private session.

None of the letters or efforts make a difference. Judge Chapman sentences Naeem to fifteen years, the maximum penalty for his crime. Pain steals Ruth's voice. She shuts down.

THE ANDERSON FAMILY TAKES THE news hard. It is unexpected, even for Mississippi, a state the family had known wasn't progressive with its criminal justice system. "He just a racist judge," William fumes through the phone. The man who was usually a model of calm and collected behavior is incensed and in pain. The fury of a father, helpless, bubbles up with nowhere to go. He is sure that Rankin County had something to do with the harshness of the sentence. He'd long ago warned the boys to stay out of specific parts of Mississippi. "I mean this is Rankin County, and he didn't have to do what he did, but he did." He can't believe that a judge could look at Naeem's background, efforts, and mistake and still give him the maximum sentence when he could have used discretion. He could understand if the crime called for a mandatory minimum, but the judge had the option to sentence him to anywhere between zero and fifteen years and Naeem had already served close to two years in jail because he couldn't afford bail.

Having been in the Mississippi prison system for nearly four decades, William has seen a lot and doesn't expect any fairness from the system, but he is still beyond shook up, near speechless at what he feels is plain cruelty. The sentence doesn't fit the crime. The lawyer's presentation, William feels, meant nothing to the judge. Naeem isn't the quintessential troubled kid with a rap sheet filled with years of crime and convictions. "I could see if he was truly a troublemaker out in the street, truly wreaking havoc on the public. If he was a troubled kid, got into something all the time, if he was robbing folks all the time. But you know, it's not the case. It's the case that you have a chance to be lenient, let a young boy correct a mistake that he made. But you give him the maximum?" William is flabbergasted. "You look at a young boy that's been working the majority of his life, and he made a mistake and you try to throw him away?"

William says he's seen people get less time on manslaughter charges. "I was maybe looking for ten, and maybe suspend some of it, you know, but fifteen; I really wasn't looking for fifteen, there was no way," he says, still shocked. "We're not saying that he was right; even though he was *wrong*, we don't feel like the punishment fit the crime. That don't mean you're weak to have a little compassion, just a little compassion for a kid who grew up without a father, who struggling."

William feels a searing sense of injustice, even for his hometown that still flies the rebel flag. Had he known just how prejudiced Mississippi would continue to be, he would have left decades earlier. Now, he is stuck. He has seen his boys, one by one, get churned up by a system that is unforgiving toward people of color, especially black men. It's hard to know for sure, but in his heart, he believes the caramel shade of Naeem's skin, the kinky coils growing from his head, and his nearly six-foot frame are attributes that invite various forms of oppression and inequality.

Naeem also believes racism played a part in his sentence. After spending nearly two years in jail, Naeem has spoken to a number of other prisoners about sentencing. "I feel like he was on some racist stuff," Naeem says of the judge. "He was really cruel though; you sit here and read my background and I ain't got no convictions." He feels like the sentence he received was fit for "people when they mess up twice, three times, four times, or something like that like. He ain't gonna suspend none of my time?"

Sellers, after working in Rankin County for a decade, doesn't believe that Naeem's race played a factor in the judge's decision. The first problem, he believes, is that Jared was sentenced first, and he received fifteen years. Jared didn't accept responsibility at first and was the mastermind, since he worked at the restaurant and set up the robbery. The judge didn't feel like it would be fair to give Naeem less time just because he played a different role in the crime. The judge, Sellers says, couldn't distinguish between who was more culpable and, therefore, decided that they were equally culpable. They were both originally charged with armed robbery, which was reduced to simple robbery. The latter charge carries a maximum sentence of fifteen years instead of life. The judge argued they received leniency when the charge was reduced in plea bargain negotiations.

The other reason, Sellers argues, is that Judge Chapman doesn't show leniency to defendants who commit violent crimes. These crimes are gun related, robbery related, invasions, anything in which fear is invoked. These are the sort of cases in which Chapman is tough, Sellers says. He metes out harsh punishments for gun crimes or even purported gun crimes. The judge argues that when someone pulls a gun on you, and you don't know if it's a BB gun or a real gun, the same amount of fear is invoked. The fear that the crime creates is what must be addressed.

Sellers says he has a lot of clients who are first-time offenders seeking leniency. "The problem you run into is anything involving a weapon, even as a first offender, is going to be a heightened sense of concern and need or want by the powers that be to punish harsher because of what can [happen]." He says he doesn't think kids consider what can happen, even if unintentionally, when a weapon is added to a scenario. It increases the likelihood that someone might be accidentally shot or killed. "What kids have to realize, you find yourself in jurisdictions where there is a zero-tolerance to crime, that's the unfortunate consequence of our younger people's actions and that's kind of what I see," Sellers says. He'd like to see more alternative sentencing in place, but admits that those sentencing options, even when they are available, aren't offered for violent offenses.

While Rankin County might be a zero-tolerance crime jurisdiction, it's hard for the Andersons to shake the feeling that Naeem's race played a factor. William has heard of and seen judges being tough, but he thinks this judge was particularly cruel. The Andersons aren't alone. Adofo Minka, a Jackson-based public defender and prison abolitionist, agrees with their sentiments. His experiences as a public defender has shown him all the ways it is impossible for Naeem's sentence to be void of race. As he sees it, the criminal justice system is rooted in racism and classism. "It's a crime to be poor in this country no matter where you are," Adofo says. His clients, who are largely poor, face an entirely different court system than the privileged. He's seen clients' lives completely destroyed from the very onset of entering the criminal justice process. The system is focused too much on being tough on crime and not enough on redemption and recovery. According to Adofo, "they see black people as less than human. They see poor people as less than human. And so-called criminality that allows them to transform you to even more of a monster than what they already think you are. So, there is no regard for the impact [of sentencing]."

For decades there has been evidence of racial disparities in sentencing. Bias at the hand of decision makers is alive at every stage of the criminal justice process. Studies have found that black people are more likely to be stopped by the police, detained pretrial, charged with more-serious crimes, and sentenced more harshly than white people.

AFTER A FEW WEEKS, the Anderson family has to move on from "why?" and start planning next steps for Naeem. Weeks after the sentencing, Ruth tries to move forward, but she keeps returning to all that she planned to explore with Naeem. "There was so much I had to teach him," Ruth says. "I didn't want the system to teach him anything." William hopes Naeem will come to his facility. Resigned to Naeem's sentence, he is ready to help him pave a future. "That's just life," he says. He will do what he can, and he can do a lot more if they are in the same prison. "So, hopefully we can get him over here, and let him do them little years and get on out of here. 'Cause, it's over and done now," he says. William would take over the duties of raising Naeem from inside. At least in the same prison, he could help Naeem transition and keep him away from the endless pitfalls of prison. Ruth could visit them both at the same facility instead of driving to different prisons across the state. Kevin, after learning of Naeem's charge, would also feel better knowing that he wouldn't be going to a particularly dangerous prison. Being next to his dad would be good. "He need a little slap on his head 'cause that was dumb as fuck. Gon do that little bit and come on out." As a coping mechanism, both William and Kevin have minimized the severity of Naeem's time.

As they wait for word about where Naeem will be transferred, William sends a message to Naeem through Ruth. He wants him to hold on. "You have to go head on and suck it up," he says. It is the same memo he sends to himself. The pain was still visceral, but he couldn't sulk in it much longer. Or if he did, he couldn't let Naeem know.

Naeem ends up being transferred from the Rankin County jail to the same prison where his father is. William has made so many friends with prison staff over the years that they were expecting Naeem when he arrived. They showed him favor, getting him processed quickly, and even scolded him gently. Officers told him they remembered him coming to see his dad when he was a boy.

When someone arrives at a Mississippi prison, they must go through initial reception and orientation, which usually lasts about four weeks. The Mississippi Department of Corrections (MDOC) is supposed to evaluate the incoming person to develop a personalized incarceration program. Naeem would be classified into a custody level, which is scored on a numerical scale to identify the type and level of risk he could likely present. He'd have to receive medical, dental, and mental health screening and be evaluated for educational, work, and housing needs.

While waiting to be processed and classified, Naeem takes it easy so that he can get settled and focused. He has to prepare to serve his time now that he knows how much it will be. Things would change. While in jail, he slept until one o'clock, watched *The Jerry Springer Show* or *The Maury Show*, played cards, and just hung out. He'd have a breakfast of oatmeal, biscuits, and bologna when he woke up early. They were mindless distractions that made the time go by but also helped him stay out of.trouble. Arguing and fighting were common occurrences. "People get beat up bad . . . eye might be swoll, lip might be swoll. People stealing, people disrespecting," he recalls. He wants to get out of limbo and be assigned to permanent housing within the prison. There, he will be able to have visits, including with his parents, possibly get a work assignment, and enroll in a GED class.

Naeem has had a lot of time to reflect on what he did, what he'd lost, and what would be in store for him. He has to contend with reality, which includes the fact that two of the people closest to him are no longer in his life. For now, he has decided to harbor the betrayal he feels from Jared's actions. He is determined to wait until he gets out of prison before he tells his former best friend that he's seen the discovery, that he's read his statement, and that he knows Jared voluntarily named Naeem as the perpetrator and placed all the blame on him. "You can't trust everybody, that's how they teach you; you can't trust everybody," he says. "That's women and all," he adds. He is referring to Brooke.

"The girl I was with for years, I get locked up three months, she up and leave; so after that you can't really trust nobody. That'll teach you a lot," he says. His girlfriend decided that she couldn't stay with him through his incarceration. At first, she was distant. Naeem had to call multiple times in order to catch her. Eventually, she told him it was too hard and that she couldn't do it. He was upset. "It ain't easy, but my mama did it for all these years," he says. "What make her different?" he asks himself. Ruth reminds him that most women aren't like her. Naeem had thought what they had could sustain them through distance, even if his expectations would change. "You come to jail and you dealing with somebody; you ain't expecting them to be faithful, like you want them to be faithful, but you ain't expecting them to be faithful." He's decided to move on. He admits that she was likely disappointed by his actions and that could have impacted her decision to end things.

His mother has been the one constant figure, and he knows he let her down the most. "My mom was shocked because I'm her baby boy and out of all, everybody of my family, she knew I was always working. Like she always see me having this job and this job and this job and this job so she wouldn't think I be out robbing," he says in one breath. He knows both his mother and father had big hopes for his future. He feels there isn't much he can say now. Sometimes during a phone call, he can tell his mom is not only hurt but still upset. He knows that Ruth is carrying an even heavier load. It's beyond understandable to Naeem. "She doing so much, she still paying our house bill, she doing stuff for me, my middle brother, and my daddy; she paying my car note and still doing other stuff for her grandkids," he admits. "It's a lot, it wear on you, and then she working all these long hours when she really supposed to be retired."

Naeem had succumbed to his environment, had taken the easy way out. Now he will have to look ahead. "I feel like I could have avoided all this stuff, like I could have, I could have stayed down, been patient and waited for my come up," he says. He feels he's on a better path now. "I've found an intelligence I didn't know I had, like if I hadn't come here, I wouldn't know I had intelligence, so it's like God put me in here for a reason." He wonders, too, whether he'll be safer in some ways, and whether "God put me in here just to avoid death." Jackson, as he sees it, is a city plagued with "house burglary, robbery, fighting, shooting, stuff like that." His assessment is credible. In 2018, Jackson had its deadliest year of homicides in two decades.

THE FIRST TIME RUTH, WILLIAM, and Naeem had a visit, Ruth scolded Naeem, her anger and sadness merging. The "why?" lingered. "We got some questions answered," William says. But he is eager to have a one-on-one with his son. "I still want to talk to him without his momma being present. He just made a serious mistake, one that he should have known better, but his momma take it a little further than that. She go a little further than me."

It's possible she did so because she feels responsible. Both Naeem and the prison system had stolen the opportunity she thought she had to mold him. "I wanted something else for him," she admits. "I didn't want the penitentiary to teach him anything." This is a crucial age for him, and she wanted to ensure he continued on the right path. "This is a time where I needed to put something in him, so he wouldn't go this path . . . to guide him away from stuff like this." Ruth reflects on her years of working multiple jobs and long hours, and she contemplates if that had played a part in Naeem going off course. He'd gotten into fights throughout school. She knew that he was hardheaded and uninterested in school, but at the time she didn't know what to do. "He didn't like school and he could have done better . . . I blamed myself, I was working. I didn't have a lot of time." But she knows it is too late to think about what could have caused it. She has to think of a way forward. She will now pass the baton to her husband; William can teach him.

The family will have more visits on Saturdays to come, and Kevin, who stopped visiting for a while, has started showing up again, alongside other family members. William is still waiting for his one-on-one. The only time Naeem and his father can see each other alone is semiannual. Family members can't be housed in the same section of the prison, but they can visit. Twice a year, prisoners with family members in the same prison get to visit one another.

William has been trying to get paroled for the last two decades, to get home to Ruth and his boys. Now, if paroled in 2020, he'll be leaving Naeem to serve the rest of his time alone. For now, he's focused on how to reduce the pressure on his wife. "She ain't but one person. She ain't young no more," he says. William is afraid that his boys don't understand the true impact their past and present incarceration has had on Ruth. "I want them to realize that it is a lot of stress dealing with this system," he says, backed by a deep sigh. "Once your momma is gone, she gone, and y'all gon put her in the grave," he says. William knows the full weight of what Ruth is dealing with. Taking responsibility and being as present as possible is all he can do from prison. "Really, it's my fault. I have to take the blame for all of it. I'm the one left her and she's been dealing with it for thirty-nine years. And then, here my boys come along and they can't seem to keep they act together and so it all comes back to the head. It's like a generational curse, you can't get rid of it."

RUTH STILL FINDS HER MOMENTS of joy. Recently she went to Dallas with her friend Pat. They went to a Saints game, went shopping, and toured the city. For Christmas, Ruth hopped in the car with her best friend and set off for the 2.5-hour drive to New Orleans. She spent the holiday with friends, forgetting reality for a day as she enjoyed oyster dressing, gumbo, cakes, pies, and honest friendship.

"This is a silent epidemic," she says about families suffering along with their incarcerated loved ones. She has seen many marriages fail over the years. People cut ties and make another life. She won't give up on her marriage or family. "It's been a long time," she admits. Her method has been to take each day as it comes, not more. And although the criminal justice system and its policies create barriers at every turn, she won't back down. "I'm a fighter, that's what I do. I can't help it. It's in me. It's just in me. That's one thing in me. I can't go down without a fight. I might be knocked down, but I'm gonna get up. I'm a try at least."

EPILOGUE

Doing the Work

Writing this book has been both rewarding and challenging. I'm honored that these families entrusted me with their stories, which then allowed me to open a lens into the life of families impacted by mass incarceration. This reporting journey also forced me to recall how my life has been impacted by imprisonment, to examine what I've seen, lost, and forgotten. It showed me that, frustratingly, life for families of prisoners has not improved much since I was the child of a prisoner.

In the end, my father served nearly twenty-seven years in California's most atrocious prisons. It wasn't until I could afford an attorney to represent him at his parole board hearing that he was finally released in 2012. I've been lucky to have him on this journey with me. Whenever I hit a rough patch with the book, my father was a free phone call away. He was a steady voice of reason, a compassionate ear, and someone who could quell the rage when it felt like it would spill out of my chest. There were a few days when I had to stop looking at the transcripts from my reporting, and there was at least one occasion when I cried into the phone, asking my father why

I'd chosen to write this book, and why our country treated so many black, brown, and poor people like shit. My father empathized with the families, but he'd seen even worse. He had mastered the art of detachment. You learn self-preservation quickly in prison. He reminded me that my job was to report what I found and to share those accounts, not internalize them, and definitely not to carry the burden of finding the solutions.

I didn't internalize the pain or sorrow these families endured, but there is no way to be welcomed so intimately into people's lives and not care about their experiences. My dad is proud of me for trying to write us closer to justice, but he'd long since become immune to the issues in the system and the horrendous experiences that families go through alongside their incarcerated family members. "That's normal, baby," he'd always say when I told him about a new appalling fact from my reporting. "Normal to whom, Dad?" I asked. He was right. For far too many families, these experiences had been normalized. Many people wanted it to get better, but no one expected better from our system. The system works to numb people until the pain is bearable.

Despite what I'd endured with my father's imprisonment, I didn't want to accept this as normal, and I wasn't resigned to the notion that the criminal justice system is irreversibly broken. As a journalist, I'm compelled to tell stories of the human experience, especially about those whom society considers to be throwaways. The lives they lead are integral to understanding the human journey, the American family. I chose these particular families because their stories are not clean-cut. It's easier for us to sympathize with nonviolent offenders, the wrongfully convicted, those serving unthinkable sentences for drug crimes. The injustices those people endure are profound, and their stories are often shared by politicians and some reform groups because they are indeed emblematic of the brokenness of our criminal justice system. But the story is actually bigger and far deeper than these experiences portray. Serious and violent crimes make up more than 50 percent of our current state prison population. Both William and Randall were convicted of murder and sentenced to life in prison. In the case of Randall, it is life without the possibility of parole. Their lives show us how impossible redemption can be inside the locked jaw of our criminal justice system, and how stripping lifelong punishment is. Naeem's story shows us how easy it is to make one mistake, to commit a first crime as a young person and be severely penalized for it. He's an example of how a young life is irreversibly changed by hard prison time when a judge had the discretion to give him a second chance and chose otherwise. The mothers, spouses, children, and extended family are their lifelines. Even though they're on the outside, they carry the enormous emotional and economic burden of their relative's confinement. These families are only a handful of those trapped in the shadow system, but they are not outliers. There are millions more.

A DISPROPORTIONATE NUMBER of poor people and racial minorities remain in our nation's jails and prisons. As Michelle Alexander so effectively illustrated in *The New Jim Crow*, the War on Drugs has been catastrophic, devastating communities of color and contributing to mass incarceration. People are still incarcerated decades after being convicted of drug crimes, and their families are suffering alongside them. Upon release, being labeled as formerly incarcerated continues to relegate them to second-class citizenship. There have been some reform efforts to reduce the sentencing disparities with regard to drug convictions. But that still leaves a huge portion of prisoners locked away with little chance at rehabilitation or redemption, and their families are shouldering the burden.

While we are making notable reforms at the federal level and incremental changes at the state level, we are not moving quickly toward reform, nor are we moving in sync as a country of wildly different state perspectives. Under the Obama Administration, the US Department of Justice started to phase out their use of private prisons because they were unsafe, more expensive, and did not provide the same level of services, programs, or resources as government-run facilities. It was a clear sign that prisoners' lives were valued and that, as a country, we wanted to turn away from a profit-driven system that rooted for the continuation of mass imprisonment. It was a milestone that would chip away at mass incarceration. Still, this progress was undone. Touting the false narrative of rising violent crime and calling for harsher sentencing, more draconian laws, and a repeat of the policies from 1980s and 1990s, the Department of Justice under President Trump reversed the decision. It was a signal to let us know who and what matters in this country, a reminder that prisoners are disposable and that their families aren't even afterthoughts.

We can't reverse the past, but we can zero in on the future. The next generation is at great risk, because children of color remain targets for incarceration. Today, one out of every three black boys can expect to go to prison at some point in his lifetime, as can one out of six Latino boys. By contrast, only one of every seventeen white boys can expect this fate. Many of our schools are too quick to apply zero-tolerance regulations that push children out of the classroom, into alternative schools, and, in too many cases, the juvenile justice system for minor school-related incidents. The school-to-prison pipeline is clipping the lives of children of color earlier and earlier. We cannot wait twenty years, until the causal impact is glaring, or until a whiter, more valued, racial demographic is impacted. This issue requires serious, ambitious intervention now.

Though more and more people are having the conversation about mass incarceration, we're not on track for meaningful change. Things won't improve simply because we acknowledge their presence and the impact they have. We won't see a monumental reduction in incarceration without meaningful criminal justice reform. The Center for Prison Reform has a list of dozens of organizations that are on the front lines of the movement. The Brennan Center for Justice, to give just one example, has specific suggestions on ways to reduce mass incarceration and in turn lift the burden that is placed on families. Their first suggestion is to eliminate prison time for low-level offenses in exchange for community-based sanctions. Their second is to reduce maximum and blind minimum sentences, especially since research indicates that longer prison sentences don't reduce recidivism. Their third suggestion is to reverse punitive laws of the 1990s by eliminating three-strikes and truth-in-sentencing laws, because both policies prohibit a judge from assessing cases based on circumstances and then issuing an appropriate sentence. Both laws hang defendants on arrival. Implementing these options is not out of reach. The Brennan Center suggests that legislators start with a 25 percent cut for six major crimes (aggravated assault, drug trafficking, murder, nonviolent weapons offenses, robbery, and serious burglary), since a huge segment of the prison population is incarcerated for these crimes. The legislative changes should also be retroactive. These are just a few examples from one organization.[1]

The Sentencing Project demystifies the reason for mass incarceration and the path to its eradication, and it advocates methods to reduce racial disparity. Such a glaring racial disparity in sentencing requires making changes that will help ensure these families, specifically, feel a measure of justice. The Sentencing Project offers suggestions on ways to help close the racial disparities, such as reducing low-level drug offenses, reducing use of cash bail, funding indigent defense agencies, developing training to reduce racial bias, and addressing collateral consequences (voting rights and a conviction's impact on housing, education, and employment). And of particular note is adopting a policy that would require federal and state legislators to use racial impact statements, a tool that would present research and findings that evaluate potential disparities in proposed legislation prior to making it law. Since 2008, Iowa, Connecticut, Florida, Oregon, and New Jersey have implemented such policies.[2]

Mass incarceration is a big part of the puzzle that needs solving. Responding to the various ways families are impacted is the immediate task at hand. Our federal government needs to step up and recognize the grave disparity of resources for families that exist from state to state. The pre-Trump federal government took a baby step and recognized those most vulnerable, namely the children. The US Department of Justice under Obama created an interagency group, Children of Incarcerated Parents (COIP). The group highlights a few issues these children face—financial instability, changes in family structure, shame, and social stigma—and pledges to evaluate the federal programs and policies that impact these children. COIP has done research and run public education programs, but federally funded programs to aid children and families directly are hard to find. Policies need to be streamlined across the country and sufficient funding must be allocated.

These families need government-funded policies, programs, and practices that help mitigate the collateral effects of mass incarceration. These families need support in maintaining their connections with their incarcerated family member. They need visitation policies that are child friendly and offer sufficient time for bonding. The trend for cutting in-person visits in favor of video visits should be curtailed. Families should not have to travel eight hours to see their family member, and they shouldn't have to choose between dinner and two collect phone calls. Mass incarceration is a lucrative business, and families need stricter regulations on the corporations that profit wildly off of them. At every turn, there is enormous profit to be made, and prisons get a kickback from many of the contracts they sign with for-profit vendors. Correctional phone companies, prison health-care companies, prison commissary suppliers, and the bail industry all exploit families of the incarcerated.

Families need reform to one of the most influential social institutions in this country, the child welfare system. They need reform to the Adoption and Safe Families Act, which currently doesn't take their circumstances fully into account, and that still relies on the draconian act of taking children from parents instead of effectively providing access to resources to alleviate the issues that brought them into the child welfare system in the first place. They need a system that uses patience when determining what steps are required to help a parent return to a condition that allows them to take care of their own children.

At multiple levels, Kentucky is exploring ways to help keep families together. After a group raised more than $400,000, Jefferson County recently reopened their Family Recovery Court. It had been closed for eight years. This specialty court offers supervised substance abuse treatment and support for individuals dealing with drug-related charges instead of locking them up. Participants have to be recommended for the voluntary one-year program. It starts with weekly one-on-one meetings with the judge. Once sobriety is established, the meetings are held less frequently. The judges collaborate with various professionals and organizations to help participants access services such as housing, employment, counseling, and even clothing for job interviews. The court aims to increase family reunification rates, lower criminal justice recidivism, and get more people to partake in treatment programs. Family Recovery Court has been proven to reduce the amount of time children spend in out-of-home placements.

The Special Project, an independent network of artists and advocates, in collaboration with the Center for Health Equity, which was established by the Louisville Metro Department of Public Health and Wellness, completed a Health Impact Assessment on the myriad ways that parental incarceration harms children's health. One of the solutions offered in the report is for Louisville courts to introduce a Family Responsibility Statement (FRS) into the criminal justice sentencing process. The FRS would allow decision makers to consider children and families when making sentencing decisions. New York State and San Francisco use FRS as a way to mitigate the impact sentencing and incarceration can have on families and children.

ChooseWell, a Louisville nonprofit, is being intentional in its community collaborations to find the right kind of support for women in recovery. One example is flexible employment. The organization found that women in recovery don't have a hard time getting a job, but they do have difficulty maintaining a position. They are often under-resourced while navigating recovery. They are often without reliable transportation or have no access to a babysitter. As well, these mothers often can't ask for time off from work if they find themselves with a sick toddler or a court date they can't miss. In response, ChooseWell started to cultivate relationships with recovery-friendly employers. They have begun a pilot job-sharing program. Their first partner is a local commercial cleaning company. The company allows the women flexibility with their schedules. If one mom needs a night off to go visit her child, or an afternoon for a court hearing, another mom can take her shift without it compromising her job.

In the meantime, states, mostly in partnership with nonprofits, are taking it upon themselves to bridge the gap to resources and to offer services to families. The umbrella of all resources is the National Resource Center on Children and Families of the Incarcerated. It is a national resource available to anyone concerned with the impact of incarceration on families. They examine policy and advocacy initiatives, as well as programs and evidence-based practices, and speak with those directly impacted to learn what they need. They also have a directory of programs for families. In some states, programming is robust while in others it's virtually nonexistent.

Programming that helps families and children is essential given the time it takes to implement and see the results of reform. But they are only gauzes to slow the bleed. We must reverse the trend.

It's hard to get legislative change when the masses don't demand it. Ambitious reform dies when it is held up against the test of political feasibility. People won't buy into something they believe is bad for them. There must be a shift in our collective consciousness when it comes to mass incarceration and impacted families. We must challenge public safety narratives and implicit and explicit racial biases about crime. As a country, we must ask ourselves why black and brown people and the poor are groups that we care the least about. What lies have we believed? If, as a country, we are to uphold our national ethos, which is supposed to promote democracy, liberty, opportunity, and equality, we have to establish a moral connectedness that crosses racial and socioeconomic lines. Public indifference, detachment, and willful ignorance can no longer be accepted standards, for they are all forms of complicity. Who are we if we don't stand up for those most vulnerable? We have a criminal justice system that doesn't just lock up people, but holds entire families and communities hostage to unbearable economic, emotional, and social tolls. We must demand that our government focus on solutions to economic, social, and political problems across the country instead of penalizing some people for experiencing them.

IN THE MEANTIME, THE FAMILIES you've come to know in this book are pushing forward. After eight years of knee problems and short-term fixes, William finally underwent a successful knee replacement surgery. Ruth is still working her twelve-hour shifts and shelling out $500 a month in costs related to having two loved ones behind bars. She has done some traveling and wants to get a puppy. They're both waiting for William's next parole hearing in the summer of 2020. They pray that after thirty-nine years, William will be coming home. Their son, Naeem, is settling into his new facility, which is two hours away from Ruth. He's no longer in the prison with his father and is using the time inside to grow. He's taking classes to earn his GED. He prefers the new facility because it has gym equipment and he's served "free world" food. He recently had a Southern dinner of fried fish, greens, potato salad, and peach cobbler for dessert. He is happy to be adding weight to his usually wiry frame.

Randall is still at the private prison and adjusting to life with less access to the law library and his daughter. The Children of Inmates program still doesn't offer Bonding Visits to his new facility. His mother, sister, and cousin have taken the eight-hour drive to visit him, but Niyah hasn't been yet. In order for Niyah to visit without her mother, Ayana needs to sign a notarized letter authorizing someone else to take her. Randall's family and Ayana haven't found time or common ground to get the proper authorization for the visits. Randall has missed out on at least three quarterly Bonding Visits. He hasn't seen his daughter since she turned eleven, and he is hoping another year won't pass before they see each other. He's planning to plead with Ayana to get the notarized document, and if he manages that he needs to convince somebody to make the eight-hour drive. For now, father and daughter are managing by speaking to each other on the phone. Niyah for the first time has started having trouble in school. Her grades have dropped. In response, her mother put her on punishment. Cynthia believes there is something serious going on that both she and Ayana need to zero in on. Ayana finally found a voucher-eligible apartment and moved in, but a short time later her apartment was broken into and trashed. She moved back in with her mother. She continues working long hours to provide for Niyah.

Dawn has moved on to a position as program coordinator at a halfway house in Louisville that oversees department of correction parolees. She's helping men with their reentry. "I might have seen myself as not good enough before," she's told me, "but it's opened up a different part of my sobriety." She has put a hold on Wesley coming to live with her because Ethan, who is now going through a divorce, has allowed her a lot more flexibility with visiting and communicating with her son.

Melissa is still doing political work to advocate for formerly incarcerated people and visiting her children. Latonya is still working at the Healing Place and taking care of her son. Christina says she was being railroaded by Kentucky DHS, so she eventually signed away her parental rights shortly before her termination of parental rights hearing. But she has a new case worker who recognizes how poorly her case was handled and is working to see if she can get her children placed with a family member and their older sibling.

My father has met a new freedom. In the time since his release, he's managed to travel to New York to see me and to Florida to see my brother. He's gone to college, taken all the classes offered in health and human services, and received certificates for each. He also volunteered at a number of organizations and has worked as an alcohol and drug counselor in his hometown. He's even started therapy to contend with decades of suppressed memories of prison. In 2017, my father completed his fifth year of parole. Upon review, his perfect record then earned him release from parole. Unlike many other ex-lifers, he doesn't have to remain on parole for the rest of his life. Finally, he is free to travel beyond fifty miles without permission, free from peeing in a cup whenever his parole officer shows up, free from the fear of any kind of police contact. When he first came home, he said he would know he was free when he opened a refrigerator door. I'm sure he has a whole new concept of freedom now.

James Baldwin wrote, "You write in order to change the world, knowing perfectly well that you probably can't, but also knowing that literature is indispensable to the world. . . . The world changes according to the way people see it, and if you alter, even by a millimeter, the way people look at reality, then you can change it."

I will continue to do my part and write. To my readers, I ask you to listen, find your place in the narrative, and move us closer to justice.

Acknowledgments

This book is alive thanks to many people. For me to trace the evolution of this endeavor, I have to honor the power of introductions and the importance of the people who believed in me. As a student at Columbia University Graduate School of Journalism, I received some funding from The Andrew Goodman Foundation. Upon graduation, I met and stayed in touch with the founders, David Goodman and Sylvia Golbin Goodman. It was Sylvia, who seven years ago, introduced me to Kelly Virella, an editor seeking journalists to contribute to her magazine. Kelly and I became friends, and she later introduced me to Esther Kaplan, then editor in chief of The Investigative Fund (now Type Investigations). Esther and I met for coffee and I told her about my plans to write a memoir. It soon became clear that I could produce a rich body of work on the collateral consequences of mass incarceration on families. For my first project, as a reporting fellow at The Investigative Fund, I wrote, "What About Us?," published as a cover story in the *Nation*. It reported on a disturbing pattern of ending extended family visits for prisoners and the impact it had on the 2.7 million children in this country who have an incarcerated parent. Thank you to the *Nation* for giving that story a home, to Kai Wright for editing it, and to Caitlin Graf, for submitting it for awards (some of which I won!).

After that first story, Esther and I worked closely on a number of stories that laid the groundwork for this book. Esther, thank you for your beautiful and thoughtful edits, for challenging, encouraging and applauding me. Sincere gratitude for knowing my value and inviting me to have a seat at the table on several occasions.

It was Alessandra Bastagli, then the editorial director at Nation Books (now Bold Type Books), who envisioned a book from that first story. To Alessandra, for enthusiastically believing in these stories, my voice, and my reporting—it meant everything. Thank you for that list of literary agents, which eventually led me to the perfect match in Tanya McKinnon of McKinnon Literary. Thank you, Tanya, for that first phone call where you kept it real, and for taking me to Kimberlé Crenshaw's Say Her Name gala, which reminded me how beautiful and powerful blackness is. Thank you for laying out all the options and thinking fully of my literary career. And thanks to Carol Taylor, who joined the team later, for being fierce, honest, and present.

I was lucky to have a stellar publishing team at Bold Type Books. Katy O'Donnell, a superb editor, thank you for your dedication and passion and letting my writing style stand; for always discussing race, class, and power explicitly and for asking me to go deeper and for letting me know that writers do miss deadlines sometimes. Your calmness has been invaluable. To the rest of the talented Bold Type Books/ Hachette team, the publisher Clive Priddle, and those who got this project to the finish line: Miguel Cervantes, Katie Carruthers-Busser, Elisa Rivlin, Mike van Mantgem, and Jocelynn Pedro, thank you all so much.

As an independent journalist, bringing a book to life requires enormous support. Thank you to Taya Kitman of Type Media Center for the fellowship that allowed me to become an independent journalist and still eat—it truly set this book in motion. And for providing the manuscript fact check—thank you, Evan Malmgren. Thank you to the Puffin Foundation for supporting the early research of *The Shadow System*. To the Logan Nonfiction Program at the Carey Institute for Global Good for providing a refuge in Rensselaerville, away from the noisy city to work on this project when it was merely a prologue. At Logan I met talented writers who believed in this book. To Adrian Nicole LeBlanc for lending her ear, advice, and French roast coffee. And to Katherine Reynolds Lewis for being an ally during that episode at lunch and becoming a friend who offered advice at different stages of this project. During the imperative, final stretch of this book, I received a Visiting Journalist appointment at the Russell Sage Foundation. It was their generous support and mission to improve the social and living conditions in this country that got my book to the finish line. Thank you to Jennifer Jennings for telling me about the foundation and for unconditionally rooting for me since I was an undergrad at Columbia. Before there was a book idea, before there were foundations supporting my work, before I landed in New York, Topher Delaney put her support behind me. Thank you all for helping ensure that it was *my* voice telling these stories.

This work would not be possible without the commitment from my interviewees, even the voices that didn't make it into the book, your perspectives and stories were essential. Thank you for sharing so fully. To S.K., for your vital research assistance and the many hours of transcribing interviews, thank you.

To my chosen New York family, the Elite Fleet, for being my hype men and women and reminding me how important this work is. For letting me miss events and be a reclusive writer for a year. For my friends sprinkled across the country who have poured into me, thank you.

For my family, I am eternally grateful. This book would not exist had it not been for my father, Vernon A. Harvey Sr., whom I love with my whole heart. For enduring a brutal system, for showing me race, class, power, inequality, perseverance, compassion, and redemption. For my late mother, Estelle Marie Harvey, for never backing down and putting her family first. To my brothers, The Harveys, for recalling stories and for surviving with me. To Quincy for letting me take over your apartment for weeks at a time while reporting, and for making me my favorite pasta. For my late brother, Vernon A. Harvey Jr., who always reminded me to keep pushing and that dark days couldn't last forever. To my cousin Monique Mills for carrying the weight of home that should have been mine, for shouldering the burden with me when deadlines called. Profound gratitude to my late maternal grandmother, Irene Williams, who unselfishly sacrificed her own life to raise a second generation of children, to give me the best life she could.

Finally, to my readers, for coming along this journey: I appreciate each and every one of you.

Notes

PROLOGUE

1. Deborah J. Vagins and Jesselyn McCurdy, "Cracks in the System: Twenty Years of the Unjust Federal Crack Cocaine Law," American Civil Liberties Union, last modified October 2006, www.aclu.org/other /cracks-system-20-years-unjust-federal-crack-cocaine-law.

2. Wendy Sawyer and Peter Wagner, "Mass Incarceration: The Whole Pie 2019," Prison Policy Initiative, March 19, 2019, www.prisonpolicy .org/reports/pie2019.html.

3. The Sentencing Project, "Report to the United Nations on Racial Disparities in the U.S. Criminal Justice System," The Sentencing Project, last modified April 19, 2018, www.sentencingproject.org/publications /un-report-on-racial-disparities; Carol B. Kalish and Marilyn Marbrook, "Prisoners in 1980," US Department of Justice, last modified May 1981, www.bjs.gov/content/pub/pdf/p80.pdf; US Department of Justice, Bureau of Justice Statistics (BJS), "Prisoners in 1988," last modified June 29, 1989, www.bjs.gov/content/pub/pdf/p88.pdf; Danielle Kaeble and Mary Cowhig, US Department of Justice, Bureau of Justice Statistics (BJS), "Correctional Populations in the United States, 2016," last modified April 2018, www.bjs.gov/content/pub/pdf/cpus16.pdf.

4. *Collateral Costs: Incarceration's Effect on Economic Mobility* (Washington, DC: The Pew Charitable Trusts: Pew Center on the States, 2010), www.pewtrusts.org/-/media/legacy/uploadedfiles/pcs_assets/2010/collateral costs1pdf.pdf.

5. Kristin Turney and Rebecca Goodsell, "Parental Incarceration and Children's Wellbeing," *Future of Children* 28, no. 1 (Spring 2018), https://files.eric.ed.gov/fulltext/EJ1179185.pdf.

6. Don Stemen, "The Prison Paradox: More Incarceration Will Not Make Us Safer," *Vera Institute of Justice*, July 2017, www.vera.org/publications/for-the-record-prison-paradox-incarceration-not-safer.

7. Ashley Nellis, *Still Life: America's Increasing Use of Life and Long-Term Sentences*, The Sentencing Project, May 2017, www.sentencingproject.org/publications/still-life-americas-increasing-use-life-long-term-sentences.

1. THE RED HAMMER

1. Sylvia A. Harvey, "2.7 Million Kids Have Parents in Prison, They're Losing Their Right to Visit," *Nation*, December 2, 2015, www.thenation.com/article/2-7m-kids-have-parents-in-prison-theyre-losing-their-right-to-visit.

2. Stephen Raher, "The Company Store: A Deeper Look at Prison Commissaries," Prison Policy Initiative, May 2018, www.prisonpolicy.org/reports/commissary.html.

3. Taylor E. Eldridge, "The Big Business of Prisoner Care Packages," The Marshall Project, last modified December 21, 2017, www.themarshallproject.org/2017/12/21/the-big-business-of-prisoner-care-packages.

4. Dan Christensen, "Florida Prison Officials Didn't Ask, Companies Didn't Tell About Hundreds of Malpractice Cases," *Florida Bulldog*, October 2, 2013, www.floridabulldog.org/2013/10/florida-prison-officials-didnt-ask-companies-didnt-tell-about-hundreds-of-malpractice-cases.

2. IN THAT PLACE

1. Author interview with COI Director Shellie Solomon, August 20, 2019.

2. Florida Kids Count, "The Burden of Incarceration on Florida Families," April 8, 2016, www.floridakidscount.org/index.php/counting-for-kids-blog/the-burden-of-incarceration-on-florida-families.

3. Sarah Blaskey, "Hard Time Gets Harder: Florida Inmates Deliberately Shipped Farther from Home, Families," *Miami Herald*, October 10,

2018, www.miamiherald.com/news/special-reports/florida-prisons/article 218689780.html.

4. Sarah Blaskey, "This Drug Is Turning Florida Inmates into 'Zombies': It's Fueling a Record Death Toll," *Miami Herald*, June 25, 2019, www .miamiherald.com/news/special-reports/florida-prisons/article215642855 .html.

5. Three infant deaths occurred within six months of each other—one from accidental drowning, one from misuse of medical equipment, and one from being dropped due to the mother's diabetic condition. Author interview with COI Director Shellie Solomon, August 20, 2019.

3. WHAT ADDICTION LOOKS LIKE

1. Eli Hager, "A Mass Incarceration Mystery," *Washington Post*, December 15, 2017, www.washingtonpost.com/news/wonk/wp/2017/12/15 /a-mass-incarceration-mystery; Ann E. Carson, "Prisoners in 2016," US Department of Justice, Bureau of Justice Statistics (BJS), last modified January 2018, www.bjs.gov/content/pub/pdf/p16.pdf.

2. Emily Hagedorn, "Funds to Fight a Drug Epidemic Cut Even As Abuse of Medicines Kills Record Number of Kentuckians," Center for Health Journalism, January 29, 2011, www.centerforhealthjournalism .org/fellowships/projects/funds-fight-drug-epidemic-cut-even-abuse -medicines-kills-record-number-kentucki.

4. BOY, THEY GON FRY YOU

1. Mississippi Department of Archives and History (MDAH), "Mississippi State Penitentiary (Parchman) Photo Collections PI/1996.0006 and PI/PEN/P37.4," accessed April 3, 2019, www.mdah.ms.gov/arrec /digital_archives/series/parchman.

2. Mississippi Department of Archives and History (MDAH), "Mississippi State Penitentiary (Parchman) Photo Collections PI/1996.0006 and PI/PEN/P37.4."

3. Hannah Grabenstein, "Inside Mississippi's Notorious Parchman Prison," *PBS News Hour*, updated January 29, 2018, www.pbs.org/newshour /arts/inside-mississippis-notorious-parchman-prison.

4. Columbus B. Hopper, "The Impact of Litigation on Mississippi's Prison System," downloaded from SagePub.com at Pennsylvania State University, March 6, 2016, http://citeseerx.ist.psu.edu/viewdoc/download ?doi=10.1.1.857.5603&rep=rep1&type=pdf.

5. Donald A. Cabana, "The History of Capital Punishment in Mississippi: An Overview," Mississippi History Now, last modified October 2004, www.mshistorynow.mdah.ms.gov/articles/84/history-of-capital-punish ment-in-mississippi-an-overview.

6. Donald A. Cabana, "The History of Capital Punishment in Mississippi: An Overview," Mississippi History Now, last modified October 2004, www.mshistorynow.mdah.ms.gov/articles/84/history-of-capital-punish ment-in-mississippi-an-overview; Parker Yesko, "Execution in Mississippi: Who Lives and Who Dies," APM Reports, July 3, 2018, www.apmreports .org/story/2018/07/03/execution-in-mississippi-who-lives-and-who-dies.

7. Alexia Cooper and Erica L. Smith, "Homicide Trends in the United States, 1980–2008: Annual Rates for 2009 and 2010," US Department of Justice, Bureau of Justice Statistics (BJS), last modified November 2011, www.bjs.gov/content/pub/pdf/htus8008.pdf.

8. Elizabeth Hinton, Julilly Kohler-Hausmann, and Vesla M. Weaver, "Did Blacks Really Endorse the 1994 Crime Bill?" *New York Times*, April 13, 2016, www.nytimes.com/2016/04/13/opinion/did-blacks-really -endorse-the-1994-crime-bill.html.

9. US Department of Justice, "Violent Crime Control and Law Enforcement Act of 1994," National Criminal Justice Reference Service (NCJRS), last modified October 24, 1994, www.ncjrs.gov/txtfiles/billfs .txt; US Department of Justice, Bureau of Justice Assistance, "Report to Congress: Violent Offender Incarceration and Truth-in-Sentencing Incentive Formula Grant Program," last modified February 2012, www.bja .gov/Publications/VOITIS-Final-Report.pdf.

10. Andrew Kaczynski. "Biden in 1993 Speech Pushing Crime Bill Warned of 'Predator on Our Streets' Who Were 'Beyond the Pale,'" CNN, March 7, 2019, www.cnn.com/2019/03/07/politics/biden-1993-speech-predators /index.html.

11. Michael Fortner, "The Clintons Aren't the Only Ones to Blame for the Crime Bill," The Marshall Project, October 7, 2015, www.the marshallproject.org/2015/10/07/the-clintons-aren-t-the-only-ones-to -blame-for-the-crime-bill.

12. Fortner, "Clintons Aren't the Only Ones."

13. Nazgol Ghandnoosh, "Delaying a Second Chance: The Declining Prospects for Parole on Life Sentences," The Sentencing Project, January 31, 2017, www.sentencingproject.org/publications/delaying-second -chance-declining-prospects-parole-life-sentences.

5. A NORMAL CHILD

1. Bill Hathaway, "Implicit Bias May Help Explain High Preschool Expulsion Rates for Black Children," YaleNews, September 27, 2016, https:// news.yale.edu/2016/09/27/implicit-bias-may-explain-high-preschool -expulsion-rates-black-children.

2. History.com editors, "Brown v. Board of Education," History.com, last modified September 6, 2019, www.history.com/topics/black-history /brown-v-board-of-education-of-topeka.

3. Sylvia A. Harvey, "How to Stop Locking Up Kids," The Root, March 26, 2018, www.theroot.com/how-to-stop-locking-up-kids-182401 9858.

4. Katherine J. Rosich, "Race, Ethnicity, and the Criminal Justice System," American Sociological Association, last modified September 2007, www.asanet.org/sites/default/files/savvy/images/press/docs/pdf/ASA RaceCrime.pdf.

5. P. A. Goff, M. C. Jackson, B. A. L. Di Leone, C. M. Culotta, and N. A. DiTomasso, "The Essence of Innocence: Consequences of Dehumanizing Black Children," *Journal of Personality and Social Psychology* 106, no. 4 (2014): 526–545, http://dx.doi.org/10.1037/a0035663.

6. Shayne Benowitz, "Historic Overtown's Black Archives History & Research Foundation," The Official Site of Miami, accessed December 20, 2018, www.miamiandbeaches.com/things-to-do/history-and-heritage /black-archives-history-foundation.

7. Francisco Alvarado, "Neighborhood Dive: Pricing Surges in Overtown," The Real Deal, last modified November 23, 2015, https://therealdeal .com/miami/2015/11/23/neighborhood-dive-pricing-surges-in-overtown.

8. Katherine Kallergis, "How Much Did David Beckham Pay for Stadium Land?" The Real Deal, last modified March 25, 2016, https:// therealdeal.com/miami/2016/03/25/how-much-did-beckham-united-pay -for-stadium-land.

9. Diana Elliott, Tanaya Srini, Shiva Kooragayala, and Carl Hedman, "Miami and the State of Low- and Middle-Income Housing: Strategies to Preserve Affordability and Opportunities for the Future," Urban Institute, March 2017, www.urban.org/sites/default/files/publication/89311/miami_lmi_2.pdf.

10. Heather Vogell, "How Students Get Banished to Alternative Schools," ProPublica, December 6, 2017, www.propublica.org/article/how-students-get-banished-to-alternative-schools.

11. Heather Vogell and Hannah Fresques, "'Alternative' Education: Using Charter Schools to Hide Dropouts and Game the System," ProPublica, February 21, 2017, www.propublica.org/article/alternative-education-using-charter-schools-hide-dropouts-and-game-system; Hannah Fresques, Heather Vogell, and Olga Pierce, "Methodology: How We Analyzed Alternative Schools Data," ProPublica, February 21, 2017, www.propublica.org/article/alternative-schools-methodology.

12. Fresques, Vogell, and Pierce, "Methodology," ProPublica, February 2017.

6. BAR BABY

1. University of Kentucky. "Kentucky Prescription Drug Abuse Summit 2012 Summary," US Department of Justice, accessed September 7, 2019, www.justice.gov/sites/default/files/usao-edky/legacy/2014/07/11/Pill%20Summit%20Revision%20summary%20Final.pdf.

2. National Center for Health Statistics, "Drug Overdose Mortality by State," Centers for Disease Control and Prevention, last modified January 10, 2019, www.cdc.gov/nchs/pressroom/sosmap/drug_poisoning_mortality/drug_poisoning.htm.

3. John Cheves, "Prison Populations Are Falling in Most States, but Ballooning in Kentucky. Here's Why," *Lexington Herald Leader*, April 26, 2019, www.kentucky.com/news/politics-government/article229666564.html.

4. Kentucky Youth Advocates, "New Data Shows Increasing Number of Kentucky Children Living with Relative Caregivers," accessed November 3, 2019, https://kyyouth.org/new-data-shows-increasing-number-of-kentucky-children-living-with-relative-caregivers.

7. MORE HUMAN

1. Sylvia A. Harvey, "2.7 Million Kids Have Parents in Prison. They're Losing Their Right to Visit," *Nation,* December 3, 2015, www.thenation .com/article/2-7m-kids-have-parents-in-prison-theyre-losing-their-right -to-visit.

2. Columbus B. Hopper, "The Conjugal Visit at Mississippi State Penitentiary," *Journal of Criminal Law and Criminology* 53, no. 3 (Fall 1962): 340–343, https://scholarlycommons.law.northwestern.edu/cgi/viewcontent .cgi?article=5106&context=jclc; Harvey, "2.7 Million Kids Have Parents in Prison."

3. US Office of Justice Programs, Minnesota Department of Corrections, *The Effects of Prison Visitation on Offender Recidivism,* Minnesota, November 2011, https://mn.gov/doc/assets/11-11MNPrisonVisitation Study_tcm1089-272781.pdf; Meghan Mitchell, Kallee McCullough, Di Jia, and Yan Zhang, "The Effect of Prison Visitation on Reentry Success: A Meta-analysis," *Journal of Criminal Justice* 47 (December 2016): 74–83, www.researchgate.net/publication/306011517_The_effect_of_prison _visitation_on_reentry_success_A_meta-analysis.

4. R. L. Nave, "State Prisons End Conjugal Visits," *Jackson Free Press,* December 31, 2013, www.jacksonfreepress.com/news/2013/dec/31 /conjugal-visits-end-parchman.

5. Jimmie E. Gates, "Chris Epps Sentenced to Almost 20 Years," *Clarion Ledger,* May 24, 2017, www.clarionledger.com/story/news/2017/05/24 /chris-epps-sentencing/341916001.

10. TIME

1. Wendy Sawyer, "How Much Do Incarcerated People Earn in Each State?" Prison Policy Initiative, April 10, 2017, www.prisonpolicy.org /blog/2017/04/10/wages; US Department of Justice, Bureau of Justice Assistance, *Prison Industry Enhancement Certification Program,* March 2004, www.ncjrs.gov/pdffiles1/bja/203483.pdf.

2. Campbell Robertson, "Mississippi Governor, Already Criticized on Pardons, Rides a Wave of Them Out of Office," *New York Times,* January 10, 2012, www.nytimes.com/2012/01/11/us/gov-haley-barbour-of -mississippi-is-criticized-on-wave-of-pardons.html.

11. THE MEANING OF LIFE

1. "The Truth About Life Without Parole: Condemned to Die in Prison," ACLU Northern California, October 18, 2017, www.aclunc.org/article/truth-about-life-without-parole-condemned-die-prison; Josh Rovner, "Juvenile Life Without Parole: An Overview," The Sentencing Project, July 23, 2019, https://www.sentencingproject.org/publications/juvenile-life-without-parole.

2. Charles J. Ogletree and Austin Sarat, eds., *Life Without Parole: America's New Death Penalty?* (New York: NYU Press, 2012), 352.

3. Ashley Nellis, *Still Life: America's Increasing Use of Life and Long-Term Sentences*, The Sentencing Project, 2017, www.sentencingproject.org/publications/still-life-americas-increasing-use-life-long-term-sentences.

4. American Friends Service Committee, "Solitary Confinement Facts," accessed April 25, 2019, www.afsc.org/resource/solitary-confinement-facts.

5. SPEAR, "Solitary Fact Sheet: Facts About Solitary Confinement," accessed April 25, 2019, http://princetonspear.com/7x9-fact-sheet.

6. Peter Wagner and Bernadette Rabuy, "Following the Money of Mass Incarceration," Prison Policy Initiative, January 25, 2017, www.prisonpolicy.org/factsheets/money2017.pdf.

7. Federal Communications Commission, "Inmate Telephone Service," last modified September 8, 2017, www.fcc.gov/consumers/guides/inmate-telephone-service.

8. Timothy Williams, "The High Cost of Calling the Imprisoned," *New York Times*, March 30, 2015, www.nytimes.com/2015/03/31/us/steep-costs-of-inmate-phone-calls-are-under-scrutiny.html.

9. Mary Fainsod Katzenstein and Maureen Waller, "Phone Calls Won't Cost up to $14 a Minute Anymore but Here's How Prisoners' Families Are Still Being Fleeced," *Washington Post*, October 26, 2015, www.washingtonpost.com/news/monkey-cage/wp/2015/10/26/phone-calls-wont-cost-up-to-14-a-minute-anymore-but-heres-how-prisoners-families-are-still-being-fleeced/?utm_term=.be68feb48d39.

10. Timothy Williams, "The High Cost of Calling the Imprisoned," *New York Times*, March 30, 2015, www.nytimes.com/2015/03/31/us/steep-costs-of-inmate-phone-calls-are-under-scrutiny.html.

11. Jason Kelly, "Records Show Increase in Confiscation of Cellphones in Florida Prisons," WFTV, November 2, 2017, www.wftv.com/news/9

-investigates/9-investigates-records-show-increase-in-confiscation-of
-cellphones-in-florida-prisons/637065013; Sandy Banks, "Allowing Phones
in the Cells Might Be a Sound Call," *Los Angeles Times*, March 26, 2011,
www.latimes.com/local/la-xpm-2011-mar-26-la-me-0326-banks-201
10326-story.html.

12. THE KIDS

1. Eli Hager and Anna Flagg, "How Incarcerated Parents Are Losing
Their Children Forever," The Marshall Project, December 2, 2018, www
.themarshallproject.org/2018/12/03/how-incarcerated-parents-are-losing
-their-children-forever?ref=hp-1-100.

2. Sylvia A. Harvey, "Stepping Up," *Virginia Quarterly Review*, Winter
2018, www.vqronline.org/reporting-articles/2018/12/stepping.

13. THE DEVIL IN HELL

1. Phil McCausland, "Mississippi Senator, Whose Runoff Opponent
Is Black, Jokes About 'Public Hanging,'" NBC News, November 12, 2018,
www.nbcnews.com/politics/politics-news/mississippi-senator-whose
-runoff-opponent-black-jokes-about-public-hanging-n935006.

2. "The Counted: People Killed by Police in the US," *Guardian*
(database), accessed April 26, 2019, www.theguardian.com/us-news/ng
-interactive/2015/jun/01/the-counted-police-killings-us-database.

3. Melissa Neal, "Bail Fail: Why the U.S Should End the Practice of
Using Money for Bail," Justice Policy Institute, September 2012, www
.justicepolicy.org/uploads/justicepolicy/documents/bailfail.pdf.

4. Katie Unger, "$elling Off Our Freedom: How Insurance Corpo-
rations Have Taken Over Our Bail System," American Civil Liberties
Union, May 2017, www.aclu.org/sites/default/files/field_document/059
_bail_report_2_1.pdf.

5. Katie Unger, "$elling Off Our Freedom: How Insurance Corpora-
tions Have Taken Over Our Bail System."

14. SOON

1. The Geo Group, "Our Locations," Accessed April 25, 2019, www
.geogroup.com/locations.

EPILOGUE

1. James Cullen, "Four Things We Can Do to End Mass Incarceration," Brennan Center for Justice, December 19, 2016, www.brennan
center.org/blog/four-things-we-can-do-end-mass-incarceration.

2. "Report to the United Nations on Racial Disparities in the U.S.
Criminal Justice System," The Sentencing Project, April 19, 2018, www
.sentencingproject.org/publications/un-report-on-racial-disparities.

Index

271

Rayon Richards

Sylvia A. Harvey is an award-winning journalist who reports at the intersection of race, class, and policy. Harvey's work has appeared in the *Nation, Virginia Quarterly Review, The Appeal, Yes! Magazine, ELLE, Colorlines, The Root, The Feminist Wire, Narratively,* AOL's Bed-Stuy, NY, Patch, where she served as the gentrification columnist, and more. Her commentary on race and the criminal justice system has been featured on WNYC, NPR, WBAI, HuffPost Live, and beyond. An Oakland native, Harvey holds a BA in sociology from Columbia University and an MS in journalism from Columbia's Graduate School of Journalism. She lives in New York City.

www.mssah.com
Twitter: @Ms_SAH